THE LEGACY OF
LIBERTY AND PROPERTY

IN THE STORY OF
AMERICAN COLONIZATION
AND THE FOUNDING
OF A NATION

DANIEL J. FORD

LEX REX PUBLISHING
Saint Louis

*For the Kingdom is the LORD'S: and He
is the Governor among the nations.*
– Psalm 22:28

Lex Rex Publishing, L.L.C.
4372 Casa Brazilia Drive
Suite 302
St. Louis, Missouri 63129
LexRexPublishing.com

ISBN 0-9724554-2-6

The author extends his deepest gratitude to the James Zes family who have
greatly assisted this work through many crucial contributions
and by their tremendous help in its editing.
– Daniel Ford

Most Scripture quotations are taken from the New King James Version.
Quotes from sources have often been updated in spelling or grammar.

Jacket art, design, layout, and typography by Daniel Ford.
Flyleaves were adapted from a nineteenth-century
illustration of important flags of
American history.

Printed in the UNITED STATES of AMERICA
First edition, First printing

This book is gratefully dedicated:

To untold thousands of the faithful in Christ who travailed
throughout the past to preserve our glorious
legacy of liberty and property.

CONTENTS

INTRODUCTION

Understanding History as a Legacy of Important Ideas

THERE is a richness to delving into history that far exceeds learning important names and events. We can pick up a book and read of interesting events and fascinating people from long ago, but if they offer little importance to our lives, it does us little good. The key, then, is reading the great stories of our past in ways that help improve our lives and, hopefully, the world around us.

Any look into our storied past is much more interesting and rewarding when we realize there are valuable lessons for us. Reading history can, in this way, be an important act of rediscovery. For example, exploring the ideas that shaped our nation's founding documents is an act of rediscovering the principles that enabled America's original success.

It is one thing, however, to know of the great exploits of historic figures and quite another to know ourselves in light of them. Exploring the ideas – good and bad, profitable and not – of those who lived long ago not only allows us to understand their contributions to the American story, but also to discover our own context within that story. Understanding our history as a legacy of important ideas helps us to see those who lived long ago not merely as interesting figures who have passed away. It helps us behold a rich inheritance of ideas that should never be allowed to pass away.

It is with a deep appreciation for the importance of ideas that this book approaches the historic subject of liberty and property. This volume investigates the roots of these key components of freedom as they stemmed from the time of the Reformation in Europe.[1] It then traces the course of those ideas as they were embraced by the early visionaries of English colonization and tracks how those ideas were applied in America by the

---

1 The Reformation was a massive movement to return European Christianity under the authority of God's written Word. It was greatly advanced in the early sixteenth century by the circulation of printed Bibles in the common European languages by those who began preaching and teaching its truths.

first English settlers. From there, our story follows the great legacy of liberty and property as it prevailed throughout the colonial era and as it eventually triumphed over the forces of tyranny in the founding of our nation. This legacy was then reconfirmed in the original state and federal constitutions that were intended to safeguard our freedoms.

The same ideas that are documented throughout this volume went on to make the United States known throughout the world as the land of the free. America was renowned as a country where her citizens were not known as subjects, but her elected officials were known as public servants. American citizens were free from the reach of invasive government and their property was known as the ground upon which they enjoyed their God-given liberty. In America, liberty and property were known as the twin catalysts of freedom – as two ideas that must remain inseparably linked for freedom to thrive in any meaningful way.

In the long run, the historic legacy that is documented in this book is not only important for an appreciation of America's past. Understanding our magnificent legacy of liberty and property is essential to our nation's very survival against the onslaught of forces always at work to undermine such a rich inheritance of freedom.

1
THE ROOTS OF LIBERTY AND PRIVATE PROPERTY IN AMERICA

An Introduction to the American Legacy of Liberty and Property

MANY books and resources are available on the subject of colonization and the founding era of the United States – about the men and the war that won our nation's independence. Few resources, however, delve topically into the basic ideas of liberty together with property as these blessings were understood in the earliest days of our nationhood.

If we were to ask Americans today what liberty means, we would get a wide range of answers. One person might express liberty as freedom from nearly all governmental control over our everyday lives. Someone else might concede to the government's economic control, but see liberty as an unquestionable freedom of choice in all other personal decisions. Still another might think of liberty as an absolute freedom from any kind of moral constraint over our lives at all. But regardless of the meanings ascribed today, they are likely quite different from the ideas of liberty that originally prevailed and made America revered as the land of the free.

The typical man on the street today might be shocked to discover how the people of America originally viewed the idea of liberty. Those views were, thankfully, well-documented. For example, in November 1776, the new state of Massachusetts published a letter of encouragement to the American Army that was engaged in an armed struggle to secure their liberties. The two thousand broadside handbills that were distributed among the troops described "*the free exercise of liberty*" as Americans' freedom "*in the worship of that almighty Being who supported them in the greatest distress.*"[1] Here, for one thing, we can see that liberty in our nation's founding era was recognized as the right to worship the God who was supporting them in the field of battle.

---

1 The broadside "*handbill*" was titled: *In the House of Representatives, November 1, 1776*, which was concurred "*in Council, November 2d, 1776*" (Boston, 1776).

The Broadside Handbill Distributed among Continental Troops Describing Americans' Principles of Liberty and Property

James Bowdoin, President of the Council of Massachusetts, with the state's handbill issued to American soldiers in November 1776

But such has been the avarice of some, and the ambition of others, amongst us, that the King and Parliament of Great-Britain have been fatally perswaded to claim this whole continent, with its three millions of inhabitants, as their own property, and to be at their difpofal.

    ❝ *But such has been the avarice of some, and the ambition of others, amongst us, that the King and Parliament of Great-Britain have been fatally persuaded to claim this whole continent, with its three millions of inhabitants, as their own property, and to be at their disposal.* ❞

       This illustrious broadside went on to encourage the army that the liberty for which they were fighting with their own toil and blood was a cause they shared with their colonial ancestors. Their own hard-fought cause of liberty was, in fact, the same as those before who *"toiled and bled, with the pleasing hope of their posterity's enjoying that freedom for which they encountered every difficulty, and braved every danger."*[2]

       The patriot soldiers who read the handbill were also reminded of the *"tyrants of the earth"* who *"exercise lawless power"*[3] over people. These *"tyrants"* were described as rulers who, instead of protecting the people's liberties, *"transgress the sacred line of property, and claim their fellow*

---

2 Ibid.
3 Ibid.

men as slaves."[4] This description is also key to our understanding of the kind of liberty that our forefathers cherished. Their idea of liberty was characterized by "*the sacred line of property*," or the "*line*" that separated *public* authority from their *private* property – the kind of property that was off-limits to the British government. This was the "*sacred*" idea of private property that these God-worshiping people were willing to defend with their own bullets, blood, and bayonets.

It should not be surprising that the same handbill reminded the soldiers why, as former subjects of Great Britain, they were then fighting as free citizens of the United States. It explained that they were in an armed struggle to secure their nation's independence so that they could continue to enjoy their "*rights*" as the "*inestimable blessings (bestowed by their all-merciful Creator)*."[5] This shows that the rights that Americans enjoyed were recognized as the distinguished blessings from a merciful God rather than mere grants by a king or any civil government. The handbill then noted that Britain's king and Parliament had "*been fatally persuaded to claim this whole continent* [North America], *with its three millions of inhabitants, as their own property, and to be at their disposal*."[6] In other words, the British government had attempted to claim both the land and the people on it as its own sovereign property.

The British government did not own these people or their property. The patriots' cause was to remain free from any government that deprived them of the God-given liberty they had in their property as well as the God-given possession they had of their liberty. Accordingly, the cause of our forefathers in becoming a nation rested on much higher principles of liberty than most Americans would recognize today.

Liberty and Property as Responsibilities under God

At the time of our country's founding, there was a deep appreciation for having become a nation that enjoyed its every freedom under God. Patriotic Americans understood liberty to be an obliging responsibility of a

---

4 Ibid.
5 Ibid.
6 Ibid.

free people to God. They knew that maintaining liberty meant respecting all *legitimate* governing authority as well as lawfully resisting any *illegitimate* exercise of governmental power. Private property was recognized as the supportive foundation upon which they enjoyed their blessings of liberty. Therefore, the property that American families had in their own land and possessions was regarded as the necessary undergirding of their freedoms.

Today little is understood about those essential components of our nation's rich and storied past. Little is therefore known of America's original character. To appreciate those blessings Americans have long enjoyed – to appreciate the blessing of freedom that has been passed onto us – it is important to know the source ideas that drove our founders to actually fight for their freedoms. It is very important for us to understand the original ideas behind the documents that our founders drafted, which were intended to guarantee the blessing of freedom that Americans still largely enjoy. For without an adequate understanding of the basis of liberty and property, we will not remain as a nation of free people for long.

Tracing the Paths of Liberty and Tyranny

Our story, however, does not begin with the most noble expressions of liberty. It begins with the advent of European dominion over America following the first exploratory discoveries in the late 1400s. Sadly, the story of American colonization begins with the story of conquest. It begins with the subjection of indigenous Americans along with their land, possessions, and resources by the Crown of Spain. We will begin our story by exploring the fundamental ideas that led to the Spanish conquest, which were diametrically opposed to the idea of liberty later planted by the English.

We will discover a sharp difference between both the ideas and methods of the Spanish conquerors and the ideas and methods of the English settlers. In fact, the two divergent models are good examples: the Spanish model is a vivid example of tyranny and excessive control by a centralized government; the English model is a vivid example of dominion retained largely in the hands of the people themselves.

Thus, America's colonial past is not only rich with great interest and intrigue, but it provides us with models of failure and success – models of dominion by the state as opposed to dominion by the people in their own liberty, land, and possessions. This latter model of liberty and private property is what led to our nation's establishment in freedom. It is the true legacy of our nation's founding – a legacy that must be understood by Americans who would like to continue enjoying the fruits of freedom.

Overview of Two Divergent Views of Earthly Dominion

The Spanish and the English methods of colonization were driven by two profoundly differing views of mankind's dominion over the earth.[7] It was thought by the Crown of Spain that it had an exclusive, sovereign right – a divine right[8] – over the land and the resources of the New World, and even over the indigenous Americans themselves. Duty to God – duty to Christ – was therefore viewed by the Spanish as the seizure of people and land in the name of their Catholic monarch. The result was sending royal fleets and armies of conquistadors to subdue the peoples and property of America in the name of a divinely authorized and emboldened Spanish Crown.

By contrast, the approach of the English was far less domineering, and their attitude and methods were based upon a divergent view of man's stewardship of the earth. It was known by Reformed Christians[9] of England

---

7 God granted mankind a stewardship dominion over the earth in Genesis 1:26, but two opposing views of that dominion developed. One view was the idea of the divine right of a dominative state, the other view was the idea of shared dominion by the people under representative government.

8 The "divine right" of kings was a political doctrine of royal absolutism. In medieval Christendom, it asserted that a given monarch was obligated more to the Roman Catholic pope (as the personal representative of Christ) than to the people of his realm. Among later Protestant and Catholic kings, divine right was viewed as a royal right to rule directly from the will of God. In either case, the king was not seen as ultimately accountable to the people or their representatives within his realm. Because God was viewed as the only judge of an unjust king, the king could supposedly do no wrong in the eyes of his subjects. The doctrine of divine right also implied that any attempt by the people or their civil representatives to restrict his power ran contrary to the will of God and might even constitute heresy.

9 The term "Reformed" applies to Protestant Christians who, beginning in the mid-1500s, pressed for thorough biblical reforms in Western Europe. They were not part of the Roman Catholic Church but part of the Protestant movement which emerged in 1517. Protestantism was based upon the return of Christianity to the supreme authority of the Bible for its teachings of godly living. The early Reformed Christians of England, for example, undertook the translation of Holy Scripture into the language of the common Englishmen so that they could understand the true nature of God's dominion.

that God granted dominion to those who were mandated by Him to multiply and fill the earth.[10] Thus, they generally sheathed the sword and used their biblical understanding of dominion to establish families, towns, and self-government in America. Their understanding of the nature of Christ's true kingdom played a key role in shaping the much more peaceable character of England's colonial homes, churches, and civil governments.

An Overview of the Path of Liberty from the Reformation to America

The English-American approach to dominion was grounded on ideas derived from the European Reformation's great expositors of Scripture. In the mid-sixteenth century, for example, Reformed Protestant authors such as John Calvin wrote strongly against all forms of tyranny exercised in the name of Christ or anyone else. Calvin spoke out not only against the divine right pretenses of Catholic monarchs, but against the pretenses of any civil magistrates as oppressive lords over people. "*Yea,*" wrote Calvin, "*and the magistrates ought with most great diligence to bend themselves hereunto, that they suffer not the liberty of the people, of which they are appointed governors, to be in any part diminished, much less to be dissolved.*"[11] In other words, to Reformed Christians, kings as well as all civil officeholders were to safeguard rather than threaten the people's liberties so that the people could then enjoy the dignity they had in their own responsibilities under God.

These were the principles of liberty that were later forged under the banner of Reformed Christianity in England, where liberty in property was regarded as the hallmark of the earthly kingdom of Christ. In the seventeenth century the cause of defending the people's freedom was taken up by Parliament, led by strongly Reformed Christians such as John Hampden, who opposed his king's attempts to abuse the liberties of Englishmen. Hampden and many other magistrates saw it as their God-given duty to defend the people whom they represented.

---

10 The dominion mandate was further described in Genesis 1:27-28: "*So God created man in His own image; in the image of God He created him; male and female He created them. Then God blessed them, and God said to them, 'Be fruitful and multiply; fill the earth and subdue it; have dominion over the fish of the sea, over the birds of the air, and over every living thing that moves on the earth.'*"

11 John Calvin, *The Institution of Christian Religion*, 2 vols. (London, 1578), vol. 2, leaf 623b, 4:20:8.

In the 1640s, Parliament Defended the Life, Liberty, and Property of the English Subjects Against a Tyrannical King

John Hampden, one of the Puritan leaders of Parliament in the 1640s, defended Englishmen's liberty and property against King Charles I. Hampden is shown here with the title page of Parliament's 1642 *Declaration* of purpose:

“ *for the preservation of ourselves, and those who have sent us hither, and entrusted us with all they have, estate, liberty, and life.* ”

The principle of lawful resistance to royal tyranny was established by freedom-loving patriots in England. Over time, the faithful principle of the interposition of the people's representatives against tyranny brought an end to any notion of absolute power in kings.[12]

Perhaps Oliver Cromwell,[13] who was one of England's most renowned champions of the people's liberty, best expressed this Reformed English understanding of the earthly dominion of Christ. Along with his older cousin John Hampden, Cromwell had resisted his English king's tyranny with great diplomatic and military skill. To say the least, he was a

---

12 Although John Hampden was killed in battle by the king's army in 1643, the principles of liberty for which he lived were again taken up by English magistrates in the later Glorious Revolution of 1688-1689. The Glorious Revolution was the overthrow of King James II by an alliance of the English Parliament and an army led by Dutch Stadtholder William of Orange. He ascended to the English throne as King William III together with his English wife Mary II. England was thereafter formally established as a "constitutional monarchy" where the people's liberties were formally recognized.

13 Oliver Cromwell, a devout seventeenth-century Puritan, was the chief executive (or the "Lord Protector") of England from 1653-1658 – a time when England was ruled without a king. Although the state religion of the realm was officially the "Reformed Church" (as Reformed Christianity had been doctrinally taught in Europe by Calvin and others), Puritans such as Cromwell faithfully continued Calvin's legacy of civic liberty and property in England throughout the seventeenth century.

powerful advocate for the reduction of royal statism. Then, as England's chief magistrate during her short-lived Commonwealth era in the 1650s, Cromwell denounced the Royalists who *"tell us, that liberty and property, are not the badges of the Kingdom of Christ..."*[14]

Oliver Cromwell's Speeches Before Parliament in 1654 Defended Englishmen's Liberty and Property

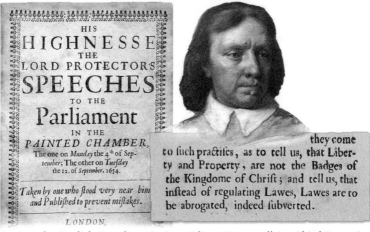

Against the English Royalists, Puritan Oliver Cromwell (as Chief Executive of the Commonwealth of England) defended liberty and property as
❝ *the badges of the Kingdom of Christ.* ❞

The republic-minded Cromwell meant that the true dominion of the earth was not the purview of powerful kings or supreme potentates in the church. Absolute dominion is Christ's alone. That dominion, then, is best retained in private families and characterized by the property they enjoy. To many Christians of earlier times, it was known that among the nations where the kingdom of Christ is genuinely respected, the enjoyment of liberty and private property also prevails.

Cromwell also recognized that these core principles of liberty and property had already been modeled by the English colonists of his time. He admired the American colonists who, rather than having their king wrest their property rights away from them in England, *"forsook their estates,*

---

14 Oliver Cromwell, *His Highness the Lord Protector's Speeches to the Parliament in the Painted Chamber ... 4 September, 1654* (London, 1654), pp. 15-16.

and inheritances here, where they lived plentifully and comfortably, for the enjoyment of their liberty, and were necessitated to go into a vast howling wilderness in New England, where they have for liberty's sake stripped themselves of all their comfort."[15]

Much of the English immigration to America during the seventeenth century was a decided attempt to establish genuine liberty upon the idea of property ownership. At times that required families forsaking everything they enjoyed in England and resettling in the untamed wilderness of America. To the English colonists, liberty and property were recognized as inseparable, and the enjoyment of their freedoms rested foremost upon the lands, the homes, and the businesses they owned.

In fact, much of the English immigration to America was a conscious attempt to counter the dominative and statist approach of Spain. For the English, a land of great opportunity was just to the north of the American colonies that were in the tyrannical grip of Spain. Though the kingdom of Spain had chosen to forcibly conquer the *geographical heart* of the Americas with its gilded riches for the taking, the more fruitful soil just to the north remained unsettled. By the gracious design of Providence, this land would, in turn, prove to be the more *fertile heart* of the Americas – a country well suited for a more peaceable and patient planting of the true kingdom of Christ and a land best suited for a lasting inheritance by industrious, freedom-loving Christians.

Thus, it was not only in Europe that the banner of the Reformation was raised upon a continent which had been previously dominated by a tyrannical model of dominion. With English immigration, the principles of the Reformation repeatedly lapped onto the eastern shores of the North American continent for over a century and a half.

"Armies" of peaceable English families went on to establish American estates of their own with a rich inheritance of liberty and property. English America then became the free and independent United States of America, as those industrious, freedom-loving Christians became the original stock of a new nation.

---

15 Oliver Cromwell, *His Highness the Lord Protector's Speeches to the Parliament in the Painted Chamber ... 12 September, 1654* (London, 1654), p. 32.

Both the illustrious era of English colonization and the triumphant era of our nation's founding provided the backdrop for America's success as a land dedicated to freedom. Our story therefore continues by explaining how the colonial legacy of property was incorporated into the foundational documents of our national republic. In all, America's story – a story that includes the fact that there is an inseparable link between the God-given blessings of liberty and private property – shows that the blessings of freedom were directly tied to her Reformed Christian inheritance. The same American story also shows that our continued enjoyment of such immeasurable blessings requires a commitment to continued vigilance.

Appreciating America's Legacy of Liberty

The question for us today remains whether we will remain true to our inheritance or be piled upon history's heap of failed governmental experiments. Americans today certainly enjoy the residual blessings of freedom that our colonial forefathers established. We still enjoy (but generally take for granted) the legacy of liberty and property that our nation's founders faithfully fought to secure for us. On this point, any proper application of the ideas in this book must take into account the sharp difference between the tyrannical policies of the Spanish colonies and the liberating policies of the English colonists. The vivid contrast between these two divergent views of the role of government gives us a timely recognition of the new face of statism that again threatens America's continued existence as a land of the free.

Understanding this all-important difference will also help free us from the blatant stereotyping that typifies our modern misinterpretations of the American colonization. Those who oppose the true Christian character of America's freedoms find it far too convenient to paint all forms of European colonization alike with the widest brush of uniform contempt. They either do not understand or fail to acknowledge the high devotion to principle that drove many faithful Christians to plant the enduring legacy of liberty and property in the western world.

2
A NEW VIEW OF THE WORLD

Christopher Columbus and the Dawn of American Colonization

THE story of sustained European colonization in America commenced with the voyage of three seaworthy ships that departed Spain on August 3, 1492. The expedition's leader, Christopher Columbus, commanded a three-masted flagship called the *Santa María* and two smaller vessels named the *Pinta* and the *Niña*. The explorers set sail with great anticipation of what they would encounter. And, armed with the widely known fact that the earth was a tremendous globe, their historic exploit was not launched in hope of finding the earth's planetary edge, but rather in hope of laying sight of the great continent of Asia, which they thought occupied the Atlantic's distant West.

The Medieval View of the World as a Globe with Three Continents

Günther Zainer published a very basic world map in 1472 showing (above left) the globe of the earth as Asia, Europe, and Africa surrounded by oceans. To the right are also fifteenth-century depictions of kings holding royal orbs, or small globes with three continents. Below is a detail of the 1436 global world map by Andrea Bianco showing the rivers of terrestrial Paradise supposedly still flowing in far-eastern Asia.

Instead of a continent, however, it was San Salvador Island – merely a dot among the greater Bahama Chain – that was first sighted by the westward explorers. They had, nonetheless, slipped through the mythical veil[1] that had long separated the East from the West as the expedition set foot in the Western Hemisphere on October 12, 1492. Flying the colors of Spain, they claimed a mere island, but in effect, they laid hold of nearly an entire hemisphere for the Crown of Spain.

Further spurred on with enthusiastic expectations, the small fleet directed its path farther to the south, soon discovering some of the more impressive islands of the Caribbean. With the encounter of island after island and a vast array of indigenous peoples, it was soon apparent that these western discoveries were of monumental importance.

Just as the triumphant fleet was preparing to depart for home in late December, however, the *Santa María* ran aground off the coast of Hispaniola in present-day Haiti. On Christmas Day in 1492, Columbus made a calculated decision to leave behind the ship's remains with just over three-dozen men, and proclaimed a small beachhead site "La Navidad." Thus by sheer default, the seed of Spain's colonial dominion was tentatively planted in the West.[2]

Discovering a Land of Grace

On his first two voyages to the West, Columbus scoured various Caribbean islands seeking out native information on where the continent of Asia might be found, but it always eluded his discovery. It was not until his third voyage in 1498 that Columbus sailed even farther south than before and at last laid sight of a vast mainland he thought to be Asia. He had, in fact, set foot upon the present-day continent of South America.

---

1 The mythical veil indicates the medieval idea that the vast, foreboding Atlantic Ocean separating Europe from Asia in the distant West could not be crossed.
2 Columbus made several attempts at settlements. Although the ill-defended La Navidad (in present-day Haiti) did not survive the year of Columbus' absence, on his second voyage in 1493 he established a larger settlement further to the east. It was named "La Isabella" in honor of Queen Isabella, the most enthusiastic backer of his ventures. That site, too, was poorly chosen and equally impossible to defend, and its survival also proved to be short-lived. But, as other better-planned and better-fortified settlements such as Santo Domingo quickly followed, sustained European colonization of the West gradually dawned under the prestige of the imperial Crown of Spain.

Even though Columbus thought he had arrived in the Far East, he did not miss an important biblical point. To him, the expedition had reached the ends of the earth and Columbus christened the landmass "The Land of Grace." He later explained that the Bible's book of Isaiah spoke vividly of the kingdom of God going forth *"to the ends of the earth."*[3] So, regardless of the particular piece of real estate he had encountered, the discoveries of Columbus were certainly a leap forward in the fulfillment of that prophetic book of Scripture.

Columbus' voyages eventually turned European Christendom's focus in an all-new direction. Before his historic discoveries, the aim of medieval Christianity had been primarily eastward to reclaim Jerusalem, the capital city of ancient Israel and the original birthplace of the Church.[4] After Columbus' discoveries, which he described by various biblical terms such as the "New Jerusalem" and even the "New Earth," Europe's attention was largely redirected from the East to the West. For Spain, there was now a whole new world to be conquered under the banner of the Roman Catholic Church. Even for Europeans in general, the name that stuck in the popular vernacular for the impressive new discoveries by Columbus and others was "The New World."

Illusions of an Earthly Paradise

Besides the misconception by Columbus that he had encountered the continent of Asia, another considerable error accompanied his view of the Atlantic's western shore. The great explorer also assumed that he was near the rediscovery of the Bible's ancient paradise called the Garden of Eden.[5] Besides calling his newly-discovered continental landmass the "Land of

---

3 The book of Isaiah has the greatest number of prophecies that the Gospel will go out to the entire world. Isaiah 24:16, 42:10, 45:22, 49:6, and 52:10 (to name just a few passages) each speak of either the kingdom of Messiah or His salvation being extended to *"the ends of the earth."* Columbus began writing his *Book of Prophecies* in 1501, explaining that he saw the western discoveries as an important part of the fulfillment of the prophecies in Isaiah.

4 Over the previous centuries, European princes and potentates had sent fleets and vast armies to the Near East in a series of Crusades. They were intended to retake what was called "The Holy Land" from the Muslims who had previously taken it from Christians by force.

5 The Garden of Eden was described in the Bible's book of Genesis as being the place where the first man, Adam, and his wife Eve lived after they were created by God. The Bible speaks of the literal garden called Eden as having been on earth: *"The LORD God planted a garden eastward in Eden, and there He put the man whom He had formed"* (Genesis 2:8).

Grace," Columbus also named the coastal region of the new continent "Paria" in line with his belief that he was near the biblical paradise.

Though the name "Paria" (or "Parias") itself did not literally mean "paradise," it accompanied a medieval legend regarding the existence of the earthly Eden.[6] In fact, the popular medieval tale indiscriminately combined an ancient Roman myth of "Paria" (a supposed utopia) with the literal account of ancient biblical Eden that once existed in the East. And, with the explorers encountering the most lush flora and fauna having yet been discovered by Europeans, many believed that the biblical paradise, along with its unfathomable riches, would soon be found in the West.

The Idea of "Parias," or a Mythical New World Paradise

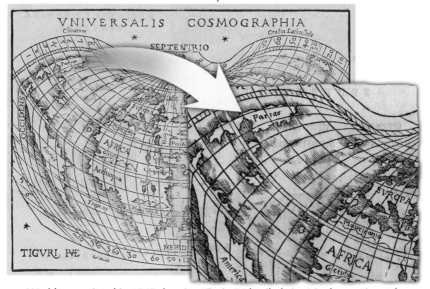

World map printed in 1545 showing "Parias" (detailed view) in the continental region of the New World that would become known as North America.

---

6 Isidore of Seville was bishop of Seville from AD 599 to AD 636. His work, *Etymologiae*, was a compilation of diverse texts incorporating Roman legends such as "Paria" with the description of the biblical Eden. His text, which was held as geographically and prophetically compelling throughout the Middle Ages, was first published in 1472, long before Columbus' discoveries. Isidore's legend popularized the view that the biblical Eden lay in far-eastern Asia, stating that "*the Lord planted a garden eastward in Eden . . . and He placed at the East of the Garden of Eden, Cherubims, and a flaming sword, which turned every way, to keep the way of the Tree of Life.*" So, at the time of Columbus' ventures west in the late 1400s, he also thought Eden was an existing geographical location. (Citation and quote from Thomas Suárez: *Shedding the Veil: Mapping the European Discovery of America and the World* (Singapore: World Scientific Publishing Company, 1992).

Such thinking entirely missed the fundamental fact that God's true paradise cannot be found in any terrestrial Eden. It missed the fact that Christ's earthly kingdom is most immediately expressed within the hearts of God's faithful. It completely missed the fact that His kingdom is then lived out by families within local communities and civil society at large by the resident influence of godly homes and churches. Such thinking also illustrates the myth that a utopian paradise of any kind could be discovered on earth and then be claimed and controlled by earthly potentates.[7]

In the medieval world, these powerful potentates were primarily those who ruled within the power structure of the Roman Catholic Church, but they also included compliant Catholic lords and princes in the state who ruled under the Church. Thus, the aspiration of Columbus and other explorers of finding an earthly paradise certainly fit with medieval misconceptions of the kingdom of Christ,[8] but it was, in reality, completely contrary to the entire nature of His true earthly kingdom.

Even after the western discoveries proved not to be part of Asia, but part of a previously unknown hemisphere, myths of a New World paradise persisted. Utopian ideas about the western discoveries prevailed, for example, in the European thinking that an American native was a "noble savage"[9] – a myth that the most primitive man was somehow closer to God than the redeemed of Christ. Beyond that error, many later explorers still persisted in hoping to discover a remnant of a physical paradise. In the early 1500s, for example, the Spanish explorer Juan Ponce de León thought that a legendary fountain of eternal youth associated with an earthly paradise

---

7 A book called *Utopia* was published by an English Roman Catholic diplomat, Sir Thomas More, in 1516. *Utopia* was a work depicting a fictional island society, but from More's viewpoint, one that had more ideal religious, social, and political customs than existed in early sixteenth-century Europe.

8 Columbus envisioned untold gold and riches accompanying the earthly Eden. He had hoped that when "Paradise" was discovered, its riches could be used to fund a great Crusade into the Middle East. By that, Columbus saw Christian dominion in terms of the Roman Catholic potentates' military triumph over Christianity's historic foe, the powerful Muslim potentates.

9 The idea of a "noble savage" expressed the sentiments that a primitive man – a native of the New World – was noble because he was unencumbered by civilization or biblical revelation. All men, whether primitive or not, had been corrupted by the sin of Adam in Eden. Although the term "noble savage" itself did not appear until it was used in John Dryden's 1672 play *The Conquest of Granada*, it was identified with the earlier mystique that virgin America was closer to God than Christianity. The idea of a noble savage also became associated with the later sentimental myth of the moral innocence of all indigenous Americans simply because of their primitive conditions, and it was also part of the mystique behind the even later notion of a metaphorical goddess of nature called "Mother Earth."

could be found in his newly discovered Florida, or "flowered land." But, like his contemporaries, Ponce de León's hopes of finding any semblance of an earthly utopia were, of course, disappointed. He, in fact, eventually died in his quest to discover eternal life in the New World.

Even as time went by, Europeans persisted in thinking of the "New World" as a distinctive setting for God's grace on earth. And though the early explorers were wrong in their expectations of finding any terrestrial utopia, the Western Hemisphere would provide many Europeans with unbridled possibilities in advancing the true kingdom of Christ. As Christians later streamed west across the Atlantic, the dream of establishing pure and undefiled Christianity on virgin soil was a key motivating factor. Consequently, in that real sense, the basic idea of the "New World" became a powerful metaphor for the enjoyment of the liberty in Christ which accompanies the genuine Gospel.

In the end, the sense of the New World as a distinctive land of God's grace had significant merit. Throngs of Europeans would eventually escape the tyranny of the Old World and find true solace and prosperity for their familial homes in the New World. And, although the promise of finding a literal paradise was merely the product of medieval fantasy, the idea of the New World as a refuge from governmental oppression afforded many faithful families the enjoyment of the genuine blessings of liberty and property that they found described in Scripture.

Continents Named "America"

As it turned out, the southern continent discovered by Columbus on his third voyage would not be named "Paria" or the "Land of Grace." It would not even be named after the aforementioned Columbus who had discovered the New World.[10] The Italian explorer Amerigo Vespucci reported that he had previously navigated the same coastline of the southern

---

10 A significant point in later American history is that honoring Columbus as the explorer who discovered the New World spread rapidly after American independence in the 1700s. During the last decade of the eighteenth century the name "Columbia" was ascribed to the new federal capital, "The District of Columbia." South Carolina's capital city, "Columbia," as well as the capital of Ohio, called "Columbus," were both named in honor of Christopher Columbus. The naming of the Columbia River and other places "Columbia" or "Columbus" were each a credit to the explorer.

continent in 1497, just before Columbus' third voyage. This, and the fact that Vespucci was also the first explorer to propose that the new discovery was a previously unknown continent, led German cartographer Martin Waldseemüller in 1507 to name it "America" after Amerigo Vespucci.

Waldseemüller's publication of Vespucci's explorations included a magnificent twelve-sheet wall map which labeled the large southern landmass "America." The map itself revolutionized Europe's concept of the whole world, not only by ascribing the name "America" to the great discovery, but by being the first map in history to confirm that there was a massive and entirely new, unexplored region of the earth.

Somewhat surprisingly, Waldseemüller's famous map also labeled a then lesser-known and ill-defined land extending to the northwest "Parias" (as in Columbus' idea of Paria). In time, explorations to the north would prove this northern land to be continental as well. It would eventually become quite a distinguished site for God's true kingdom extending to the ends of the earth, as was promised in the book of Isaiah.

The New World Named "America" after Amerigo Vespucci

Martin Waldseemüller's 1507 world map was the first to show the new discoveries as separate continents. "America," for Amerigo Vespucci, is named on the southern continent (lower left and on detail). "Parias" is indicated on the large landmass in the northern New World (upper left arrow).

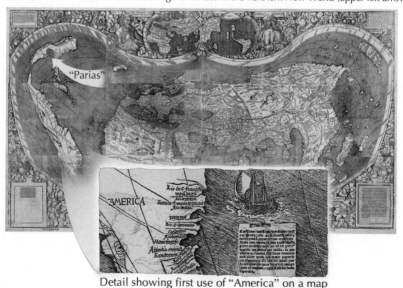

Detail showing first use of "America" on a map

The New World's northern continent would indeed fulfill the idea of a figurative paradise – at least as a refuge longingly sought out by later Protestants following the European Reformation.[11] Then, in God's good timing, the true promises of the Gospel of Christ would be extended to the proverbial "ends of the earth," and they would find fertile soil in the distinctive part of the New World known as "North America."

A Revolution in Europe's World View

Martin Waldseemüller's map, printed at Strasbourg, France in 1507, revolutionized the thinking of Europeans regarding the physical makeup of the world. That, however, would not be the only revolution in the minds of early sixteenth-century Europeans. It was exactly ten years after the publication of Waldseemüller's map that another revolution commenced in nearby Germany. This, however, would be a revolution enlightening Europeans' hearts as well as their minds.

In late 1517 the European Reformation commenced with the bold protests of an Augustinian monk named Martin Luther. Before that time, Luther had been a devout Roman Catholic theologian, but like others, he had begun to protest the Church's numerous theological and administrative corruptions. Luther particularly disputed the claim that "indulgences"[12] purchased by individuals from the Roman Church could free them from God's punishment of sin. Luther and those who read the Bible with hearts having been opened toward God and His eternal Word knew that He alone grants any and all blessings of an afterlife.

The hand-written *Ninety-five Theses* that Luther quite literally nailed to the door of All Saints' Church in Wittenberg, Germany on October 31, 1517, boldly confronted the immorality of selling the disgraceful paper

---

11 The Protestant Reformation in Europe began in the early 1500s as an attempt to reform the Roman Catholic Church. Particularly troubling was the Church hierarchy of authority known as the "Magisterium," which claimed that all power emanated from Rome over every aspect of Christian living. Protestants rejected that claim of authority and practiced the Christan faith apart from the Church of Rome.

12 An indulgence was a full or partial remission of punishment for sin in the afterlife. It was believed that before a Christian entered eternal rest, temporal punishment was required after one's physical death to make payment for sins that had not been absolved. An indulgence that was granted (or most often sold) by the Roman Church supposedly drew upon the merits of prior saints (or even Christ) from a "Treasure House of Merit," allowing a penitent sinner to escape this kind of temporal punishment and to readily enjoy the bliss of the afterlife.

indulgences. This action was simply emblematic of an ever-widening European disgust with the audacious practices of Rome. That single act of protest against Church corruption therefore unleashed a much wider protest known as Protestantism. Luther had, in effect, begun a sweeping cultural protest against the medieval Roman Church by implementing the more lively and invigorating principles of God's Word.

At the time, Luther's actions may have appeared much less momentous than sending royal fleets to the New World, but its effects would be every bit as monumental. Luther's stance for biblical truth provided the spark that ignited a sweeping Christian movement not only throughout his native Germany, but throughout the rest of central and northern Europe. Luther's resolve and continued unwillingness to compromise resulted in the larger cultural movement now known as the Reformation. This resulted in local churches and even nations completely severing themselves from the Roman Church's control, and with it, the entire medieval order of vassal slavery under that Church gradually unraveled.

The driving force for it all was the authority of God's printed Word, known as "la Biblia" (the Bible), coming into the hands of scholars and merchants alike. The Roman Church had before suppressed and even forbidden the common laity's access to Holy Scripture. The introduction of the printing press by Johannes Gutenberg in the mid-1400s changed everything. Mass-produced Bibles became available on the open market in a most astounding demonstration of the triumph of free enterprise.

Edition after edition of the Bible poured from the first European presses by the end of the fifteenth century. And, with the Bible becoming even more widely read in the sixteenth century, tens of thousands of souls were being turned from religious superstition to truth and faith. Following the onset of the Reformation, Bibles began to be published in the languages that the common people could read and understand. As the principles of God's Word were more widely studied and applied, hundreds of thousands of souls were then freed from their former vassal servitude to earthly lords unto a godly sense of familial dignity and private industry amid Reformed Christian communities.

Printed Bibles and the Rediscovery of God's Written Word

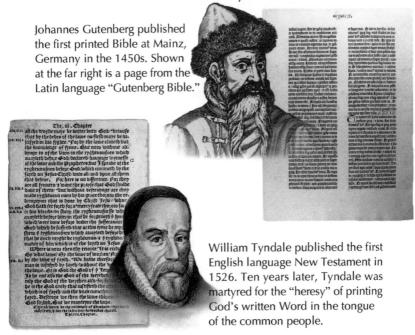

Johannes Gutenberg published the first printed Bible at Mainz, Germany in the 1450s. Shown at the far right is a page from the Latin language "Gutenberg Bible."

William Tyndale published the first English language New Testament in 1526. Ten years later, Tyndale was martyred for the "heresy" of printing God's written Word in the tongue of the common people.

Consequently, two concurrent revolutions reshaped Europe's understanding of its importance in the world. The first was the discovery of a geographical "New World," and the second was the rediscovery of God's written Word. And, with both coming on the heels of the invention of mass publication, the two revolutions commenced in unison and ushered in a worldview that changed the entire course of subsequent world events.

3
A FAILED MODEL OF DOMINION

The Medieval Idea of Dominion

BY the time of the first European discoveries in America, the authority
of the medieval Church had become nearly absolute. It alone sat atop the
power structure of feudal Europe. It alone reigned over individual souls
and the property of families as well as the realms of nobles and princes.
In fact, during the centuries leading up to the Reformation, the Roman
Church claimed to be God's voice in all matters public or private, with its
pontiff having the final say over all the kings and kingdoms of Western
Europe.[1]

The typical European monarch could do little to resist this medieval
"Vicar of Christ," who was known as the "pope" – a term which simply
meant "father." A nearly-deified father is a good description for the kind
of earthly honor that this single potentate was afforded over European
homes and monarchs alike. When the pope demanded conformity to the
dictates of his Church, it came with an implied threat of excommunication
by which any man or any prince could lose his eternal soul. For private
men this also meant, in effect, becoming an outlaw. To a prince it meant
losing his entire public dignity as well as his nation's respect among the
other Crowns of Europe.

---

1 Feudalism was the social order that existed in the Middle Ages under the medieval Roman Catholic
Church. The feudal order was composed of a set of reciprocal legal and military obligations that involved earthly lords and their vassal subjects. The Church confirmed the key positions of lordship (including the monarch), and it was the lording nobility who owned the land. A vassal was a person who
was granted conditional possession of a piece of property by the lord through pledging his allegiance
in homage, paying fees, and providing military service to him. The common peasant under the vassal
had no standing in the feudal system, but he provided needed labor in exchange for a right to exist on
a small plot of land owned by his superiors.
The Catholic Church hierarchy, which supposedly had dominion over the eternal souls of the lords,
vassals, and peasants alike, was central at every level of feudal society. The local parish church and
regional cathedral were places where everyone came to offer their regular homage to their heavenly
Lord, and the Catholic Church defined the terms of everyone's religious service to Him. Beyond that,
the earthly lord-vassal relationship was not restricted to civil positions, as Church bishops and clerics
also acted as lords over vast tracts of land of their own and played a significant role in the civil policies
of all Western European principalities.

Power politics, as they were practiced in the Middle Ages, occasionally brought England's own Crown into conflict with the Roman Church. For example, England viewed the appointment of English bishops and archbishops as a matter of her own national concern rather than Rome's. The Church, however, viewed such appointments as a matter of its exclusive Catholic, or "universal," right. When, in 1207, King John asserted England's rights by trying to influence the appointment of the local Archbishop of Canterbury, he quickly provoked the ire of the Roman pontiff. A papal legate (or political representative) soon presented the English king with a clear ultimatum to either fully capitulate to the Roman pope or be excommunicated from the Catholic Church.

King John Offers the English Crown to a Roman Legate in 1213, Indicating His Submission to the Pope as England's Overlord

The submission of England's King John to the papal legate Pandulph, as illustrated in the 1570 edition of John Foxe's *Actes and Monumentes* (later known as *Foxe's Book of Martyrs*).

Pressed to the point of choosing between grace and disgrace, the reluctant king finally submitted for the sake of preserving both his soul and his realm. In a profoundly poignant ceremony in May of 1213, King John relinquished his rule, literally handing the crown on his head over to the papal legate. However, the crown was promptly handed back to

John as a formal gesture confirming that the king and his realm alike were vassals of supreme Roman authority. The whole ordeal provided a powerful example to other European monarchs of the coercive strength of the sovereign dominion – both temporal and eternal – that emanated from the pontiff in Rome.

Dominion and the Crusades

Such threats of excommunication drove the most powerful principalities and powers to submit to Rome's ecclesiastical dominion over Europe. Although under the banner of papal supremacy, many of those same kingdoms developed a significant military prowess, even undertaking great military exploits on behalf of the Roman Church. For example, as military power began to accumulate in Europe during the Middle Ages, Western Christendom began a series of armed Crusades against the Muslims who had dominated the Middle East for centuries.

The city of Jerusalem – the capital of the ancient kingdom of Israel and the very birthplace of the Christian faith – had fallen under the grip of the Islamic religion. It was from that beloved region known as the "Holy Land" that the Lord Jesus Himself had commissioned His disciples to "*Go therefore and make disciples of all the nations*."[2] Now that same site had fallen, not just to any outside oppressors, but to the fiercest opponents and most dreaded persecutors of the historic Christian faith.

Beginning in the eleventh century, various European monarchies began an historic series of prolonged campaigns to recapture the Holy Land and restore it to the sole domain of Christendom. These "Christian" Crusades were in large part a military reaction to the violence of the Islamic religion. With the objective being to reestablish the medieval model of forced dominion, however, the crusaders violated the very nature of the peaceable Gospel Commission given by the Lord. In other words, the use of offensive force and plunder perfectly mirrored the Muslims' methods of subduing large numbers of people and vast tracts of land, but it hardly reflected the peaceable dominion of the true kingdom of Christ.

---

2 See the "Great Commission" found in Matthew 28:18-20.

The European Crusades to Reclaim the Middle East

Contemporary manuscript of the recovery of
Bethlehem from the Muslims in AD 1099

Crusader coin minted in Jerusalem honoring Europe's victory

Another no-less important error employed by the medieval Church also began with the Crusades. Early on in the Crusades, the Church of Rome began to grant indulgences for absolution (or pardon) of sin as an ecclesiastical function of the pope. At first, limited indulgences for sin were granted to troops who engaged in various forms of violence – not only against armed opponents, but against peaceable people, families, and whole communities that were forcefully subdued.

The earliest record of a *plenary* indulgence (or a "complete" pardon from the penalties of sin) was Pope Urban II's decree in 1095 that such an indulgence was to be granted to the crusaders. Some believed that forgiveness applied to all who enlisted and participated in a Crusade. Others believed that a crusader must actually fight Muslims or even die in battle for the pope's forgiveness to apply. But, regardless of the specific way a pardon might be credited, it was, in effect, borrowing from another erroneous tactic used by their Islamic opponents: to associate an engagement in an armed religious battle with benefits in the afterlife.

As time went by, the proliferation of indulgences became a significant source of revenue for a Church hierarchy that was ever-growing in its dominion over the land and the people of Europe. And, by associating eternal forgiveness with military conquest in distant lands, indulgences contributed immensely to the popularity of the Crusades as well as to the illusion of the necessary political supremacy of the Roman Church.

Over time, both royal and financial backers of the Crusades were also offered forgiveness through indulgences, allowing for economic as well as military support of the Church to be associated with a meritorious pardon of sin. Hence, the whole scheme of papal decrees and indulgences not only contributed to the opulence of the Catholic Church in Europe, but its supposed power of forgiveness emboldened European kings in their sense of a divine right of foreign conquest.

The Crusading Spirit Turns Toward the West

Recapturing the Holy Land was the chief military objective of Europe's crusading spirit before the voyages of western discovery. However, from then on, the medieval idea of crusading became less a matter of taking back the Middle East and more a matter of taking full advantage of the possibilities in the more distant West. The Western Hemisphere held untold riches for a Catholic realm that could subdue America and dominate the Atlantic trade. And with those riches abundantly confirmed by Columbus and the other explorers flying the Spanish flag, Spain, of course, seized her opportunity.

Just before launching the first exploratory expedition by Columbus in 1492, the Spanish Crown had expelled the remnant of an invasive Muslim dynasty from within her own southernmost borders. Spain was motivated to now expand her imperial horizons and increase her foreign revenue stream. It was then not entirely coincidental that Columbus sailed westward across the Atlantic the same year that the Muslims were expelled by Spain's co-reigning monarchs, Ferdinand ("Ferdinand the Catholic") and his wife Isabella (Queen of Castile).[3] From that time on, the same

---

3 In 1469, the Roman Catholic Crowns of the kingdoms of Aragon and Castile were united by the

kind of supposed divinely-sanctioned power that had been previously flexed against the Islamic powers in the Middle East was now unfurled in massive fleets to conquer the New World in the West.

The Spanish Idea of Dominion in America

For Spain, American colonization meant the same kind of conquest and dominion as in the prior Crusades. It also meant gold, silver, and native subjects for the Spanish Crown along with souls for the Roman Church. The Spanish approach to conversion therefore amounted to sending armies of conquistadors to subdue the peoples, their resources, and their lands on behalf of both the king and the pontiff.

The justification for Spain's claim of absolute supremacy in the West came in the form of papal decrees and bulls. The first official edict handed down from Rome regarding the New World was the 1493 *Bull of the Inter Caetera*. As soon as the news of Columbus' maiden voyage arrived in Europe, Pope Alexander VI affirmed Spain's sovereignty over her discoveries. Before the nature or extent of those discoveries could be known to Spain, Rome, or anyone else, the pope sanctioned the Spanish Crown with a divine right of dominion over all land and people in the following words:

> [B]*y the authority of Almighty God conferred upon us in blessed Peter and of the vicarship of Jesus Christ, which we hold on earth, do by tenor of these presents, should any of said islands have been found by your envoys and captains, give, grant, and assign to you and your heirs and successors … forever, together with all their dominions, cities, camps, places, and villages, and all rights, ju-risdictions, and appurtenances* [significant amendments], *all is-lands and mainlands found and to be found, discovered and to be discovered towards the west and south…*[4]

marriage of Ferdinand II of Aragon and Isabella I of Castile. In early 1492, they captured Granada on the southwestern corner of Europe, ending the last remnant of the 780-year Muslim dominion of that area of the continent. Ferdinand and Isabella centralized royal power at the expense of local nobility, and the word España ("Spain" in English) began to be used for designation of the unity of the two kingdoms. With her far-reaching military and religious exploits, Spain then emerged as one of the leading powers of Europe.

4 Francis Gardiner Davenport, ed., *European Treaties Bearing on the History of the United States and its Dependencies to 1648* (Washington D.C., Carnegie Institution of Washington, 1917), pp. 77. The

Bull *Inter Caetera Divinae Maestati* of 1493
Granting the Spanish Crown a Divine Right
of Dominion Over Land and People

Pope Alexander VI and a copy of the Bull granting Spain's King Ferdinand
and Queen Isabella exclusive "divine" right over the newly discovered
peoples and lands in the West due to the explorations
of Christopher Columbus in 1492.

This historic bull also included a papal mandate to convert the indigenous people for the glory of the Roman Church, and it was interpreted by the Spanish Crown as a divine right – a divinely sanctioned justification of forced conversion, conquest, and plunder. In effect, it was a sweeping decree to subdue all of the native families, tribes, and property by military might and forceful conversion to a Catholic king and his Church. And, according to the methods employed during the prior Crusades, conversion to the medieval Catholic religion was neither a matter of personal conviction nor finding freedom in Christ. Implemented at the point of a sword, the conversion of the native Americans was a matter of imperial policy and forceful surrender into vassal subjection.

Mass slavery, theft, and even butchery therefore characterized Spain's methods of American colonization. To the natives, the arrival of Spanish Christendom was indeed more synonymous with an all-out Crusade than

text in the original Latin: Francis Newton Thorpe, ed., *The Federal and State Constitutions, Colonial Charters, and Other Organic Laws of the States, Territories, and Colonies Now or Heretofore Forming The United States of America Compiled and Edited under the Act of Congress of June 30, 1906*, vol. 7 (Washington, D.C.: Government Printing Office, 1909), pp. 41-43.

with any semblance of liberation from their former tyrannical rulers. Though the American Indians were freed from the often-tortuous brutality of their own native masters, those who survived Spain's onslaught were simply incorporated into her colonial regime with a status of conquered foes rather than as converts with any degree of Christian dignity.

The "Bull of Crusade" in America Granted to King Philip II of Spain by Pope Gregory XIII in 1572

Decree by Pope Gregory XIII granting Philip II divine right of conquest in the New World, with details of the title and the indulgences for services performed for the Spanish king and the Church.

Later in the sixteenth century, additional papal bulls with many added features reconfirmed the divine right of the Spanish king. The *Bulla de Cruzada* ("Bull of Crusade") of 1572 issued to Philip II[5] included the kind of indulgences indicative of the earlier Middle Eastern Crusades against the Muslims. This bull granted by Pope Gregory XIII offered the same indulgent forgiveness, but now for services performed in behalf of Spain's

---

5 Philip II, who lived from 1527 to 1598, was King of Spain, Naples, and Sicily, and when he married Mary I, he was King of England from 1554 to 1558. His international policy was a combination of Catholic devotion and imperial self-interest. He considered himself the defender of Catholic Europe against the forces of the Protestant Reformation. He engaged in frequent wars against what he saw as heretical nations and waged a bitter campaign against a Dutch uprising. In 1588 the English defeated Philip's Spanish Armada, thwarting his invasion of the then Protestant realm.

further conquest of America. The decree was the death knell for the remnant Incan Empire in South America,[6] bringing the last of its gilt-laden lands into Philip's hands. Philip also used his divine right pretenses to further tighten his grip on his other Spanish holdings, squeezing as much additional revenue as possible from each of his American colonies.

The added revenue was not without a pointed objective. At the time, Philip II was also in the process of prosecuting an aggressive campaign against Protestantism in Europe. The "Counter-Reformation" was an explosive and expensive effort to halt the growing influence of Reformed Christianity on continental Europe. This effort employed an aggressive Inquisition[7] to root out all so-called "heretics" of a non-Catholic persuasion. It required a vast network of informers, interrogators, prosecutors, and at times, even armies. Thus, the papal bulls that encouraged a more vigorous western Crusade in the later 1500s and provided Philip the religious cover for his increased plunder of Central and South America, also helped to fund the most aggressive warfare against faithful European Christians since the ancient martyrdoms under the pagan Caesars of Rome.[8]

From the 1570s on, Philip II worked diligently to control every facet of life in Spain's dominions across the Atlantic. His Crown agents in America not only called into question the titles to all American lands formerly granted to the conquistadors in payment for their service, but they imposed a more rigorous stream of administrative regulations. In that

---

6 Spanish conquistadors led by Francisco Pizarro explored southward from Central America, reaching Inca territory on the western side of South America by 1526. The Inca Empire was a wealthy land and a source of great treasure for Spain. Pizarro conquered much of the empire in the early 1530s, and in the 1570s the last Inca strongholds were conquered. When the last of their rulers were captured and executed, the Incan Empire came to an end.

7 An Inquisition was an organized and brutal prosecution of the opponents of the medieval Roman Church. Early on, the suppression of so-called "heresy" involved confiscations of property and imprisonment, and then later, torture or execution. In the 13th century, Pope Gregory IX authorized aggressive Inquisitions to root out and suppress hidden, anti-Catholic heresies. In the name of the pope and with his full authority, inquisitors worked secretly to spy out heretical offenses and then used local authorities to establish a public tribunal and to prosecute all offenders as infidels.

8 The Reformed English scholar John Foxe published several editions of his *Actes and Monumentes* (later known as *Foxe's Book of Martyrs*) in the late 1500s. It was an exhaustive account of the waves of tyranny inflicted upon Christians since the apostolic times. Beginning with Foxe's 1570 edition, the book included a large "Table," or illustrated chart, that implicitly compared the Roman Catholic Inquisition in Europe by despots such as Philip II to the "*heathen Tyrannies of Rome*" of earlier centuries. In other words, the persecution of Reformed Protestants by Philip and other Catholic potentates was compared to the tactics of the ancient "heathen" Roman emperors against the earliest Christians.

way, the central government of Spain tightened its grip over both her own colonists and the indigenous Americans alike. And, by controlling the land as well as the people on it, Philip sought to satisfy his ever-increasing thirst for empire and reap a very purposeful reward by the ongoing plunder of America's vast resources and revenues.

Dominion by an Absolute State

By the late 1500s Spain's dominion in America was in nearly every way absolute and despotic. The king controlled the entire governmental apparatus of the colonies, and his colonial administrators controlled almost every aspect of Spanish-American life.

Thus, we have an instructive example of governmental tyranny on an exceptional scale. In effect, the regime of Philip II in America marked the epitome of absolute statism west of the Atlantic. His despotic policies came in the name of divine right, which violated every principle of true biblical dominion. His tactics of controlling all people, property, commerce, and resources represent the very trademark of governmental tyranny. Under Philip II, there were few rights of property or the kind of heaven-blessed dominion that should reign within peaceable, private homes. Any absolute governmental regime – whether it comes with the claim of divine right or in the form of godless humanism – is ultimately characterized by an ignorance of God's biblical mandates and a drive for its own domination, regulation, and control of the people's lives, liberty, and property.

In contrast to the methods of Spain, the biblical principles of the Reformation were being applied in Protestant communities of Europe, and a divergent view of dominion was emerging. This was the kind of dominion derived by applying heavenly principles to every aspect of earthly life. It began to yield the kind of meaningful liberty in which the people enjoyed both their private and public blessings under God. The result was the rise of civil rule where governing officials were viewed as public servants – as the protectors of the people's interests and as guardians of the property and resources that families themselves owned.

Truly Christian Principles of Sovereignty

The English model of colonization would be quite different from that of Spain. According to the tenets of the Reformed Christian faith, England's idea of sovereignty set a course quite the opposite to that of statist Spain. The Reformed Christian approach to sovereignty was, after all, based upon a wholly different Sovereign. The true kingdom of Christ would be planted home-by-home, town-by-town, and colony-by-colony on the soil of North America as the ever-lengthening effect of the European Reformation.

The Reformed Christian faith found its divine sanction in the decrees of Scripture rather than in bulls and indulgences from Rome. Here we must again give due credit to the astute Protestant expositors of the Bible such as the bold theologian John Calvin. For example, in his 1536 dedication of one of the most enduring of all the Protestant publications, *The Institution of Christian Religion*, Calvin encouraged the reigning monarch of his native France to put truly royal principles first. *"This consideration constitutes true royalty,"* Calvin implored his king, *"to acknowledge yourself in the government of your kingdom to be the minister of God."*[9]

At that time, the king of France was the devout Catholic Francis I, and he was being anything but a civil minister of God. Francis had, in fact, just undertaken the first sweeping wave of persecution against the Protestants in his realm – towns and communities of loyal but Reformed Christians were being targeted. To Calvin, the entire legitimacy of the French monarchy was now at stake, and in the dedication of his *Institutes*, he therefore boldly admonished Francis in no uncertain terms:

> *For where the glory of God is not made the end of the government, it is not a legitimate sovereignty, but usurpation, and he is deceived who expects lasting prosperity in that kingdom which is not ruled by the scepter of God, that is, His Holy Word...*[10]

---

9 John Calvin, *The Institution of Christian Religion* (London, 1578), vol. 1, leaf iii3a. Dedication: *To the Most Mighty and Noble Prince Francis ...* 1578. But with wording updated as per John Allen's translation, 1930 edition, pp. 22-23. The biblical passage to which Calvin was referring regarding a civil ruler was Romans 13:4: *"For he is God's minister to you for good."*
10 Ibid.

For Calvin and those who revered that Holy Word as the true scepter over all the potentates of the world, the true objective was respecting God's glory and dominion. Calvin knew that true sovereignty resided with one – and only one – absolute Potentate. It would be the exclusive character of that Sovereign's dominion spelled out in His written Word that would give Reformed Christianity (and the Reformed Christians who came to America) a distinctive strength of character.

John Calvin's *The Institution of Christian Religion* with the Dedication to the King of France

 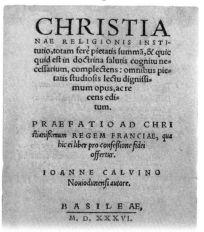

Later commemorative portrait of John Calvin with title page of the 1536 (first) edition of *Christianae Religionis Institutio,* which became known in England as Calvin's *Institutes.* The title page indicates the "Praefatio" (or introductory dedication) to the king of France.

To adequately appreciate the distinctively English approach to American colonization, it is first necessary to understand the Reformed Christian view of earthly dominion. Frankly, it is impossible to grasp the heart of England's whole approach to American colonization without an adequate understanding of the views of Christ's dominion that awakened her earliest colonial visionaries. To understand those instrumental ideas, the following chapter offers a rough framework of some of the core Reformed Christian ideas of biblical dominion and godly civil government.

4
THE BIBLICAL IDEA OF DOMINION

The First Protests Against Invasive Dominion

IT was an amazing timing of Providence in that the European discovery of vast new lands and peoples in America predated the Reformation by only a few decades. With the Protestant Reformation, the abusive medieval ideas of dominion began to be discredited, and the recovery of biblical ideas of dominion began to turn Europe in a new direction.

As we have already seen, to those who read the Bible – to those who understood what it said – the whole idea of granting a papal indulgence as a pardon for sin was recognized as preposterous. To Martin Luther and many other Protestants, the invasive nature of the Crusades was as unbiblical as the indulgences that funded them. In his *Explanations of the Ninety-five Theses* printed in 1518, Luther condemned the offensive use of force by so-called "Christian Europe" which had, in fact, victimized Middle Eastern cities and families in the name of the Savior.

That being said, shortly after Luther spoke out against the Crusades, a sweeping Muslim invasion into Europe itself seemed to undermine his arguments, at least against Christian militarism. With the fall of Hungary to the Turks in 1526 and the Muslim siege of Vienna, Austria in 1529, Luther was scapegoated. His criticisms of the Crusades were blamed for Europe's inability to successfully resist Christianity's historic foe.

Luther was thus compelled to explain his position on biblical dominion and to address the idea of a "just war." In his 1529 treatise *On War Against the Turks*, Luther addressed the offensive nature of the Islamic religion itself, stating that it was, most of all, an outright apostasy against the Triune God. Islam's military inroads into Europe were also (obviously enough) an invasive affront to peaceable cities and innocent families. To Luther, a Muslim invader was lawless *"like a pirate or highwayman, he seeks to rob and ravage other lands."*[1] In laying out the biblical sanction

---

1 Martin Luther, *Selected Writings of Martin Luther*, 4 vols., ed. Theodore Tappert (Philadelphia: Fortress Press, 1967), vol. 4, p. 18.

for military resistance to such a godless invasion, he condemned the Muslim conqueror who *"does not fight from necessity or to protect his land."*[2] In biblical terms, Luther laid out the justification for a defensive and truly Christian war. And, with equal fervor, he condemned the godless and invasive approach to taking dominion by the Muslim hoards and the Catholic crusaders alike.

Luther's *Ninety-Five Theses* Published in the Autumn of 1517 Set the Protestant Reformation in Motion

– 1517 Latin Edition of *Ninety-Five Theses*

Luther Opposes Muslims' Invasive Dominion in his 1529 *Sermon Against the Turks*

Affirming the principle that a defensive war against tyrannical invaders is a just war.

– 1529 *Sermon Against the Turks*

With this important clarification of the Protestant position, Luther helped set a proper Christian posture for the military defense of Europe. Protecting and defending Christian homes and cities against armed invaders was, in fact, recognized as an obliging biblical cause. For Luther there was no contradiction in using the power of the sword (military or civil) in defending the Christian institutions of Europe. It was a matter of the proper use of that force. For Protestants, the issue with the Muslims was one of using arms in a godly, defensive war against ravenous invaders.

---

2 Ibid.

Luther also strongly affirmed Christians holding positions of civil authority, saying: *"Would to God they were all Christians, or that no one could be a prince unless he were a Christian!"*[3] Thus, for the early Protestants, there was no opposition to Christians serving in positions of civil authority and then using that protective authority to safeguard the faith. The issue remained one of employing only biblical (and thus legitimate) means in a defense of the institutions of family, church, and state that were ordained by God.

Many Protestants continued to oppose the use of aggressive, invasive force; *"for Christ's name,"* Luther explained, *"is used for sin and shame and is thus dishonored."*[4] In advancing Christ's true dominion, the core issue was propagating His kingdom through means that brought glory to God and honor to the true faith. There were biblically prescribed means in both the spiritual and earthly connotations of the holy text. Those means were spelled out in Scripture, and those connotations were best described by a later contemporary of Luther named John Calvin.

John Calvin and the Dominion of Christ

Even though Luther's dynamic reforms preceded those of Calvin, their careers overlapped considerably. Martin Luther was born in 1483 and died in 1546. John Calvin was born in 1509 and died in 1564. With Calvin's conversion in the early 1530s (somewhat after Luther's), their active careers coincided for about a decade and a half. And, although each man's theology differed in some ways, their published works together largely defined the key points that advanced the cause of Protestantism.

Both Luther and Calvin certainly agreed that the Roman Church's pretense to world dominion was unbiblical. They both recognized that its methods of enforcing its dominion were also immoral and tyrannical. Both men also agreed that grace was a divine act of mercy from God alone. Luther's central protest against Rome in his *Ninety-five Theses* pointed out that Rome's real concern was not for eternal souls at all, but in obtaining

3 Ibid., p. 14.
4 Ibid., p. 13.

the monetary property of those souls: *"the treasures of indulgences are nets with which one now fishes for the wealth of men."*[5]

Calvin strongly agreed with Luther, describing papal indulgences as *"those most filthy buyings and sellings that they have used, while the world was in such gross senseless ignorance."*[6] He included an entire chapter in his landmark work *The Institution of Christian Religion* on the errant use of indulgences that *"run so far forth into madness, ... which the Pope deals abroad by his Bulls."*[7] For such Reformers, the idea of the Church using the name of Christ to spread its own dominion across the earth while keeping the world in ignorance of His free grace was blasphemous.

Calvin was, however, among the strongest advocates of advancing the genuine dominion of Christ. In his *Commentary on the Epistle to the Colossians*, Calvin noted Christ's preeminence over *"the whole world."*[8] Whereas the Apostle Paul had written that Jesus Christ was preeminent over *"all things"* including *"thrones, or dominions, or principalities, or powers,"*[9] Calvin added the implications: *"He places the Son of God in the highest seat of honor, that he may have the preeminence over angels as well as men, and may bring under control all creatures in heaven and in earth."*[10]

Psalm 2:12 also made the issue of Christ's dominion over civil rulers clear, directing earthly potentates to *"Kiss the Son,"* meaning God's Son. In his *Commentary on the Psalms*, Calvin said: *"Kiss refers to the solemn token or sign of honor."*[11] Calvin, as well as many other Reformed Christian writers, thereby understood that the kingdom of Christ was more than a matter of saving eternal souls. There is also an administrative lordship of Christ in the here and now, and all earthly authorities are commanded to submit to His dominion.

---

5 Luther, *The Selected Writings of Martin Luther*, vol. 1, p. 57.

6 Calvin, *The Institution of Christian Religion*, vol. 1, leaf 277a, 3:5:10.

7 Ibid. leaf 271a, 3:5:1.

8 John Calvin, *Commentary on the Epistle to the Colossians* (Grand Rapids: Baker Books, 2005), p. 152.

9 Ibid., p. 145, citing Colossians 1:16.

10 Ibid., p. 152.

11 John Calvin, *Commentary on the Book of Psalms*, vol. 1 (Grand Rapids: Baker Books, 2005), p. 22.

Reformed Christianity on Mankind's Dominion of the Earth

Another key point in Reformed dominion theology was that God not only reigns supreme over all the earth, but He has delegated to man some of His governing authority. Calvin explained: *"It is certainly a singular honor, and one which cannot be sufficiently estimated, that mortal man, as the representative of God, has dominion over the world."*[12]

God's representative dominion was vested with mortal men in Genesis 1:26, saying: *"let them have dominion over the fish of the sea, over the birds of the air, and over the cattle, over all the earth."* The Lord thereby blessed all men in the sense of providing mankind with a rich, earthly inheritance. *"Thus,"* Calvin explained, *"man was rich before he was born."*[13]

To biblical expositors like Calvin, such a blessed dominion was not seen as delegated to a few select potentates. To Reformed Protestants, man's dominion over the earth clearly had its limitations. Calvin, for instance, qualified his interpretation of God's dominion mandate by adding: *"He appointed man, it is true, lord of the world; but he expressly subjects the animals to him."*[14] In other words, man was certainly unique in enjoying dominion over the earth and all of its creatures, yet he has not been given an unlimited lording dominion over his fellow men who also have their own God-given share in that same dominion mandate.

According to the Reformed Christian expositors of Scripture, all mankind has a part in the dominion of the earth. This is because each human being has been given a sanctified property in his *own person* as well as his possessions that he owes first to God. This is at the *heart* of God-given liberty! No authority is to be used by those in positions of power to dominate their fellow men as if they are mere creatures of their own self-interest. Consequently, to Reformed Christians, the legitimate dominion of the earth was not regarded as a divine right to tyrannical power in either church or state.

---

12 Ibid., p. 105, citing Psalm 8:6: *"You* [God] *have made him* [man] *to have dominion over the works of Your hands; You have put all things under his feet."*
13 John Calvin, *Commentaries on the First Book of Moses Called Genesis*, vol. 1 (Grand Rapids: Baker Books, 2005), p. 96.
14 Ibid.

John Calvin Describes the Nature of God's Dominion Mandate

Contemporary portrait of John Calvin with the title page of the first English edition of
A Commentary of John Calvin upon the First Book of Moses Called Genesis (1578)

The Biblical Idea of Godly Rule Versus Tyranny

With God alone as the absolute Lord over the earth, He alone has absolute sovereignty over all men. Reformed Christians therefore recognized that any legitimate government is limited by mankind's mutual accountability to God. This implied a sense of mutual self-government shared by men. It also meant that a distinctive, though always qualified, reverence was to be paid to civil rulers by those who were ruled.

Calvin thus defined good civil rulers as a kind of *"excellent men"* who *"cultivated equality with their inferiors, who yielded them a spontaneous rather than a forced reverence."*[15] In other words, godly civil rulers were to maintain a sense of equality with the people they served. Rulers were, in fact, to be regarded as public servants. They were to use their authority in ways that cultivated a genuine reverence for civil government, rather than exercising a forced dictatorship upon those they were supposed to serve.

---

15 Ibid., pp. 316-317.

There are, of course, many examples in Scripture of ungodly lording rulers – the kind of rulers who disregarded the bounds of true reverence for God and man. In the book of Genesis, the foremost of these men was Nimrod, who, Calvin said, *"disturbed and broke through the boundaries of this reverence."*[16]

Nimrod was the prototype tyrant – a despotic man who ruled over others as if they were beasts to be subdued according to an inflated sense of his personal dominion. Thus, in explaining the fact that Nimrod *"attempted to raise himself above the order of men,"* Calvin noted that he was called in the Bible *"a mighty hunter,"* which could be interpreted as *"seizing upon prey."*[17]

Calvin described the conceit behind such a lofty attitude in rulers: *"as proud men become transported by a vain self-confidence, that they may look down as from the clouds upon others."*[18] He described the virtuous character of godly civil government by also pointing out, *"how highly pleasing to God is a mild administration of affairs among men."*[19]

For Reformed Christians, governmental power was seen as protective rather than invasive. The duty of government was not to subdue the people, but to safeguard those who possessed their own property and enjoyed the blessing of God in what they owned. Calvin thus explained the accountable stewardship that accompanies all private property and possessions, saying *"that all earthly things are so given us by the bountifulness of God, and appointed for our commodity, that they may be as things delivered us to keep, whereof we must one day yield an account."*[20]

God's Blessing upon Family Dominion

That idea of the earth as *"the bountifulness of God"* was to Reformed Christianity the picture of God's gracious provision. Christians recognized

---

16 Ibid., p. 317.
17 Ibid. (Referencing Genesis 10:9).
18 Ibid.
19 Ibid.
20 Calvin, *The Institution of Christian Religion*, vol. 1, leaf 294a, 3:10:5.

a sacred blessedness placed upon man and woman together in Genesis 1:28, which adds the fact that *"God blessed them."*[21] This wording was seen as God's blessing upon the sacred dominion of the family, and from there, His blessings upon all mankind. The union of husband and wife, Calvin noted, *"may be regarded as the source from which the human race has flowed."*[22]

To Reformed Christians, the family was the basic building block of all human society, and they recognized a special, sacred dignity of the home. In his comments on Genesis 2:24, Calvin explained: *"that among the offices pertaining to human society, this is the principal, and as it were the most sacred, that a man should cleave unto his wife."*[23] By planting homes and by generations of families growing, spreading, and populating, God gave the means for mankind to fill the earth. Taking possession of the earth was the object of God's benediction upon the first marriage. Calvin noted: *"that Adam with his wife was formed for the production of offspring, in order that men might replenish the earth."*[24]

It was this idea of the family being the sacred foundation of all human society, which brought Europe out of the slavish system of vassal feudalism.[25] Rather than viewing a family as the doormat for the more pronounced, public institutions of church and state, Reformed Christianity

---

21 Calvin, *Commentary on Genesis*, vol. 1, p. 97.

22 Ibid.

23 Ibid., p. 136. Genesis 2:24 describes God's institution of the family as a covenantal bond, that: *"a man shall leave his father and his mother and be joined to his wife, and they shall become one flesh."*

24 Ibid., p. 98.

25 In the Middle Ages, the feudal order incorporated a "manor" or "manorial" system of property ownership based upon lordships of nobility. The term *noble* originally referred to those who were the "knowable" or "notable" within the feudal order in Western Europe. The lord's seat of authority was his manor house (or "mansion"), which served as his residence and the site from which he ruled his land and tenants. The nobility were the primary landowners in the feudal system, having a civic and social status above the commoners along with their privileged (usually hereditary) titles that were contractually granted or confirmed by a monarch to his vassals. The peasants (who lived under the vassals) did not own property of their own, so their liberties were tied to the graces of those who owned or managed the manorial property upon which they lived. The manor house was typically set slightly apart (and on higher ground) from the surrounding manor lands. A commoners' village often grew up just beyond the outskirts of the immediate property of the manor house while the tenant lands stretched well into the countryside. The surrounding peasant tenants enjoyed limited legal rights that were tied to the specific manorial custom and had some recourse regarding their private household possession through locally enforced laws. They, however, could not be viewed as having the power that typifies the rights of property ownership, and therefore they did not have the status of free men. Thus, the principle holds that property ownership is power, and liberty is the free enjoyment of one's possessions!

viewed the principal society of the family as essential to the others. The institution of the family resident in private homes was regarded as foundational to spreading true godly dominion over the face of the earth.

To Subdue the Earth

According to the societal ideas of the Reformers, the home was the setting from which people possess and enjoy the bounty of the earth. It was not enough to merely possess a piece of ground, it was important to render it useful for the greatest godly good. Consequently, although the mandate of God was put in terms of the multiplication of families, their fruitful possession and enjoyment was put in terms of subduing the earth.[26]

Calvin explained that the clause in Genesis 1:28 for man to "*subdue*" the earth was an important part of the dominion mandate. He wrote that by this, "*at length, he is put in possession of his right.*"[27] This involved the productive use of what God has provided. Calvin saw man as obligated by God "*to nurture the things provided for thee.*"[28] Calvin also explained Adam's original stewardship responsibility, and from that he drew our obligations to be productive stewards of our own private possessions:

> [T]*he custody of the garden was given in charge to Adam, to show that we possess the things which God has committed to our hands, on the condition, that being content with a frugal and moderate use of them, we should take care of what shall remain.*[29]

Adam's charge of custody of the garden was therefore synonymous with our use of the land and things we possess. That level of care, then, did not mean leaving nature untouched, but to put it to good use for the benefit of man and the improvement of the earth. In other words, we do not possess the earth by idolizing it as an untouchable goddess or worshiping it as a self-contained ecological ideal. Subduing the earth means working to yield an appropriate bounty from God's blessing of property ownership.

---

26 The passage in Genesis 1:28 is referred to as the "dominion mandate": "*God said to them, 'Be fruitful and multiply; fill the earth and subdue it; have dominion...'*"

27 Calvin, *Commentary on Genesis*, vol. 1, p. 98.

28 Ibid., p. 99.

29 Ibid., p. 125.

In short, we do not neglect but embrace our responsibility to subdue the earth, as Calvin put it:

> *Let him who possesses a field, so partake of its yearly fruits, that he may not suffer the ground to be injured by his negligence; but let him endeavor to hand it down to posterity as he received it, or even better cultivated. Let him so feed on its fruits, that he neither dissipates it by luxury, nor permits to be marred or ruined by neglect.*[30]

This was a key to man's responsible dominion: that each man with his family are to take active and industrious possession of their private property. Our blessings from God are to be used in ways that yield a sufficient provision for us, but with adequate care and improvements that secure their continued blessedness to future generations.

Families and Domestic Stewardship

To the Reformed Christians, godly government certainly involved the diligent stewardship of a family's property and possessions. *"With respect to those good things which God has given us to enjoy,"* Calvin explained, *"let every one regard himself as the steward of God in all things which he possesses."*[31] This meant that a faithful householder was one who governed his home for the glory of God as well as one who provided for the material necessities of those under his roof.

Calvin noted that a man's personal labor was not to stem from covetousness or selfish ambition: *"God more esteems care to rule a household godly, when a holy householder being loosed ... from all covetousness, ambition, and other desires of the flesh, travails* [labors] *to this purpose to serve God in a certain vocation."*[32] Thus, for Calvin, the dominion mandate meant that the family governor was to be active in a productive calling: *"that the Lord bids every one of us in all the doings of his life, to have an eye to his calling."*[33]

---

30 Ibid. Commentary on Genesis 2:15: *"Then the LORD God took the man and put him in the garden of Eden to tend and keep it."*

31 Calvin, *Commentaries on Genesis*, vol. 1, p. 125.

32 Calvin, *The Institution of Christian Religion*, vol. 2, leaf 529b, 4:13:16.

33 Ibid., vol. 1, leaf 294b, 3:10:6.

The Geneva Bible and Domestic Responsibilities

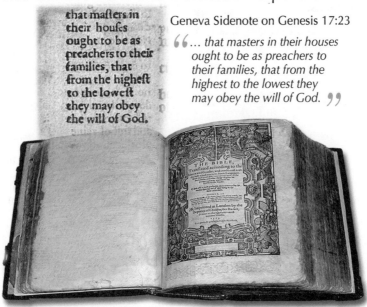

that masters in
their houses
ought to be as
preachers to their
families, that
from the highest
to the lowest
they may obey
the will of God.

Geneva Sidenote on Genesis 17:23

❝ … that masters in their houses
ought to be as preachers to
their families, that from the
highest to the lowest they
may obey the will of God. ❞

A calling, in the context of a man's responsibility toward his family, did not allow for disinterest or passivity toward his home; it meant being employed diligently in productive work for his family's benefit. Among the most obliging of all biblical directives for men to work was the Apostle Paul's straightforward charge in II Thessalonians 3:10: "*If anyone will not work, neither shall he eat.*" With such a charge facing all men, Calvin admonished them to the responsible government of their homes – including both personal "*industry*" as well as "*ruling his family.*"[34]

Families and Private Possessions

In II Thessalonians 3:12, where Paul also recommended men to "*eat their own bread*," Calvin advocated the responsible use of one's own property: "*This is the first law of equity, that no one make use of what belongs to another, but only use what he can properly call his own.*"[35] Such ideas of individual responsibility countered the idea that society at large

---

34 John Calvin, *Commentary on the Second Epistle to the Thessalonians* (Grand Rapids: Baker Books, 2005), p. 355.
35 Ibid., p. 358.

was responsible to put bread on a man's table. Families were obligated to care for their own as well as those of their extended family; charity beyond that was a gift freely given, but it was never a social or governmental entitlement that was owed.

Families were also to honor the Lord in their increase, meaning to give back to the Lord a portion of what the land had produced. This was the same principle of "tithing" to the Lord that was employed by the ancient Israelites when they entered the "Promised Land" of Canaan.[36]

Understanding the Reformed Christian idea of private stewardship completely discredits a statist approach to dominion as it is viewed today. The societal or governmental control of household property violates the foremost principles of familial dominion.[37] Calvin explained that only those who walk in humility before God know how to rightly possess anything. In commenting on Jesus' words: "*the meek will inherit the earth*" in Matthew 5:5, Calvin denounced the pride of potentates "*who claim for themselves the dominion of the earth.*"[38] He therefore observed the vanity of those who think they can possess anything under the dominion of pride: "*While they lead so stormy a life, though they were a hundred times lords of the earth, while they possess all, they certainly possess nothing.*"[39]

In other words, earthly potentates who put the quiet and peaceable realm of the home within their own grip are really oppressors rather than possessors. The possession of anything honors God only through rightful title, ownership, and godly management. Tyrants, who presume they have a vested entitlement to what belongs to others because of their supposed superiority or even divine right, really "*possess nothing.*" It was "*in contrast with the fury and violence of wicked men,*" Calvin concluded, that Christ "*declares, on good grounds, that the meek will be the lords and heirs of the earth.*"[40]

---

36 Leviticus 27:30 explained to the Israelites: "*And all the tithe of the land* [one tenth of one's increase], *whether of the seed of the land or of the fruit of the tree, is the LORD's. It is holy to the LORD.*"

37 The dominion mandate was given by God in Genesis 1:28 to families who were to multiply, take possession of, and subdue the earth, not for civil governments to dominate and subdue the liberty and property of private families.

38 John Calvin, *The Harmony of the Evangelists*, vol. 1 (Grand Rapids: Baker Books, 2005), p. 262.

39 Ibid.

40 Ibid.

Safeguarding Private Dominion and Property

According to the Reformed Christians, there was a very significant role for civil government, and that role was to safeguard the people's wealth and property. In Calvin's commentary on I Timothy 2:2, which admonished the people to *"pray for those in authority, that we might live a quiet and peaceable life,"* he wrote a very insightful discourse. On one hand, Calvin affirmed the people's duty to pray for their rulers to do well in governing, and on the other, he wrote that rulers were to *"restrain all acts of violence, and maintain peace"*[41] on behalf of the people. Governments were, in fact, *"appointed by God for the protection ... of the peace and decency of society, in exactly the same manner that the earth is appointed to produce food."*[42]

In other words, there was a fruitful purpose in God ordaining civil government. To Calvin there were *"fruits which are yielded to us"* in the proper use of *"a well regulated government."*[43] Those fruits were the benefits of the people who were protected under godly laws, *"when everyone obtains what is his own, and the violence of the more powerful is kept under restraint."*[44] The purpose, then, for governments bearing the sword of justice was to defend the people's liberty in the quiet and peaceable use of their own property and possessions.

Godly government thus defends the people's liberties from encroachments by either private criminals or by public rulers acting criminally. In commenting on the Apostle Paul's designation of a civil magistrate as a *"minister of God for thy wealth,"*[45] Calvin wrote that the role of all such public ministers was not to be a threat to that wealth: *"nor are they endued with unbridled power, but what is restricted to the well being of their subjects."*[46] The fact that God authorized rulers as civil

---

41 John Calvin, *Commentaries on the Epistles to Timothy, Titus, and Philemon* (Grand Rapids: Baker Books, 2005), p. 53.
42 Ibid., p. 52.
43 Ibid., p. 51.
44 Ibid., p. 52.
45 Geneva Bible version on Romans 13:4.
46 Calvin, *Commentaries on the Epistle of Paul the Apostle to the Romans*, trans. and ed. John Owen,

ministers also meant they were obliged to govern civil society according to His purpose and not to their own advantage. The Apostle Paul's comments in Romans 13:1-4 that obliged people to honor civil power also affirmed the officeholders' indebtedness toward the people they served, as Calvin explained:

> [T]*he ministration which God has committed to them has a regard to their subjects, they are therefore debtors also to them. And private men are reminded, that it is through the divine goodness that they are defended by the sword of princes against injuries done by the wicked.*[47]

Once again, we see that the function of civil government as it was biblically defined is to protect and defend the people in their persons and property against the violence and wickedness of all men. While civil government's obligation is to enact and enforce laws that safeguard the people and their property, private citizens then have an obligation to submit themselves under their ruler's power toward that end.

Another key duty for civil rulers was to administer justice evenly and without partiality under the law. Their job was certainly not to favor one person or group over another. The key was to establish equal justice and to prevent all injustice. In commenting on Exodus 23:6,[48] Calvin cautioned against the propensity of governments to become licentiously liberal:

> *For, although the poor is for the most part tyrannically oppressed, still ambition will sometimes impel a judge to misplace compassion, so that he is liberal at another's expense. And this temptation is all the more dangerous, because injustice is done under the cloak of virtue.*[49]

Those who read Calvin's writings understood both the godly purpose and the godly limitations of civil government. Government's role was not

---

(Grand Rapids: Baker Books, 2005), p. 481. Romans 13 begins: *"Let every soul be subject to the governing authorities. For there is no authority except from God, and the authorities that exist are appointed by God."*

47 Ibid.

48 Exodus 23:6: *"You shall not wrest the judgment of thy* [your] *poor in his cause."* (KJV)

49 John Calvin, *Commentaries on the Last Four Books of Moses*, vol. 3 (Grand Rapids: Baker Books, 2005), page 139.

to adjudicate social compassion nor redistribute property or wealth. Its role was certainly not to be *"liberal at another's expense,"* but simply to ensure the people's liberty, to protect their property, and to maintain the kind of civil dignity in which all will find impartial justice under the law.

The Biblical Legacy of Liberty

A key discourse that greatly defined the Reformed Christian view of civil government was Calvin's chapter "Of Civil Government" included in his *The Institution of Christian Religion*. That highly influential chapter laid out the fundamental role of civil power as it was defined in Scripture, spelling out both the people's duties toward legitimate civil power as well as the lengths and limits of that power.

Particularly important to the Reformed Christian legacy of liberty was that Calvin's chapter on civil government addressed the essential role of civil government toward our God-given freedoms. That role was not to accumulate absolute lording power in the state, but for civil officers to use their vested authority to protect and maintain the liberty of the people:

> *Yea, and the magistrates ought with most great diligence to bend themselves hereunto, that they suffer not the liberty of the people, of which they are appointed governors, to be in any part diminished, much less to be dissolved; if they be negligent and little careful therein, they be false faithbreakers in their office, and betrayers of their country.*[50]

For Reformed Christians, the issue of genuine governing authority was one of ruling faithfully under God. They were therefore diametrically opposed to the idea of a state that dominates either the liberty or the property of the people. Such observations might appear strikingly astute to us in light of the licentiousness of the civil governments of our age. Governments have indeed become liberal at others' expense; they have also become extravagant in both their taxation and their spending. Thus, by disregarding the people's liberty and discounting their private property, governments violate the most fundamental purpose of godly civil rule.

---

50 Calvin, *The Institution of Christian Religion*, vol. 2, leaf 623b, 2, 4:20:8.

Calvin's *The Institution of Christian Religion* Published in England

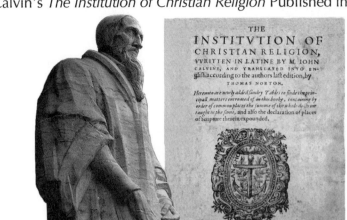

Title page of the sixteenth-century edition of what became known as Calvin's *Institutes,* one of the most influential books in early English publishing.

In earlier times, the principle of linking God's overall dominion with man's stewardship dominion helped shape the successful and enduring legacy of the Reformed faith in England. That key principle, grounded in the mandates of Scripture, certainly became the hallmark of political thought in later Reformation-era England.

The Reformed English expositors of Scripture informed and then reformed Britain's view of the overall kingdom of God. Calvin's writings, immensely influential in England, also played a key role in reshaping that nation's political climate. In the late 1500s, for example, Calvin's *Institutes* became required reading for students of law at Oxford and Cambridge Universities, ensuring that his views of godly government would impact future generations of English magistrates.

Such a devotion to the first principles of Scripture would also inspire the early visionaries of English colonization in America. Both a growing national devotion to Scripture and the ongoing influence of the Reformed Christian faith fueled England's ever-widening sense of obligation to open up vast frontiers for that faith in the New World, as we will see in the following chapter.

5
ENGLAND'S CALLING TO COLONIZE AMERICA

Ambassadors of the True Kingdom

THE dominion established by Spain in America provided a stark contrast to the Reformed Christian model of colonization. Whereas Spain's conquistadors had subdued vast tracts of land for their king, Reformed Christians saw America (and the whole world) in light of a much greater kingdom. When Calvin, for example, interpreted the phrase: "*Your kingdom come*" in the Lord's Prayer,[1] he explained that Jesus Christ would "*gather to Himself churches out of all the coasts of the world.*"[2]

Such a view of Christ's kingdom involved evangelizing rather than terrorizing the world. The Great Commission given to Jesus' disciples in Matthew 28:19 was, after all, to "*teach all nations.*" That commission, Calvin wrote, gave Jesus' disciples "*their embassage* [ambassadorship] *when He commanded them to go and teach all nations, all those things He had commanded.*"[3] A dignified and truly Christian ministry was not advanced through brutality or overpowering military force, but rather through faithfully preaching and teaching God's Word. Christ's commission to His disciples, as Calvin also explained, was given "*to all ministers what rule they ought to follow in teaching.*"[4] And, with the entire evangelistic mission of the true Church[5] being *liberating* rather than *domineering*, the cultural effect of that mission would be positively life-changing from one person, family, church, and nation to the next.

Isaiah and Planting Christ's True Vineyards

It was not without historic importance that John Calvin's *Commentary on Isaiah* was dedicated to Elizabeth I of England on the date of her

---

1 Matthew 6:10.
2 John Calvin, *The Institution of Christian Religion,* vol. 2., leaf 373b, 3:20:42.
3 Ibid., leaf 478b, 4:8:4.
4 Ibid.
5 The true Church is the universal body of true believers in Christ rather than a physical institution.

coronation in 1558.[6] For one thing, Elizabeth's coronation marked the return of Protestantism to England, putting an end to the tight grip of tyranny during the reign of her sister Mary I with her despotic husband Philip (the aforementioned king of Spain).[7]

Calvin's *Commentary on Isaiah* Dedicated to Elizabeth I on the Day of Her Coronation in 1558

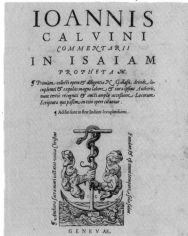

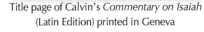

Title page of Calvin's *Commentary on Isaiah* (Latin Edition) printed in Geneva

Coronation portrait of Queen Elizabeth I showing England's Royal Orb, representing Christ's dominion over the earth

Of equal importance in Calvin's dedication to Elizabeth I was that, more than any other prophetic text of Scripture, the prophecies of Isaiah pointed to the true Church's worldwide mission. That book contains reference after reference to the kingdom of God extending to *"the ends of the earth."*[8] In Isaiah 24:16, for example, where the Scripture declares: *"From the ends of the earth we have heard songs,"* Calvin observed in his comments on that passage that it meant spreading the true Christian faith:

---

6 Elizabeth I was Queen of England from November 17, 1558 until her death in 1603. Sometimes called the "Virgin Queen" or "Good Queen Bess," Elizabeth was the last monarch of the Tudor dynasty. As the daughter of the Reformed Christian Anne Boleyn, princess Elizabeth was raised as a Protestant even after her mother's execution in 1536. Following the death of her older sister Queen Mary I in 1558, Reformed Protestantism was formally established in the reign of Elizabeth.

7 Queen Mary I reigned in England from 1553 until her death in 1558. She is remembered for her marriage to the despotic Philip of Spain. After their marriage in 1554, "Bloody Mary" had about 300 Protestants burned at the stake.

8 We have seen the reference to Isaiah's prophecy in Columbus' view of his discoveries in Chapter 2.

But here he [Isaiah] *speaks of spreading the true religion through the whole world; and this makes it still more evident that the prophecy relates to the kingdom of Christ, under which true religion has at length penetrated into foreign and heathen nations.*[9]

Similarly, when the English turned to the same passage of Isaiah in their beloved Geneva Bible[10] (the most popular version in the Elizabethan era), they read in its margins: "*Meaning to God, who will publish His gospel through all the world.*"[11] To the faithful in England who were weaned on God's Word and who fed on such voluminous Bible commentaries, evangelizing America appeared as a calling upon their own island realm.

Such a calling, however, did not mean that they were to deposit the Gospel in America and then leave for home. They were to *plant* homes. The Bible's book of Isaiah also addressed the *means* by which God's true kingdom would be spread among the nations. For example, by using the metaphor of planting vineyards, the text of Isaiah 65:21 explained: "*they shall build houses and inhabit them; they shall plant vineyards and eat their fruit.*" Calvin addressed the implications of this passage:

[T]*he prophet, speaks not only of life, but of a peaceful condition of life; as if he had said, "You shall plant vineyards, and shall eat the fruit of them; and you shall not be removed from this life before receiving the fruit, which shall be enjoyed, not only by yourselves, but by your children and posterity."*[12]

To many English, God had placed such a mantle upon the true faith – the Reformed Christian faith – to send families rather than conquistadors to distant lands. And, although properly speaking, the biblical idea of planting vineyards refers to Christ's kingdom in its spiritual connotation, the *means* by which the Lord accomplishes that end involves planting the

---

9 John Calvin: *Commentary on the Book of the Prophet Isaiah*, vol. 2 (Grand Rapids: Baker Books, 2005), p. 177.

10 The Geneva Bible was the most significant early translation of Scripture in the English language, preceding the King James version by over 50 years. First published in 1560, it coincided with Elizabeth I's reign in England and was the primary Bible of the sixteenth and early seventeenth centuries.

11 Geneva Bible footnote on Isaiah 24:16.

12 John Calvin: *Commentary on the Book of the Prophet Isaiah*, vol. 4 (Grand Rapids: Baker Books, 2005), p. 402.

dominion of quiet and peaceable families both at home and abroad.

The Reformed Christians of England saw God's original dominion mandate and Christ's evangelizing commission working in unison. For them, the metaphor of *planting vineyards* unified the idea of establishing faithful homes with the spiritual mission of expanding the kingdom of Christ. For the English, sending large numbers of well-governed families to America was the perfect response to the biblical calling to carry God's redemption to the ends of the earth.

Under Reformed Christianity, Queen Elizabeth I Affirms the Liberty and Property of English Subjects in 1575

A most Excellent and Remarkable

SPEECH,

DELIVERED

By that Mirrour and Miracle of Princes,

QUEEN ELIZABETH,

Of famous memory, in the Honourable the High Court of PARLIAMENT, in the seventeenth yeere of her REIGNE;

...rein shee fully expresseth the duty of Princes to their Subjects, and that of Subjects to their Princes:

Dan Ford, 2002

Queen Elizabeth I and the title page of her speech on the duty of princes to their subjects:

❝ Surely what Monarch in England that shall at any time go about to alienate the property of the subject, or impose on their immunities any innovation or diminishment, can ever boast himself to ... enjoy his Crown and dignity, with well wishes and affections of his Subjects, for so large is the charter of the English Subjects liberty, ... that they are a free people, if compared with other nations, who groan under the yoke and heavy burdens laid on their servile necks by their sovereigns. ❞

The English View of Household Government

Influenced by the Reformed faith, Queen Elizabeth acknowledged the responsibility of families in their own property as well as the duty of English monarchs to respect their private domain. Elizabeth told her Parliament in 1575 that no English monarch "*shall at any time go about to alienate the property of the subject.*"[13] By that, the queen meant that

---

13 Queen Elizabeth I, *A Most Excellent and Remarkable Speech, Delivered by That Mirrour and*

the people had *"immunities"*[14] from the Crown laying taxes or making any *"diminishment"*[15] of the people's private estates without the consent of their representatives in Parliament. She also boasted of *"the English Subjects liberty"* among Europeans, saying *"that they are a free people, if compared with other nations, who groan under the yoke and heavy burdens laid on their servile necks by their sovereigns."*[16]

With both liberty and property as core tenets of the Reformed Christian faith in England, there was an obligation for each family to understand its own internal responsibilities. Accordingly, the leaders of the late sixteenth-century Puritan[17] movement encouraged Englishmen not only to embrace their biblical duties within their country's wider civil society, but especially their governing responsibilities within their own homes.

The late sixteenth-century Puritan authors John Dod and Robert Cleaver, for example, collaborated in writing one of the first works dedicated to biblical responsibilities of English families. Their groundbreaking work called *A Godly Form of Household Government* was a masterpiece of Reformed theology concerning the home, explaining first that *"the governors of a family, be such as have authority in the family by God's ordinance."*[18] By that, the authors were referring to the God-ordained governors of husband and wife – those who had been delegated His exclusive rule within the private realm of their homes.

In line with the views of John Calvin, *A Godly Form of Household Government* also described a home's wider societal implications. In commenting on I Timothy 3:4, Calvin had explained that the Christian man must be *"a good and praiseworthy master of a household."*[19] He had also

---

Miracle of Princes, Queen Elizabeth, of Famous Memory, in the Honourable the High Court of Parliament, in the Seventeenth Year of her Reign (London, 1643), p. 5.

14 Ibid.

15 Ibid.

16 Ibid.

17 Puritans were devoutly Reformed Christians who sought to restore the entire English culture in family, church, and/or state to the precepts of God's written Word.

18 John Dod and Robert Cleaver, *A Godly Form of Household Government: for the Ordering of Private Families, According to the Direction of God's Word* (London, 1603), p. 15.

19 John Calvin, *Commentaries on the First Epistle to Timothy*, p. 82. I Timothy 3:4 described a necessary quality of a Christian leader as being: *"one who rules his own house well, having his children in submission with all reverence."*

described the biblical principle: *"that he who does not know how to rule his family, will not be qualified for governing the church."*[20] Dod and Cleaver expanded on this principle, applying it to the civil sphere, saying: *"It is impossible for a man to understand how to govern the Commonwealth, that does not know* [how] *to rule his own house, or order his own person, so that he* [who] *knows not* [how] *to govern, deserves not to reign."*[21]

Simply put, a well-governed nation needs well-governed homes to provide it with well-equipped public servants. Thus, under the influence of the Reformed faith, the institution of the family not only gained new respect in its own right, but the home became revered as the seedbed for the kind of well-trained rulers needed to lead England to greatness in the succeeding centuries.

Puritans Dod and Cleaver on Self-Government in the Home

A GODLY FORME OF HOVSEHOLD GOVERN-MENT : FOR THE ORDE-ring of priuate Families, according to the direction of Gods word.

John Dod

Parentes alſo are commaunded to bring vp their children in the *inſtruction and information of the Lord.* By all which places it is euident, that Religion muſt be ſtirring in Chriſtian families, and that good gouernment looketh to bring godly behauiour into families, as well as thrift and good husban-drie.

Parents also are commanded to bring up their children in the instruction and information of the Lord. By all which places it is evident, that religion must be stirring in Christian families, and that good government looks to bring godly behavior into families, as well as thrift and good husbandry.

A property of good go-uernment. 1.Tim.3.4 It is in poſſible for a man to vnderſtãd how to gouerne the Common-wealth, that doth not know to rule his owne houſe,or order his owne perſon,ſo that he that knoweth not to gouerne, deſerueth not to raigne.

It is impossible for a man to understand how to govern the Commonwealth, that does not know [how] to rule his own house, or order his own person, so that he that knows not [how] to govern, deserves not to reign.

Excerpts from *A Godly Form of Household Government*, first published in 1598

---

20 Ibid.
21 Dod and Cleaver, *A Godly Form of Household Government*, p. 16.

This new appreciation for familial self-government also had implications for the importance of English families in the Church. By reading the Bible, common Englishmen learned that regular worship and even preaching were not duties reserved only for the leaders of their churches. The Geneva Bible's footnote on Genesis 17:23, for example, expressed a mandate placed on every householder, that *"masters in their houses ought to be as preachers to their families, that from the highest to the lowest they may obey the will of God."*

For the Puritans of England, the home was the only setting for the regular, daily worship of God. It was there that God's Word was read on a daily basis and taught to children in regular devotions. Only by privately pursuing God's holiness in the home would He be truly honored when those families then joined together to worship Him in their public congregations. Dod and Cleaver therefore warned English householders with typically Puritan candor:

> *Where, therefore, holiness is not sought for in families, there God has no friends, nor lovers, nor walkers with him, howsoever they will sometime come visit him in the church.*[22]

The idea of only occasionally visiting God weekly at church was revealing. The Puritans recognized that the Lord deserved friendship throughout the week, and families needed His guidance daily. And with the heart of Christ's kingdom established in regular family worship, the evangelization of the lost began within the mission field of every faithful English home.

The First Visionary of English Plantings

The fundamental shift toward a healthy respect for biblical family government, of course, worked beautifully with the English idea of American colonization. The Reformed Christian view of the family, in fact, was key to the distinctive methods that the English used in settling America. To the English, planting godly homes would become the centerpiece of

---

22 Ibid., pp. 18-19.

planting Christ's kingdom itself, and responsible government in homes would be the foundation of self-government in their wider societies of church and state.

The year 1582 marked the ninetieth year since Christopher Columbus had first planted the Spanish flag in the New World, but England had yet to plant a permanent presence of any kind. That year, however, marked the publication of Richard Hakluyt's landmark book *Diverse Voyages*. In it, the devoutly Reformed English author lamented that "*since the first discovery of America (which is now full fourscore and ten years), ... we of England could never have the grace to set fast footing in such fertile and temperate places....*"[23] The point was that after such a long stretch of time, the planting of a faithful English colony was still awaiting God's providential timing.

Born in England in 1553, Richard Hakluyt was educated at the time when Reformed theology was taking hold in England's two institutions of higher education. By the late 1570s the Puritan movement had become firmly entrenched at Cambridge University. And in 1578, the year that Calvin's *Institutes* became mandatory reading for Oxford University students, Hakluyt received his pension (or scholarship) to pursue a degree in divinity there.

At Oxford, Hakluyt immediately began speaking out against the prideful and brutal character of Spanish colonization, calling Spain's regime repugnant to the Gospel of Christ. By the end of 1578 he had written letters urging England's more peaceable colonization on behalf of a particular group of American natives: "*the Symerones, a people detesting the proud governance of the Spaniards.*"[24]

This was the first of Hakluyt's many callings for England to defend the true interests of Christ in America. His intention for sending English families to settle among the natives was therefore more than extending a one-time hand of charity. His motive was to establish the kind of self-

---

23 Richard Hakluyt, *Diverse Voyages Touching the Discovery of America and the Islands Adjacent,* London, 1582. Hakluyt Society edition, London, 1850, p. 8.

24 E.G.R. Taylor, ed., *The Original Writings and Correspondence of the Two Richard Hakluyts*, vol. 2 (London: Hakluyt Society, 1935), p. 142.

sustaining government that the natives lacked, and so for them to become *"well lodged and by our nation made free from the tyrannous Spaniard, and quietly and courteously governed by our nation."*[25]

Here we see the theme developing that English colonies were to counter Spain's tyranny by planting well-governed families and communities among the natives of America. Hakluyt also recognized that any planting of a free people would also give them a sense of independence from England, warning: *"that the English there would aspire to government of themselves, yet it should better be so than the Spaniard."*[26]

Although Hakluyt's first proposed mission among the Symerones was never undertaken, his vision of English colonization was a step toward planting a godly seed to counter the dominion of Spain. And, considering the later course of English colonization in America, his caution *"that the English there would aspire to government of themselves"* also proved to be profoundly prophetic.

Hakluyt's Discourse Concerning Western Planting

It was two years after Hakluyt's first proposal for an American colony that Sir Francis Drake accomplished a great feat for England. In 1580, Drake succeeded in circumnavigating the earth. In Drake's courageous undertaking he sailed around the southernmost straits of America and made several discoveries along the northern Pacific coastline, which he promptly claimed for England. Drake's mission, though an effective thorn in the side of colonial Spain, was like all the prior English explorations in one important way. Like the previous English ventures, Drake's mission brought England a noteworthy level of fame, but it failed to plant a permanent English presence in America that would truly counter the kind of statist dominion imposed by Spain.

At the time, another notable English adventurer named Sir Walter Raleigh was also staking New World claims. It was while Raleigh was on one of his own famed missions of discovery in 1584 that Hakluyt drafted

---

25 Ibid. p. 143.
26 Ibid.

a manuscript of greatest historical importance. Hakluyt's *A Discourse
Concerning Western Planting* was specifically directed to the attention of
Queen Elizabeth, and it amounted to a Reformed manifesto for permanent
English colonization. Hakluyt first called for the English queen to stake
England's own worthy claim *"for the enlargement of the Gospel of Christ,
whereunto the princes of the Reformed Religion are chiefly bound."*[27]

Richard Hakluyt's *Discourse Concerning Western Planting*

Stained window depiction in Bristol Cathedral of Richard Hakluyt,
with opening manuscript (above right) of his 1584 *Discourse*,
and (below) Hakluyt's statement on colonists' liberties.

❝ [Colonists] *should enjoy as great freedom, liberty, and security as they
do in their native country: the havens, towns and villages in those parts
being occupied and possessed by their fellow subjects, which
freedom and liberty will greatly encourage them ...* ❞

Hakluyt's *Discourse* was written as if he had taken Calvin's dedication
to Elizabeth in his *Commentaries on Isaiah* to heart as England's own
divine mandate. To the visionary Hakluyt, England should fully embrace
the Great Commission to plant Christ's scepter in the West. In citing
Romans 10, Hakluyt quoted the argument first made by the Apostle Paul
for evangelizing the nations of the world. Now, Hakluyt asked his English
queen:

---

27 Richard Hakluyt, *A Discourse Concerning Western Planting* (Cambridge, 1877), p. 7. Opening
chapter head in the manuscript version of the treatise.

But how shall they call on Him whom they have not believed? And
how shall they believe Him whom they have not heard? How shall
they hear without a preacher? And how shall they preach except
they are sent?[28]

Hakluyt's fervent appeal was for England to extend the spiritual
kingdom of Christ where it was desperately needed. His argument also
pointed to the fact that the Spanish Crown had completely subverted the
true calling of the faith: *"For the kings of Spain have sent such hellhounds*
and wolves thither as have not converted, but almost quite subverted
them."[29] Hakluyt then pointed to the hard, hellish realities of Spain's
colonial government: *"by these devilish doings of the Spaniards, don* [put]
to death unjustly and tyrannically more then twelve million souls, men,
women, and children."[30] It was equally clear that the Spanish had not only
vanquished people, but as ravaging conquerors *"touching that main land,*
... their cruelties and cursed doings, have despoiled and made desolate
more than ten realms greater than Spain."[31]

Hakluyt was most of all appalled at the papal bulls that granted Spain
her supposed claim of divine right. *"But none of the prophets,"* Hakluyt
argued, *"made bulls or donations in their palaces, under their hands and*
seals and dates, to bestow many kingdoms which they never saw nor knew...
as the Pope has done in giving all the West Indies to the kings of Spain."[32]
Hakluyt was contrasting true prophets like Isaiah with the pretenses of the
pope – that even those who truly spoke for God never claimed an authority
in themselves to grant whole regions of the earth to anyone.

To Hakluyt, it would be the English families settling in America who
"should enjoy as great freedom, liberty, and security as they usually do in
their native country; the havens, towns, and villages in those parts being

---

28 Ibid., p. 8. Hakluyt was quoting from Paul's Epistle to the Romans (chapter 10, verses 14-15), asking: *"How then shall they call on Him in whom they have not believed? ... ."* Verse 15 also answers
prophetically: *"How beautiful are the feet of those who preach the gospel of peace, who bring glad*
tidings of good things!" (NKJ)

29 Ibid., p. 145.

30 Ibid., p. 74.

31 Ibid.

32 Ibid., p. 133.

occupied and possessed by their fellow subjects."[33] In this statement, we find not only a consistent articulation of the Reformed Christian legacy of liberty, but its all-important application to American colonies as self-governed families and communities.

The First Attempts to Colonize

In 1584, Hakluyt personally presented his English queen with his manuscript *A Discourse Concerning Western Planting*. The presentation was strategically timed to secure a patent for his colleague Walter Raleigh, who was pursuing royal permission to colonize along the eastern coast of North America. Hakluyt bolstered his own aim in advancing the faith by writing to Francis Walsingham, one of the most influential men at Elizabeth's court. Hakluyt offered Walsingham his personal services to accompany Raleigh: "*I am most willing to go now,*" Hakluyt pledged, "*in the service of God and my country to employ all my simple observations, readings, and conference whatsoever.*"[34]

Due in part to Hakluyt's persuasion, Elizabeth authorized Raleigh's mission of colonization in 1585. Walsingham, however, chose Thomas Hariot to accompany Raleigh in Hakluyt's place. It was therefore Hariot rather than Hakluyt who went on to document the landmark venture. Although the first Raleigh colony was ill-planned and soon abandoned, in 1588 Hariot published a marvelous account entitled: *A Brief and True Report of the New Found Land of Virginia*.

Raleigh's colony, called the "Dominion of Virginia," had been a bold first step in England's efforts to permanently plant her flag on North American shores. As historically significant as the mission was in naming the eastern coastline of America "*Virginia*" in honor of Elizabeth (England's *virgin* queen), equally important was Hariot's recording of the first English effort to evangelize the natives of North America:

Many times and in every town where I came, according as I was able, I made declaration of the contents of the Bible; that therein was set

---

33 Ibid., p. 94.
34 Taylor, *The Original Writings*, pp. 208-210.

forth the true and only God, and His mighty works, that therein was contained the true doctrine of salvation through Christ...[35]

The Founding of Virginia and the First English Effort to Evangelize the Natives of America

Title page inset from Thomas Hariot's 1590 account of America: *A Brief and True Report of the New Found Land of Virginia, of the Commodities and of the Natural Inhabitants Discovered by the English Colony There Seated ... in the Year 1585*, and an illustration of a village including (at its center) pagan worship under the Pomeiooc Chief

Such declarations characterized the Reformed, evangelistic approach to colonizing. These straightforward proclamations of Christ expressed God's grace toward the natives of America. They spoke of His liberating kingdom rather than the yoke of tyranny. The cause of that superior kingdom gave Hariot full confidence to look beyond England's initial failure and express his optimism regarding the further work of the Gospel among the natives: *"that there is good hope they may be brought through discreet dealing and government to the embracing of the truth."*[36]

In 1587, Walter Raleigh attempted a second colony on Roanoke Island nearer the Chesapeake Bay. Under Governor John White, the large

---

35 Thomas Hariot, A *Brief and True Report of the New Found Land of Virginia ... at the Special Charge and Direction of the Honorable Sir Walter Raleigh Knight... Illustrated by Theodore De Bry* (1590). Republished as *The First Plantation of Virginia in 1585* (London, 1893), p. 40.
36 Ibid., p. 43.

company of English settlers now included many committed families. A blessed result was that the first English child was born in a colonial settlement – the governor's granddaughter who was appropriately named Virginia Dare.

All of that being said, the fine art of successful, sustained colonization was far from perfected. The site for Raleigh's second colony on Roanoke Island had not been well-positioned to either provide adequate crops or to sustain a proper defense. The supplies soon waned as the Indians kept the settlers confined to their quarters. The hapless colony was at last forced to return Governor White to England for needed provisions.

The timing, however, could not have been worse for the fledgling colony due to England's own emergency that arrived off her southern coast. In the summer of 1588 the Spanish nemesis, King Philip II, launched his "invincible Armada" – an immense crusading fleet of Spain's finest and best equipped ships – to conquer England.

The Magnificent "Protestant Wind" Saves England from the Invasion of the Spanish Armada in 1588

Thanksgiving medal minted in 1588 showing an English family's gratitude: 66 *Man Proposes, but God Disposes.* 99 ("*Homo Proponit, Deus Disponi*" in Latin)

Map of Britain showing the Armada's invasion route through the English Channel from the South. Its defeat came by being providentially blown to the North. Vanquished, it fled up around Scotland.

Miraculously, Philip's invasion was thwarted. Although by remarkable bravery, skill, and cunning, England's smaller fleet had an amazing series of successes against the Armada, it was a turn in the weather, or rather, it was the magnificent "Protestant Wind" that saved the island realm. By God's good graces, Philip's Armada was blown disastrously adrift from its carefully plotted objective. Thus the Roman Church[37] as well as the rest of Europe saw how the Lord Himself had sunk Philip's pride along with much of his so-called "invincible" fleet.

England's triumph over the Armada, however, came at the price of a grave disappointment in America. By the time Governor White was able to secure provisions and return to his beloved Roanoke in 1590, little was found of the so-named "lost colony," with no trace of the ninety men, seventeen women, and eleven children, including White's granddaughter Virginia.[38]

A New Wind of Providence

As events so often turn in the hand of Providence, it was the defeat of the Armada that gave England her best encouragement to colonize. The grip of Spain in America would certainly be no more invincible than the Armada, and the "Protestant Wind" had turned again toward the West.

In 1589, the year after England's miraculous success over Spain, the ever-persistent Hakluyt published one of the greatest works of early English prose. Hakluyt's book, *The Principal Navigations, Voyages, and Discoveries of the English Nation,* used eyewitness records to present a sweeping account of England's long history on the seas. Hakluyt's argument was that England's storied history of navigation gave her as much right as any nation to pursue her interests across the seas. His conclusion was obvious as well – that England's story of navigation must not end.

Hakluyt dedicated the enlarged 1599 second edition of *Principal Navigations* to his chief patron and Secretary of State, Sir Robert Cecil.

---

37 Pope Gregory XIII (who died in 1585) and then Pope Sixtus V urged Philip to conquer England.

38 The Roanoke colonists disappeared without needed supplies from England. On his return in August 1590, Governor White found that the settlement had been dismantled. White's party found no trace of the families or any sign of a battle. Their only clues were the words "Croatoan" carved on a post of the fort and "Cro" carved on a nearby tree, leading to the mystery known as "The Lost Colony. "

That dedication (pointedly signed *"Richard Hakluyt, preacher"*[39]) pressed Cecil to pursue England's course in the virgin land that still lay *"under our noses."*[40] Hakluyt described this land as *"the great and ample country of Virginia; the inland whereof is found of late to be so sweet and wholesome a climate…"*[41] By the end of the sixteenth century, England had yet to plant a single successful colony in America. But, due to Reformed Christian visionaries like Hakluyt and Raleigh, her sights remained fixed upon planting a permanent colony on the shores of Virginia.

Richard Hakluyt's Repeated Call to Colonize America

Map published in 1590 showing England's claim to Virginia (oriented with North to the right)

Title page of Hakluyt's *Principal Navigations, Voyages, and Discoveries of the English Nation* published in 1589 describing England's place and purpose in the New World

It would be in the early seventeenth century under a new English monarch that England would gain a determined foothold in the New World. Throughout the seventeenth century, Virginia, as well as colonies to its north and south, would slowly begin to prosper under wave after wave of faithful English immigrants.

---

39 Richard Hakluyt, *The Principal Navigations, Voyages, Traffics and Discoveries of the English Nation*, vol. 1 (Glasgow: James MacLehose and Sons, 1903), lxxiii.
40 Ibid., p. lxvi.
41 Ibid.

6
THE FOUNDING OF JAMESTOWN COLONY

A New Political Climate in England

WHEN the century that witnessed the glorious rays of the Reformation shine upon England had come to an end, it was apparent that the illustrious reign of Queen Elizabeth I was also drawing to an end. At the dawn of the seventeenth century, it was equally clear that England would be illuminated with many new blessings and cast under the shadows of many new trials.

It was but a few days after Elizabeth's death in March of 1603 that her eagerly awaiting successor (James VI of Scotland) was proclaimed James I of England. Expectations were high as his royal procession moved slowly southward from James' native Scotland, and his new subjects gathered along the way for a curious glimpse of England's new king.[1] Upon entering London, James was also joyously met by the subjects of his new realm, many who anticipated that he would pursue the principles of the Reformed faith with even more enthusiasm than had their former queen.

Any hopes for a further Reformation soon vanished. James, in fact, chided his first Parliament (England's legislative body) regarding the Puritans who had been patiently pushing the government of England in a more representative direction. In James' opening speech before Parliament, he denounced the Puritans as those he said "*do not so far differ from us in points of Religion, as in their confused form of policy and parity, being ever discontented with the present government.*"[2]

With those words, James' governing demeanor was made abundantly clear. Though England's new king viewed the Puritans' private faith as consistent with his own, he regarded any attempt to move the government in a more representative manner as seditious. To James, such political views made the Puritans simply intolerable. Put in his own autocratic

1 James had become King of Scotland in 1567 at the age of thirteen months, succeeding his mother Mary, Queen of Scots. Though born Roman Catholic, James was educated under a Reformed tutor, George Buchanan. As a strong advocate of limited monarchy, Buchanan sought to cultivate James as a king who accepted the limitations of government.

2 James I, *The Kings Majesties Speech, as it was delivered by him in the upper house of the Parliament to the Lords ... 1603* (London, 1604), leaf B4.

terms, the Puritans' public policy made them *"unable to be suffered in any well-governed commonwealth."*[3]

James I's 1603 Speech Calling for a Passive Parliament

THE
Kings Maiefties Speech, as
it was deliuered by him in the vpper
houfe of the Parliament to the Lords
Spirituall and Temporall, and to the
Knights, Citizens and Burgeffes
there affembled,
On Munday the 19.day of March 1603.

The Puritanes & Nouelifts, doe not fo farre differ from vs in points of Religion, as in their confufed forme of Policie and Parity, being euer difcontented with the prefent Gouernement, and impatient to fuffer any fuperioritie, which maketh their Sect vnable to be fuffered in any well gouerned Common wealth.

Dan Ford,
2002

❝ *The Puritans and Novelists* [Separatists], *do not so far differ from us in points of Religion, as in their confused form of* [public] *policy and parity, being ever discontented with the present government, and impatient to suffer any superiority, which makes their sect unable to be suffered in any well-governed commonwealth.* ❞

The intention of the king's opening speech had been to silence all meaningful opposition to his rule and even reduce England's historic Parliament to no more than an advisory body. The effect, however, set England's legislative court (the High Court of Parliament) at odds with a king hell-bent on imposing his unqualified royal prerogative. Like a Spanish king, James saw his governing authority as a grant from God, but unlike Spain's monarch under the pope, England's new king saw his rule as a direct entitlement from heaven. Such presumption, more akin to the pretenses of Babylon's Nimrod than to a godly Christian king, gave rise to great opposition by a people weaned on the rich milk of God's Word.

The king's presumption, in fact, provoked an all-new sense of purpose in England's House of Commons (the lower House of Parliament). In that body lay the representation of the people's liberties and their rights of private property, and from the beginning of the reign of James I, the

---

3 Ibid.

Commons began asserting those rights against their grossly errant king. The emboldened Commons was now willing to stand on principle against what they recognized, biblically speaking, as a tyrant. Successive Parliaments then resisted the king's every attempt to subvert England's constitution and the truly Christian principles of a *"well-governed commonwealth."*

Sir Edwin Sandys, a leading member of the House of Commons, was one of the most outspoken proponents of the people's liberties. Sandys led a coalition of members that opposed James' divine right pretenses over the liberty and property of his subjects. In 1611, for example, the English Commons asserted that *"impositions* [taxes] *laid upon merchandise, or other goods of the subjects of this Realm, by the King's Majesty, without the free consent of the Subjects in Parliament was not lawful."*[4] In the Commons, Sandys and his Puritan allies repeatedly pushed for legislation that halted James' divine right attempts to subdue the people and property of his realm.

The Puritans and the Parliament of 1611: No Taxation of the People's Property or Goods without their Consent

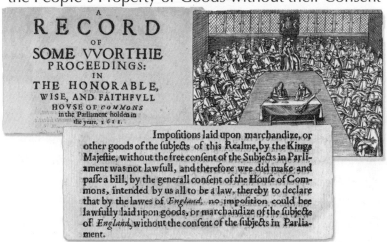

A
RECORD
OF
SOME VVORTHIE
PROCEEDINGS:
IN
THE HONORABLE,
WISE, AND FAITHFVLL
HOVSE OF *COMMONS*
in the Parliament holden in
the yeare, 1 6 1 1.

Impofitions laid upon marchandize, or other goods of the fubjeﬆs of this Realme, by the Kings Majeﬆie, without the free confent of the Subjeﬆs in Parliament was not lawfull, and therefore wee did make and paﬆe a bill, by the generall confent of the Houfe of Commons, intended by us all to be a law, thereby to declare that by the lawes of *England,* no impofition could bee lawfully laid upon goods, or marchandize of the fubjeﬆs of *England,* without the confent of the fubjeﬆs in Parliament.

❝ [By] *a bill, by the general consent of the House of Commons, intended by us all to be a law, thereby to declare that by the laws of England, no imposition [taxes] could be lawfully laid upon goods, or merchandise of the subjects of England, without the consent of the subjects in Parliament.* ❞

4 English House of Commons, *A Record of Some Worthy Proceedings in the Honorable, Wise, and Faithful House of Commons in the Parliament Holden in the year 1611* (London, 1641), p. 6.

The Key to Colonial Failure and the Keys to Success

Sandys, who opposed the divine right pretenses of all kings, also became one of the chief proponents of English colonization in the New World. His aim was to both promote the Reformed faith and to counter the tyranny of the Spanish king. James, however, was determined to make peace with England's historic foe, and in 1604 he oversaw negotiations that brought an end to the long, drawn-out Anglo-Spanish war. That armed contest was due in part to England's prior efforts under Elizabeth I to advance Protestantism in America. It had continued long after Philip II's attempt to subdue England with his Armada in 1588, and for England's new King James, the time for reconciliation with Spain had arrived.

Soon after the ink had dried on James' treaty with Spain, Edwin Sandys' small volume titled *A Relation of the State of Religion* was clandestinely printed. Sandys' *Relation*, first published in 1605, sent a new and unwelcomed volley across the bow of England's old opponent Spain, reminding his English readers that Spanish kings had led "*the most cruel inquisition that ever the world had.*"[5] It also characterized Spain herself as "*a nation that aims so apparently at the monarchy of the whole West.*"[6]

Such charges made by an influential leader of Parliament could not have been more unwelcome to a king who was courting cordial relations with Spain. According to Sandys, Spain's approach to colonization was a disaster not only to the natives of America, but to Spain's own domestic families: "*their country being so generally exhausted of men, what eaten up by long war, what transported into their huge number of Indian Colonies, that their cities remain now wholly peopled with women, having some old men among them, and many young children ....*"[7]

Sandys' point was that Spain's attempt at dominion abroad had come at the expense of her intrinsic strength at home. Her heartiest men had been sent on far-flung missions of plunder, while Spain's domestic families were being deprived of necessary manly virtue. Of her remaining

---

5 Edwin Sandys, *A Relation of the State of Religion*, leaf P4b.
6 Ibid., leaf Qa.
7 Ibid.

"*old men*" and "*young children*," Sandys observed with typical English sarcasm, "*the grave attends the one, and foreign service the other.*"[8]

One might suppose that with such an astute criticism of Spain, Sandys would disdain any scheme of English colonization abroad. However, Sandys knew that if colonization was undertaken according to biblical principles, it would benefit England and English families alike. In fact, faithful Christian colonies would not only counter the divine right pretenses of Spain's dominion in America, but provide an outlet for those who could not suffer the divine right pretenses of their English king.

Edwin Sandys and Spain's Formula for National Failure

Dan Ford
2010

Sir Edwin Sandys
1561-1629

Title page of Edwin Sandy's 1605:
A Relation of the State of Religion

❝ [Spain] *aims so apparently at the monarchy of the whole West, ... their country being so generally exhausted of men ... transported into their huge number of Indian Colonies, that their cities remain now wholly peopled with women, having some old men among them, and many young children, whereof the grave attends the one, and foreign service the other.* ❞

In Sandys' *Relation*, he explained the only means of success for any faithful people. "*The first and chief means*," Sandys wrote, "*whereby the Reformed religion prevailed in all places, was their singular assisitude* [assistance] *and dexterity* [aptitude] *in preaching....*"[9] In other words, the liberating kingdom of Christ triumphed amidst people who were

8 Ibid.
9 Ibid., leaf Ha.

continually steeped in the precepts of Scripture. *"A second thing,"* Sandys added, *"whereby the Protestant part has so greatly enlarged itself, has been their well-educating of youth, especially in the principles of Christian religion and piety..."*[10] This was Sandys' astute observation of the centrality of God-honoring families in any successful societal endeavor. These two distinctive features of the Reformed Christian faith – skillful preaching and family education – would prove to be the keys to both success and self-government in English colonial America.

The 1606 Charter of Virginia

With the possibilities of English colonization having been first awakened by the writings of visionaries such as Richard Hakluyt in the sixteenth century, England's grand adventure into America commenced with new determination in the seventeenth century.

Several commercial ventures had emerged in the late sixteenth century for the purpose of trading with distant countries in the East. Most prominent was England's widely successful East India Company chartered in 1600, with its remarkable success giving rise to hopes that well-financed corporate enterprises might also be successful in the West. Accordingly, in 1606 two companies were formed through which England's claim of Virginia was divided into two parts: the southern part was granted to the London Company and the northern to the Plymouth Company. They each obtained a royal charter which enabled them to found a colony and granted them a right to make Company laws, but each was also under the oversight of the king.

James' stated objective in chartering the companies was *"to make habitation, plantation, and to deduce* [lead] *a colony of sundry of our people into that part of America commonly called Virginia."*[11] The use of corporations was an important feature that distinguished England's

---

10 Ibid., leaf H2, side b.

11 Francis Newton Thorpe, ed. *The Federal and State Constitutions, Colonial Charters, and Other Organic Laws of the States, Territories and Colonies Now or Heretofore Forming the United States of America*, vol. 7 (Washington: Government Printing Office, 1909), p. 3783.

colonies from those of Spain. The Companies afforded English investors and settlers an opportunity to make a profit on the patient cultivation of the land, rather than the king reaping the immediate rewards in the pillage and plunder of the American natives. It also meant that the free enterprise of the investors and settlers, rather than the king, would take personal responsibility for both funding and securing the venture. In other words, with a distinctly Reformed Christian understanding of the stewardship of the earth, the English were motivated to settle peaceable and profitable colonies without the use of overpowering and domineering royal armies like those of Spain.

A less invasive, less aggressive approach certainly aided the spirit of Protestant colonization. King James (though likely motivated by the fact that private investors were risking their own necks and capital) consented to the London Company's 1606 charter that specified of the investors: "*that they shall have all the lands, woods, soil, grounds, havens, ports, rivers, mines, minerals, marshes, waters, fishings, commodities, and hereditaments* [inheritable estates]."[12]

Although establishing Virginia by means of free enterprise was the stated corporate objective of the London Company, the mission of Christian evangelism was certainly not overlooked. According to those who drafted the 1606 charter (including Richard Hakluyt), the mission of advancing the kingdom of God was central to their venture: "*in* [the] *propagating of Christian Religion to such people, as yet live in darkness and miserable ignorance of the true knowledge and worship of God...*"[13] In all, conveying goodwill to the natives, bringing glory to God, and securing a healthy profit to the settlers and investors were the core objectives of the English venture into the Virginian wilderness. The English mission was thereby decidedly peaceable, and it included bringing the natives "*to human civility, and to a settled and quiet government,*"[14] rather than bringing them under the tyrannical grip of European despotism.

---

12 Ibid., p. 3784.
13 Ibid.
14 Ibid.

Trials of Early Jamestown

The first Englishmen to make a successful foray into the woodlands of North America were those representing the London Company of Virginia. In December of 1606 three ships bearing one hundred and five hopeful souls marked the first of many English immigrations to America. The winter's trip, however, was as long as it was grueling, and the one hundred forty days' journey across the Atlantic was simply a foretaste of the trials lying ahead for the English in Virginia.

Planting a New Britain upon the Virgin Soil of America

To the left is the title page of Robert Johnson's 1609 tract: *Nova Britannia, Offering Most Excellent Fruits by Planting in Virginia*, calling English settlers to Jamestown colony.

To the right is Minister Samuel Purchas and the title page of his 1613 volume titled: *Purchas, His Pilgrimage*, a work recalling the purity of England's mission to Virginia:

❝ Let us draw nearer the sun to New Britain, whose virgin soil not yet polluted with Spaniards' lust, by our late Virgin-Mother [Queen Elizabeth I], was justly called Virginia. ❞

In April of 1607 the expedition finally arrived at the mouth of the Chesapeake Bay. Their first territorial claim was made by designating the two prominent points on the flanking sides of the bay's entrance "Cape Henry" and "Cape Charles" after the sons of the English king. As the ships approached one of the largest rivers flowing into the bay itself, the Company promptly named it the "James River" after the king himself.

Then, following the James for some thirty miles upriver, on May 14 they finally arrived at a site equally safe from either the salty tidal backwash or any sudden surprise by Spanish invaders. Their chosen site, with a clear view up and down the river and with a channel still deep enough to accommodate their seafaring ships, was named "Jamestown," also in honor of their English king.

Against expectations of laying hold of all the bounty of Virginia, the ill-prepared adventurers found themselves encompassed by nearly every kind of trouble. On one hand, the Indians, who saw the English as a decided threat, proved not to be as welcoming as was hoped and immediately penned them within the walls of a makeshift palisade. On the other hand, succumbing to the noxious diseases of the surrounding lowland swamps, the English began to die at a rate of more than two per week. Then, finding neither local game for hunting nor suitable land for planting, the adventurers resorted to expending their remaining rations.

The London Company's resident council in Virginia, headed by Captain Edward Maria Wingfield, was unsuited to govern such a starving lot. Their common discontent soon turned to internal quarreling and ultimately to outright despair. By the time a supply ship arrived with welcomed provisions and settlers in January of 1608, less than forty of the original colonists had survived.

Just as the new supplies sustained them, the added settlers served to stabilize Jamestown's desperately declining population. The settlement's numbers gradually increased with the new arrivals and needed stores – that is, until the dreaded "starving time" of the 1609-1610 seasons. The Indians had by that time become openly hostile and a new and growing plague of disease began to dwindle Jamestown's population from its peak of five hundred to a mere sixty souls in all. By June 1610 it was apparent that another growing season had been lost, and the few beleaguered survivors resigned themselves to abandon Jamestown altogether. This was, at best, a desperate attempt to save whoever they could from a total loss. The despondent English then gathered all supplies suitable for an ocean voyage to England and floated down the James River toward the Chesapeake Bay.

While at last making preparations to cast their fate upon the Atlantic, Providence intervened and stopped the retreat in its tracks. With total amazement by the evacuees, an English fleet captained by Lord De La Warr (or "Delaware") suddenly appeared at the mouth of the great Chesapeake Bay.

With a healthy stock of hearty men as well as an abundance of desperately needed supplies, the English settlement had yet again been miraculously saved. Ruin had been staved off and hopes raised as the colonists returned to Jamestown. It was now apparent that from the deepest valley of earthly despair, the heavenly smile of Providence had again visited the English with His hand of favor. It was certainly evident to all who were blessed to witness their marvelous deliverance that a truly divine Sovereign had plans for Virginia far greater than having Jamestown become another failed English venture.

7
SUCCESSES IN ENGLISH VIRGINIA

Edwin Sandys and the First Improvements in Jamestown

FOLLOWING the early starving times, colonial Jamestown survived, but under the constant strain of both external and internal trials. The new resident governor, Lord De La Warr, vigorously fought back against the Indians, and for a time, greatly suppressed the outside threats to the colony. De La Warr also brought news of administrative reforms from the London Company in England which would better accommodate the internal needs of colonial Jamestown as well.

As we have seen, one of the most devoted proponents of English liberty and English colonization was Sir Edwin Sandys. When news had arrived in London of endemic problems in Virginia, Sir Edwin took immediate note and began to intervene. And, as might be expected, he did not intervene on behalf of royal interests, but in the interests of Virginia's long-term health and prosperity.

Sandy's first contribution was lending a hand in drafting Virginia's new 1609 charter. This charter's key improvement was in the London Company gaining a further measure of independence from the Crown. Whereas (according to the previous charter) the king appointed all Company officers, with the new charter the London Company (although still managed in London) was now at liberty to elect its own officers. King James conceded to allow the voting members, as was stated in the 1609 charter, "*to nominate, make, constitute, ordain and confirm, by such name or names, stile or stiles, as to them shall seem good.*"[1]

Another important feature was the London Company's ability to draw up a more efficient means of supervising an ever-growing colony. Along with sending Governor De La Warr, Company administrators were also sent to Virginia with "*patents and indentures*" to allow for much larger

---

1 Thorpe, *The Federal and State Constitutions, Colonial Charters, and Other Organic Laws of the Territories and Colonies*, p. 3798.

"*tituled*" (titled) property holdings by the Virginian residents.[2] With these more generous landholdings titled in private hands, the resident settlers gained a further measure of independence from the core settlement of "James City" (or Jamestown). They were also advised to experiment with a variety of crops (planted away from the disease-ridden lowland swamps). In all, though the Jamestown colony was still supervised by a governor and agents who were accountable to London, the colonists began to enjoy a greater sense of the Company's encouragement of their private industry. With such governmental respect for privately owned and managed landholdings eventually came the blessings of true free enterprise and ever-expanding private estates.

Calls for Reformation and Prayer

Jamestown continued to remain a monetary drain rather than a positive return for the London Company, and by 1613 its stockholders were becoming weary. Experimental crops often failed to produce adequate profits, and a popular (though exaggerated) refrain by those in London was to ask: "*when they come there* [to America], *are they not starved, and do they not die like dogs?*"[3]

The Virginian venture, however, did have advocates in England such as William Crashaw, a Puritan preacher who was also a strong proponent of Christian colonization. Crashaw rebuffed such "*slanders raised upon our colonies, and the country itself.*"[4] To him, what was lacking in Virginia was not adequate monetary backing or increasing numbers of willing settlers, but those with the proper zeal for advancing Christ's kingdom.

That, Crashaw wrote, meant sending those who had a vision for building a genuinely Christian society and planting them as a hearty stock in both church and state. "*Magistracy and ministry are the strength and*

---

2 *Susan Myra Kingsbury, ed., The Records of the Virginia Company of London. The Court Book, From the Manuscript in the Library of Congress*, vol. 1 (Washington: Government Printing Office, 1906), pp., 346-347.

3 Alexander Whitaker, *Good Newes from Virginia. Sent to the Counsel and Company of Virginia, resident in England* (London, 1613), leaf A4a.

4 Ibid., leaf A2a.

sinews; nay the very life of being a Christian body politic," explained
Crashaw, *"therefore seeing without these, all emptying of purses here* [in
London], *and venturing of persons thither* [to Virginia], *is of no purpose."*[5]

In other words, Crashaw's recommendation for Virginia's success was
to send the best stock of devoted Christians that England could provide,
and have them form a genuinely *"Christian body politic"* (or Christian civil
government). Against all those who held contrary opinions, Crashaw had a
resolute faith that God would supply that needed provision, reminding all
those concerned with monetary profits *"that assuredly God Himself is the
founder and favorer of this Plantation."*[6]

Good News From Virginia: Investing in the True Kingdom

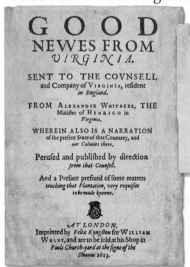

Title page of Alexander Whitaker's tract, *Good
News From Virginia,* published in 1613. Puritan
preacher and missionary Whitaker exhorts his
fellow Englishmen that the trials of Virginia
are part of a sound investment in
the true kingdom of Christ:

❝ *Awake you true hearted English men, you servants of Jesus Christ,
remember that the Plantation is God's, and the reward your country's.* ❞

Besides England's William Crashaw, there were also those in Virginia
who advocated advancing Christ's kingdom more assertively. Alexander
Whitaker, the so-called "Apostle to Virginia" who was instrumental in

5 Ibid., leafs A4a and A4b.
6 Ibid.

the conversion of the renowned Indian princess Pocahontas, also urged prayer and a genuine reformation. Within a year of baptizing Pocahontas in Virginia, Whitaker's tract *Good News From Virginia* (1613) was published in London. His purpose was to call those on both sides of the Atlantic to restore the Virginian planting to the first principles of English colonization, "*that the predicate* [presumptuous] *opinion of some and the disheartened mind of others may be reformed.*"[7]

As an avid Puritan preacher, Alexander Whitaker was an advocate of discipling the lost in America – both the original natives and the newly resident colonists. Because Whitaker (like Crashaw) believed that England's work in Virginia was the Lord's work, his advice was for all English brethren to fortify their common resolve: "*Awake you true hearted Englishmen, you servants of Jesus Christ,*" Whitaker urged those in his native England to "*remember that the Plantation is God's and the reward your country's.*"[8] Then, cautioning against expectations for immediate monetary return, Whitaker pointed his fellow Englishmen to their greater investment:

> *Wherefore, aim not at your present private gain, but let the glory of God, whose Kingdom you now plant, & good of your country, whose wealth you seek, so far prevail with you, that you respect not a present return of gain for this year or two: but that you would more liberally supply for a little space, this your Christian work, which you so charitably began.*[9]

Thus, for Whitaker, a true investment was put in terms of England's ongoing charity toward the work in Virginia, and as always, put in the definitive terms of advancing God's glorious kingdom.

Edwin Sandys and a Reformation of Colonial Virginia

Any faith professed must be faithfulness put into practice on a practical and tangible basis. Hence, when Edwin Sandys was elected to the leading

---

7 Ibid., leaf D2b.
8 Ibid., leaf H3a.
9 Ibid.

position as the Treasurer of the London Company in 1618, he proceeded
with a more vigorous agenda in securing financial backing for the work
in Virginia. One aim was for a long-term investment in *"the collecting of
monies to erect and build a College in Virginia."*[10] Sandys' intent was to
use a place of learning as a missionary endeavor to train native converts
in the *"true knowledge of God and understanding of righteousness."*[11]
In this, Sandys' goal was consistent with the terms of the original 1606
charter: the *"propagation of Christian Religion to such people, as yet live
in darkness and miserable ignorance of the true kingdom of God..."*[12]
Sandys' proposal for a college was, however, initially set aside pending
adequate funding.

The formal college mission was completely abandoned following an
unprovoked and vicious attack by the Indians against the English in 1622.
The devastation brought not only an end to plans for a college mission,
but it nearly brought the entire Jamestown venture to ruin. Many families
and estates were decimated. From then on, the work of missions among
the Virginian Indians would be pursued without the advantage of a formal
institution. Any hopes for a college in Virginia would have to wait for
another seven decades, though the work of propagating the dominion of
Christ in America was certainly carried on by other means.

Planting Godly Homes

Upon becoming Treasurer of the London Company of Virginia in
1618, Sandys led other efforts for widespread reforms in Virginia. For
example, when the Company's goals of receiving outside funding fell short,
Sandys at times provided the needed revenue from his own pocket. On one
occasion in 1619 he arranged for the transport of over three hundred new
settlers, including women and families, at his private expense. Sir Edwin
was later pleased to receive news of significant agricultural success,
reporting: *"plenty of corn that God this year has blessed them with, the*

---

10 Kingsbury, *Records of the Virginia Company of London*, vol. 1, p. 220.
11 Ibid.
12 Thorpe, *The Federal and State Constitutions*, vol. 7, p. 3784.

like never happened since the English was there planted."[13]

These efforts by Sandys confirmed to the London Company that permanent success would be achieved only by planting an abundance of English homes in Virginia – and what was most lacking was an adequate supply of wives. After repeated attempts to reinvigorate the colony with male replacements, an indicting report to the Company admitted:

> [T]*he people thither transported, though seated there in their persons for some few years, are not settled in their minds to make it their place of rest and continuance, but having gotten some wealth there, to return again into England.*[14]

The London Company's new policy was then to anchor the ambitions of the male adventurers to the soil by importing English ladies. In November 1619, Sandys requested: "*to send them over one hundred young maids to become wives; that wives, children, and family might make them less movable and settle them, together with their posterity in that soil.*"[15]

Another Company report stated that because of a lack of wives, "*sprang the greatest hindrances of the increase of the plantation.*"[16] The same report then happily added that the cure was on its way:

> [That] *the planters' minds may be the faster tied to Virginia by the bonds of wives and children, care has been taken to provide them young, handsome, and honestly educated maids whereof 60 are already sent to Virginia....*[17]

The Jamestown colony would not have survived long without domesticating the ambitions of the resident adventurers. A home provided an anchor for the ambitious soul, and a man's family provided the moral underpinning that a successful colony needed. The man who wed and then rooted his family in the soil was often amply rewarded for his wise investment, and his colony was certainly blessed with the godly increase of lasting virtue.

---

13 Kingsbury, *The Records of the Virginia Company of London*, vol. 1, p. 310.
14 Ibid., p. 269. This report was delivered to the London Company's managers in 1619.
15 Ibid.
16 Ibid., p. 566.
17 Ibid.

Planting Godly Government

The crowning achievement of Sandys' reforms was the authorization of an assembly of colonial representatives. The new resident governor in Virginia, Francis Yeardley, was directed to issue writs for the election of a Virginian assembly. On July 30, 1619, the House of Burgesses – the first elected representative body in the New World – met in the church building at Jamestown. A prayer by the minister at the beginning of the proceedings was recorded in the official report sent back to Sandys:

> *But foreasmuch as men's affairs do little prosper, where God's ser-vice is neglected, all the burgesses took their places in the quire* [the general pulpit and lectern area of the church], *till a prayer was said by Mr. Bucke the Minister, that it would please God to guide & sanctify all our proceedings to His own glory, and the good of this plantation.*[18]

The Account of the First Self-Governed Assembly in America: Report from the Virginian Assembly to Edwin Sandys in 1619

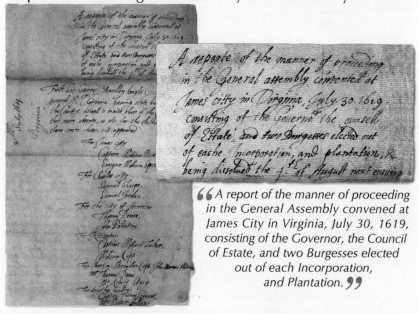

❝A report of the manner of proceeding in the General Assembly convened at James City in Virginia, July 30, 1619, consisting of the Governor, the Council of Estate, and two Burgesses elected out of each Incorporation, and Plantation.❞

---

18 Elizabeth Hallam & Andrew Prescott, *The British Inheritance* (Berkeley: University of California Press, 1999), p. 47.

With their footing set upon first things first – namely God's glory and guidance – the example of free representative government was established in America. This feature was significant because it would be the hallmark of the later colonial governments and would yield beneficial fruit throughout the colonial era. Liberty and property would find protection under representative colonial legislation, and the security of private property rights would then continue as an essential part of the American character well beyond the founding era of our republic in the late 1700s.

The basic purpose of self-representation in Jamestown was to protect the resident's private interests from outside encroachments. Most importantly, because all legislation was initiated within the body of local representatives, impositions or taxes on the property of the Virginian landowners could only come from within the colony itself. The colonists could then safeguard their own private interests within this most prosperous model of colonial government.

In effect, Sandys had transferred a significant part of the London Company's own independence from King James to the colonists. At least for the time being, the colonists were as politically and economically safe from an autocratic English king as possible, which is what Sir Edwin had been seeking for all English subjects in his beloved House of Commons.

It was said at the time that Virginia's Burgess system of local rule was more akin to Calvin's republic in Geneva than to the English government under King James. Whether Sandys had that in mind or not has been a matter of considerable speculation. It is known that during his tenure as Treasurer of the London Company, a contemporary of Sir Edwin reported him to have asserted: "*if our God from heaven did constitute and direct a form of government it was that of Geneva.*"[19]

King James and his associates grew to dislike Sandys' growing influence both at home and abroad. James' allies at court accused this liberty-minded London Company Treasurer of having devious designs, saying that "*his intent was to erect a free state in Virginia.*"[20]

---

19 Alexander Brown, *The First Republic in America* (Boston: Houghton, Mifflin and Company, 1898), p. 529. Quoting a letter dated May, 1623 to the commissioners by Sir Nathaniel Rich.
20 Ibid., p. 530.

The Virginia Company and Self-Government in America

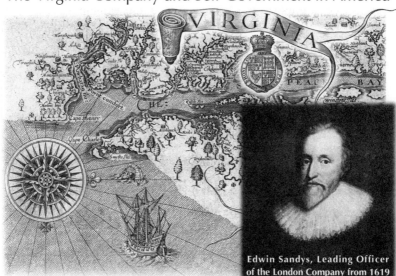

Edwin Sandys, Leading Officer
of the London Company from 1619

By the time of the demise of the London Company of Virginia in 1624, Edwin Sandys had seen that the colony was stocked with English families grounded on private estates and fortified with representative government.

Sandys' opponents, even within the London Company, increased in proportion to his resolve to promote the interests of the Virginian colonists over those of the English Crown. In the end, it was a combination of the growing strife among the Company's factions in England and a sudden and disastrous attack by the Indians against the dispersed plantations in Virginia that resulted in the demise of the London Company of Virginia in 1624.

In an advantageous move, King James then placed the supervision of Virginia directly under his own charge. For the colony itself, it was a great providence of God that James died before acting on his intention to also abolish the Virginia House of Burgesses. It was then another magnificent providence of God that when James' son was crowned Charles I in 1625, England's new king somewhat reluctantly allowed for the continuation of representative assemblies in America under another revised royal charter.

Ultimate Success in Colonial Virginia

It was the planting of families, churches, and representative government, rather than discoveries of gold or plundering of native riches, that ultimately ensured the success of Virginia. Consequently, the English colonies were not seen as places for temporary profit or fleeting gain. They were seen as England's own society planted in America, which secured a more rewarding and enduring possession of liberty and property.

This model of colonization, with dominion in private hands and local representation, would provide the greatest adornments to both Mother England and her daughter Virginia. The English families in America became as fruitful as possible. In time, their increased numbers and bountiful resources would provide the whole British realm with wealth enough to become a highly respected economic power among the nations of Europe.

8
A NEW PLYMOUTH IN A NEW ENGLAND

The Despised Separatists

THERE was one type of Puritan that King James despised more than all
the others. Although Puritans in general strove to reform the ritualized
Anglican Church, to some, its hierarchy of bishops and formalized
worship were so unbiblical that they separated from the national Church
altogether. These were the "Separatists" who considered themselves as
*"witnessing against human inventions, and additions in the worship of
God."*[1] To King James, who was perched atop the entire Anglican order,
these nonconformists were regarded as the *"Novelists"*[2] – as simply
troublemakers whom he thought were making a mere novelty of religion.

The Separatists were not only the object of James' personal scorn
but were targeted for official punishment and persecution. Their land
and possessions were often the objects of seizure and their persons the
objects of imprisonment or banishment from the realm. When Separatist
congregations met for worship, they gathered in secret. Even at that,
although they were temporarily outside the notice of royal authorities,
they were never far from ultimately losing everything they held dear.

The most historically renowned group of Separatists was a relatively
small congregation of English families driven by James to Holland in 1608.
Many of these Separatists became known as the famed American "Pilgrims"
who later planted New England's Plymouth Colony in 1620. These God-
fearing saints became the first stock of all the European refugees who
would eventually escape to America for the sake of Christian liberty. This
particular group of English Separatists will always be remembered as the
first among Christ's truly faithful who, for the sake of their own Christian
consciences, sailed to New England and made America renowned as the
land of the free.

---

1 Nathaniel Morton, *New-England's Memorial or a Brief Relation of the Most Memorable and Remarkable Passages of the Providence of God, Manifested to the Planters... With special Reference to
the First Colony Thereof, Called New-Plymouth* (Cambridge, New England, 1669), p. 2.
2 James I, *The Kings Majesties Speech*, leaf B4.

Trying Times in Holland

The core of the group that would come to be known as the "Pilgrims" were those who had originally gathered for worship north of London at the Scrooby Manor House in Nottinghamshire, England. This residence had been owned by the father of Sir Edwin Sandys and was at the time being leased by his brother. The Sandys family welcomed the Scrooby congregation, led by their elder William Brewster and others. Once news of their gathering reached the authorities in London, however, pending persecution made survival in England impossible. And, choosing freedom over persecution, many of the Separatists secretly fled to Holland over the span of 1607 and 1608.

The decade that the Pilgrims then spent as refugees in Holland was a time of hardship for a majority of the congregation. At first, there were cultural differences including a language barrier that brought difficulties in gaining employment. It was, however, the *"great licentiousness of youth in that country, and the manifold temptations of the place"*[3] that the later Pilgrim author Nathaniel Morton recorded as the main concern of the English families in Holland. The liberalism of the Dutch was the greatest threat to the English children, who, as Morton explained, were *"departing from their parents."*[4]

Losing both their family integrity and their national identity were prime factors for many of the refugees wanting to leave their temporary haven in Holland for a safer cultural environment. Some families, in fact, returned to England and reluctantly conformed to the Anglican Church as the lesser of the two evils. Others, having heard news of the successful English settlements of the London Company in Virginia, set their future hopes on America.

Securing Legal Passage

It would be a major feat for a people who had been expelled from their homeland and were despised by their king to then obtain his permission

---

3 Morton, *New-England's Memorial*, p. 3.
4 Ibid., p. 4.

to settle anywhere under an English flag. Facing a Church establishment that vigorously opposed them and a king who fervently despised them, the situation of these English sojourners stranded in a foreign nation appeared even more desperate. But here again, that same familiar friend of liberty, Sir Edwin Sandys, would lend his hand. The later governor of Plymouth Colony, William Bradford, documented Sandys' attempts to intervene on their behalf. His manuscript chronicle *Of Plymouth Plantation* recorded the refugees' Holland pastor John Robinson and elder William Brewster giving enthusiastic thanks to Sandys. In a letter from December of 1617, they expressed their personal thanks, saying: *"above all persons and all things in the world, we rely upon you, expecting the care of your love, counsel of your wisdom and the help and countenance of your authority."*[5]

Sandys had, in fact, worked diligently behind the scenes to arrange for the Pilgrims to obtain a patent to immigrate to America. But, because he was despised by James I, Sandys secured the help of Robert Naunton, the king's chief Secretary of State, to negotiate on their behalf. The more agreeable Naunton pressed the king, *"that such a people might enjoy their liberty of conscience under his gracious protection in America."*[6] And, being astute of the pride of royalty, Naunton made sure his argument included the most prestigious jewel for the crown of James by adding that the immigrants *"would endeavor the advancement of his majesty's dominions."*[7] King James' somewhat surprising and satisfying reaction was: *"it was a good and honest motion."*[8]

Secretary Naunton's argument had apparently hit its mark by linking the Pilgrims' objective to secure their liberty in Christ with the king's interest in enlarging his personal prestige. Edward Winslow[9] also

---

5 William Bradford, *Of Plymouth Plantation*, ed. Samuel Eliot Morison (New York: Alfred A. Knopf, 1996), p. 32.

6 Cotton Mather, *Magnalia Christi Americana: or the Ecclesiastical History of New England, from its First Planting in the Year 1620, Unto the Year of our Lord, 1698*, Book 1 (London, 1702), p. 6.

7 Ibid.

8 Ibid.

9 Edward Winslow was one of the most prominent Pilgrims who came to America in 1620. At New Plymouth he was the colonists' diplomatic agent to the natives and succeeded in winning the friendship of Chief Massasoit. He was one of the colony's civil magistrates for the greater part of two decades and governor in 1633-1634, 1636-1637, and 1644-1645. In 1643 Winslow was also a commissioner of the United Colonies of New England. On several occasions he was sent to England to look after the interests of both the Plymouth and Massachusetts colonies.

recorded the secretary's effort to persuade the king. Winslow added that when James further inquired about the nature of the settlers' employment, Naunton replied, "*By fishing.*"[10] The king's affirmation was even more enthusiastic in exclaiming: "*So God save my soul, 'tis an honest trade, 'twas the apostles' own calling.*"[11]

At this point, hopes were high among the Pilgrims and their representatives, with their mutual interests allied behind the true cause of "*the enlargement of the interests of the Gospel.*"[12] But, though King James may have been inclined toward granting a license for immigration, his bishops were not. The Anglican bishops rejected any semblance of granting liberty to worship God apart from their authority – especially granting formal liberty to the detested Separatists who would then be officially sanctioned as free and separate from the Anglican Church. The king conceded this critical point to the bishops. Then, in a gesture of sheer royal prerogative, James flatly refused a license for the nonconformists to immigrate anywhere within his realm under a formal grant of liberty of worship.

The patient Pilgrims were delayed but not defeated. During negotiations with Secretary Naunton, James had gestured that he would no longer molest them if they immigrated under a patent previously granted to others for commercial reasons. And thus, even though Sandys' personal objective had fallen short, significant ground had been gained.

The king's pledge not to interfere was enough for the Pilgrims to seize upon the opportunity to escape to America as loyal Englishmen. They first encountered many trials and delays by negotiating with often-disingenuous merchants who desired to translate the Pilgrims' faithful hopes into their own financial gain. In 1620, under the leadership of William Brewster, the Pilgrims were at last able to contractually align themselves with a legitimate company of commercial adventurers (merchants authorized by the Crown to seek profits in the New World).

---

10 Bradford, *Of Plymouth Plantation*, p. 30 (footnote relating Edward Winslow's account in *Hypocrisie Unmasked*, 1646, p. 89).

11 Ibid.

12 Mather, *Magnalia*, Book 1, p. 6.

The Pilgrims entered into an arrangement to secure their transport in exchange for working off their debt in contracted service upon their safe arrival in America. Although their passage came at the price of added financial burdens, eventual freedom for their beloved families and church at last lay before them upon a foreseeable horizon.

A Vine into the Wilderness

Aboard the *Mayflower* there were many family Bibles – the book that had served the Pilgrims so well during the trials of their past. That "Good Book" would certainly be needed during the many trials in their future. Aboard were also copies of the great Reformed Christian expositors of Scripture. Perhaps among the most noteworthy volumes was William Brewster's copy of John Calvin's *Commentary on Isaiah*.

William Brewster's Copy of John Calvin on Isaiah Carried Aboard the *Mayflower* to Plymouth Colony

William Brewster, 1566 - 1644, Plymouth Colony Church Elder

Brewster's ownership signature on the title page of Calvin's *Commentary on Isaiah*.

This volume was a fitting tribute to the mission of the Pilgrims, for in Isaiah were found the great prophecies of taking the Gospel to the ends of the earth. The fact that Calvin had dedicated that work to a Protestant monarch of the English realm was also a providential tribute to the Pilgrims' mission. These were the Christian planters from that realm who truly sought to give Calvin's vision of civil liberty a fitting home.

These Pilgrims were, after all, Reformed Christians – a people of covenantal commitments (meaning, everything they did took on proportions of significance greater than themselves). And fittingly, before disembarking at the chosen site for Plymouth Colony in America in the frigid autumn of 1620, the men of the *Mayflower* committed themselves in a formally binding civil covenant.

First Self-Governed Body Politic in New England, 1620
The Mayflower Combination as recorded by Plymouth Colony's William Bradford:

❝ [We] in the presence of God and one another, Covenant and Combine ourselves together into a Civil Body Politic; for our better ordering and preservation, and furtherance of the ends aforesaid; and by virtue hereof, to enact, constitute, and frame such just and equal Laws, Ordinances, Acts, Constitutions and Offices, from time to time, as shall be thought most meet and convenient for the general good of the Colony ... ❞

This document is now popularly known as the Mayflower Compact, but it was what Pilgrim Nathaniel Morton more accurately described as a "*solemn combination*."[13] This term denoted much more than a contractual agreement like the financial arrangement they had made with the merchant investors. The Mayflower "*solemn combination*" was a conscience-

---

13 Morton, *New-England's Memorial*, p. 16.

binding engagement to serve one another in their civil affairs under God. Its phraseology was similar to the mutually binding covenant which they had undertaken years before in forming themselves as an independent church. Its key was in uniting one another under their only absolute Sovereign, as their "combination" began with the indelible phrase: "*In the name of God, amen.*"[14]

The legal reason for drafting this document was the fact that the Pilgrims had landed north of the territory covered by their patent and outside any previous English civil establishment.[15] The Combination of 1620 expressly joined them as a "*civil body politic.*"[16] It served as the basis for the future free government of the colony, as was stated in its wording: "*by virtue hereof, to enact, constitute and frame such just and equal Laws, Ordinances, Acts, Constitutions and Offices, from time to time, as shall be thought most meet and convenient for the general good of the Colony.*"[17]

The phrase "*general good*" was indicative of the Puritans' idea of a commonwealth – of a people free to govern themselves by principles much higher than sheer royal eminency. Morton explained this "*body politic*" as "*more orderly carrying on of their affairs ... by mutual consent.*"[18] This document as "*the first foundation of the government of New Plymouth*"[19] formed the second self-governing body in English America, following the first such body established at Jamestown, Virginia the year before.

Such a noble "*body politic*" had been explained to the Pilgrims in a letter they had received from their former Leiden, Holland pastor, John Robinson, just before their departure from England. Robinson wrote:

> *Whereas you are to become a body politic, using among your-selves civil government, and are not furnished with special eminen-cy above the rest, to be chosen by you into office of Government; let your wisdom and godliness appear ... in choosing such persons as do entirely love, and will promote the common good...*[20]

14 Ibid. For further reading, see Daniel Ford's book *In the Name of God, Amen* (Lex Rex Pub., 2003).
15 Ibid. Morton wrote that their location resulted in "*their patent being made void and useless...*"
16 Ibid.
17 Ibid., pp. 16-17.
18 Ibid., p. 16.
19 Ibid.
20 Ibid., pp. 9-10.

The Mayflower Combination (Compact) reflected this idea of a civil body. Any lordly *"eminency"* that their leaders may have lacked was indeed their greatest asset. They were now free to govern themselves as a representative body under the higher principles of *"wisdom and godliness."* They could now enact laws that would best honor God and benefit the families living directly under Him.

The whole endeavor was, after all, God's work, as Nathaniel Morton attested to *"those many memorable and signal demonstrations of God's goodness, viz. the first beginnings of this plantation in New England."*[21] It is worth noting that the common evangelistic phraseology used in colonial America perfectly mirrored that of the Reformation era as well as that of the first English visionaries of the former century. That same calling was now being accomplished as Morton also attested: *"that God brought a vine into the wilderness."*[22]

Public Testimonials of the Only True Sovereign

The Pilgrims' first winter was more than merely trying and difficult. It was brutal and devastating. The winter season of late 1620 to early 1621, marking their first months at New Plymouth, took the lives of about half of the total one hundred and two original immigrants. Bitter cold, starvation, and disease crippled efforts to obtain adequate food and shelter, and by the spring of 1621, a scant seven of their intended nineteen dwellings had been constructed. And, as many past trials had strengthened their character, their resolve to endure even such devastating hardships had been settled long before. It should therefore be noted that upon the *Mayflower*'s return to England in the spring of 1621, not one of the nearly starved survivors chose to abandon the colony.

According to Governor William Bradford's account, the new year brought new hopes. In 1621, their faithfulness and diligence then began to pay off in an adequate supply of fowl, fish, turkey, venison, and even corn, as Bradford reported: *"they took good store, of which every family*

---

21 Ibid., p. vi.
22 Ibid.

had their portion."[23]

The Pilgrims' many new blessings (and undoubtedly their very survival) were accompanied by an appropriate public thanksgiving in the autumn of 1621. Pilgrim Edward Winslow recorded that the colonists' celebration included an invitation to the surrounding natives, *"whom for three days we entertained and feasted."*[24] It was an exuberant expression of the colonists' thankfulness, which their native guests certainly witnessed as the public celebration of the mercies of the only true and living God.

The whole event was unlike the formal Thanksgiving Days in England that were decreed exclusively by the king and celebrated with the pomp of his High Church formalities. The Pilgrims' celebration was a genuine outpouring of gratitude by a people who were free to worship the King of kings on His terms. Winslow's account which described the Pilgrims' celebration was, in fact, written to friends in England. He recommended that they come and join in on such an abundance, saying: *"yet by the goodness of God, we are so far from want, that we often wish you partakers of our plenty."*[25]

The following year marked another remarkable outpouring of gratitude to God. In July of 1622 Plymouth Colony *"set apart a solemn day of humiliation, to seek the Lord by humble and fervent prayer in this great distress."*[26] This *"great distress"* was a severe summer drought. Following nearly two months *"without any rain, and with great heat of weather,"* on the very afternoon of their fast, a soaking rain commenced *"without either wind or thunder, or any violence, and by degrees in that abundance, as that the earth was thoroughly wet and soaked therewith."*[27] The Pilgrims had witnessed God's remarkable deliverance once again.

Nathaniel Morton recorded the concerns of an Indian living among

---

23 Bradford, *Of Plymouth Plantation*, p. 90.
24 *A Relation or Journal of the Beginning and Proceedings of the English Plantation settled at Plymouth in New England, by Certain English Adventurers both Merchants and Others* (London, 1622), pp. 60-61. Referencing a letter from Edward Winslow dated 11th of December 1621.
25 Ibid.
26 Morton, *New-England's Memorial*, p. 42. Morton put this under that date of 1622; other accounts place the date at 1623.
27 Ibid.

them who had before remarked of the English: *"I am afraid they will lose all their corn ... and so they will be all starved."*[28] After witnessing the miraculous Fast Day's rain, that same native then confessed: *"surely your God is a good God."*[29] The natives were again duly impressed at season's end in the *"fruitful and liberal harvest, to their great comfort and rejoicing."*[30] The English families therefore again *"solemnized a Day of Thanksgiving unto the Lord."*[31]

Those who chronicled the events of Plymouth's early years were careful to recognize that their deliverances were answers to public prayers and open acknowledgments of God. Morton observed: *"He was pleased to give them a gracious and speedy answer, both to their own and the Indians' admiration."*[32]

The First New England Day of Humility and Prayer, 1622: God's Gracious Mercy and Power Astonished the Local Indians

Upon which they set apart a solemn day of humiliation, to seek the Lord by humble and fervent prayer in this great distress: And he was pleased to give them a gracious and speedy answer, both to their own and the Indians admiration, that lived amongst them; for all the morning, and the greatest part of the day, it was clear weather, and very hot, and not a cloud nor any sign of rain to be seen, yet towards evening it began to be overcast, and shortly after to rain, with such sweet and gentle showers, as gave them cause of rejoicing and blessing God: It came without either wind or thunder, or any violence, and by degrees in that abundance, as that the earth was thoroughly wet and soaked therewith, which did so apparently revive and quicken the decayed corn and other fruits, as was wonderful, and made the Indians astonished to behold.

Title page of the 1669 edition of Nathaniel Morton's *New England's Memorial* with a description of Plymouth Colony's 1622 Day of Humiliation and Prayer and the remarkable rain that commenced that day.

❝ [The Lord] *was pleased to give them a gracious and speedy answer, both to their own and the Indians' admiration, that lived among them; for all the morning, and the greatest part of the day, it was clear weather, and very hot, and not a cloud nor any sign of rain to be seen, yet towards evening it began to be overcast, and shortly after to rain, with such sweet and gentle showers, as gave them cause of rejoicing and blessing God.* ❞

---

28 Ibid.
29 Ibid.
30 Ibid., 43.
31 Ibid.
32 Ibid., p. 42.

The point was that the land the colonists occupied was recognized as the Lord's possession. God's profound demonstrations in securing the lives and property of these first New England planters were clearly indicative of His exclusive sovereignty over them. In other words, the Lord alone was their Landlord, and their English king was nowhere near to superintend their everyday lives. Thus, for centuries Americans regarded the success of Plymouth Colony as a powerful testimony to the enjoyment of liberty and property as coming from God rather than human potentates. And, in a wider sense, such public expressions of thanksgiving are always indicative of those who gratefully acknowledge their dependence upon heaven rather than upon mere human potentates who might try to exhibit god-like sovereignty in their seats of authority.

The Pilgrims' openness with their public thanksgivings was also an important part of evangelizing the natives. Publicly crediting God's hand of mercy upon their Christian homes was an impressive aid in the presentation of the Gospel to those who had not yet heard the glorious news of Christ. Men such as Plymouth's Edward Winslow were deliberate in acknowledging the Lord's mercies toward the English, and he was thereby successful in negotiating treaties of friendship and peace between the colonists and the local tribes.[33] Thus, unlike the Spanish, the English colonists did not resort to forced conversion. They demonstrated the truly liberating dominion of the Almighty without the use of conquistadors or the scourge of tyranny. These English trusted in the power of God and His Word and then relied upon their own examples of submission under Him to demonstrate the Lord's genuinely gracious, saving character.

Days of Fasting with humiliation and Days of Thanksgiving with feasting then became staples of the New England colonies. Each occasion served as a standing declaration that the dominion of the true Sovereign of the earth had arrived in America.

---

33 Edward Winslow was delegated by Plymouth Colony as its agent to the natives of America in the vicinity of their settlement, and he succeeded in winning the friendship of their chief, Massasoit of the local Pokanoket Indians. A common grievance of the English settlers was that the natives of America would often want English families to raise their children. When Winslow returned to England during her Commonwealth era, he noted that grievance and was at the forefront of establishing the Puritans' first formal evangelistic effort, called *The Society for the Propagation of the Gospel of Jesus Christ in America*.

The Mercy of God in the Survival of Plymouth Plantation

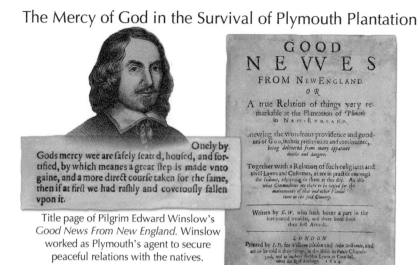

Onely by
Gods mercy wee are fafely feated, houfed, and fortified, by which meanes a great ftep is made vnto
gaine, and a more direct courfe taken for the fame,
then if at firft we had rafhly and covetoufly fallen
vpon it.

Title page of Pilgrim Edward Winslow's
Good News From New England. Winslow
worked as Plymouth's agent to secure
peaceful relations with the natives.

GOOD
N E V V E S
FROM NEW ENGLAND.
O R

A true Relation of things very remarkable at the Plantation of *Plimoth*
in NEVV-ENGLAND.

ʃhewing the wondrous providence and good-
nes of GOD, in their preʃervation and continuance,
*being delivered from many apparant
deaths and dangers.*

Together with a Relation of ʃuch religious and
civill Lawes and Cuʃtomes, as are in practiʃe amongʃt
the *Indians*, adjoyning to them at this day. As alʃo
*what Commodities are there to be rayʃed for the
maintenance of that and other Plantations in the ʃaid Country.*

Written by *E. W.* who hath borne a part in the
fore-named troubles, and there lived ʃince
their firʃt Arrivall.

L O N D O N
Printed by *I. D.* for *William Bladen* and *Iohn Bellamie,* and
are to be ʃold at their ʃhops, at the *Bible* in *Pauls*-Church-
yard, and at inoʃince Golden Lyons in Corn-hil,
neere the *Royal Exchange.*   1 6 2 4.

66 *Only by God's mercy we are safely seated, housed, and fortified, by which means
a great step is made unto gain, and a more direct course taken for the same,
than if at first we had rashly and covetously fallen upon it.* 99

Economic Reformation and Prosperity at Plymouth

The Pilgrims' idea of economic liberty was consistent with the
Reformed Christian principles of personal hard work and reaping personal
rewards. That model of a healthy economy was therefore centered on the
biblical idea of individual industry and private property ownership.

The business contract that the Plymouth colonists had entered into
with the English investors, however, created a completely different set
of circumstances. The contract itself, in fact, forced the colonists into a
communal economy by decreeing that *"all profits and benefits that are
got by trade, traffic, trucking, working, fishing, or any other means of any
person or persons, remain still in the common stock until division."*[34] That
idea of a *"common stock"* associated with all they produced, in effect,
created a common or socialistic ownership of the colony.

For the first two years at Plymouth there was neither private property
nor a division of labor. Everyone worked as a unified conglomerate of
laborers, as produce was grown for the town and provisions of food

---

34 Bradford, *Of Plymouth Plantation*, p. 40.

were distributed equally. The result was the suppression of individual incentive and family responsibility. The colony was soon suffering under an economic environment showing no sign of prosperity nor any hope of paying off their corporate debt. Governor Bradford complained that the economy of *"all being to have alike"* (holding all things in common) was to him *"a kind of slavery."*[35] The fact was that those who worked hardest benefited no more than the lazy who lived off the sweat of the others.

The communal economy was most of all destructive to the biblical family, as Bradford explained, with *"men's wives to be commanded to do service for other men, as dressing their meat, washing their clothes, etc."*[36] Nathaniel Morton, as the later secretary of Plymouth, added that it was akin to the *"Spaniards"* in America who, at their victims' expense, *"seemed to go to a bride feast, where all things are provided for them."*[37]

With complete failure facing the colony, Governor Bradford explained: *"they began to think how they might not ... still thus languish in misery."*[38] The solution advised by Plymouth's leaders was a total reformation of the economy, *"that they should set corn every man for his own particular, and in that regard trust to themselves."*[39] In other words, prosperity would come when they abandoned the unbiblical model of economic socialism, and instead, each man worked his own ground and his *domestic* family benefited from the fruit of his labor.

By allotting private plots of land in Plymouth, the colony's productivity took a remarkable turn for the better. With personal responsibility and incentive restored, each family's industry benefited itself and improved the vitality of the commonwealth as a whole. Governor Bradford duly praised the result, saying:

> *This had very good success, for it made all hands very industrious, so as much more corn was planted than otherwise would have been by any means the governor or any other could use...*[40]

---

35 Ibid., p. 121.
36 Ibid.
37 Nathaniel Morton, *Memorial*, p. 48.
38 Bradford, *Of Plymouth Plantation*, p. 120.
39 Ibid.
40 Ibid.

With a privately based economy secured, Plymouth began to prosper as well as to pay off its contracted public debt. It prospered even more when the colony's land distribution was enlarged. Prior to 1627 the colonists had only been granted tightly grouped plots, *"having had hitherto ... every person one acre allowed to him as to property, besides their homesteads, or garden plots."*[41]

The introduction of a number of cattle into the colony in 1627 put an added strain upon such restrictive landholdings. Similar to the successful land reforms undertaken in Virginia, the private estates in Plymouth also *"necessitated to lay out some larger proportions."*[42] These *"larger proportions"* (or more accommodating private landholdings) were naturally plotted outside the town of Plymouth. Thus, what had formerly been a colony sustained by relatively small private plots began to thrive as healthy familial estates when it was *"allotted to every one in each family twenty acres to be laid out..."*[43]

This was the seed of the township system in New England. The outskirts consisted of private farms and estates, providing the livestock, produce, and resources for the private industry and commerce within the central town. And, with the dominion of the land in private hands, the inseparable link between liberty and property had been confirmed by yet another gracious providence of God.

The Economic Model for New England

The successful land system modeled in Plymouth was, to a large extent, employed by the later Puritan settlements. A prominent feature of the New England system was to get as much land into private hands as possible, which resulted in as much productivity as possible.

In New England a civil community of like-minded families was typically formed around a church community. Local proprietors (as the

---

41 Morton, *Memorial*, p. 72.
42 Ibid.
43 Ibid.

representatives of the church community) would petition the larger colonial government for recognition as a town. Then the central town would sell the wider township land to the citizens, securing it in private hands. The larger township, now extending well beyond the central village, fortified the entire economy, composed of private farmers, tradesmen, shopkeepers, investors, and others with any calling worthy of an industrious community.

In all, a thriving economy based on private property and private interest was then the greatest benefit of the public good at large. Consequently, the local towns formed by an industrious people, an agreeable faith, and a common respect for private property became an important feature of free and independent colonial life.

Plymouth Governor William Bradford Drafts a Detailed Account of the Pilgrims' Trials and Successes

Opening page of William Bradford's manuscript *Of Plymouth Plantation,* a work describing the first Reformed Christian planting in New England.

Drafted between 1620 and 1647, the purpose was stated in the sixth chapter:

❝ *that their children may see with what difficulties their fathers wrestled in going through these things in their first beginnings, and how God brought them along, notwithstanding all their weaknesses and infirmities.* ❞

Stewardship Dominion Ordained by God

The legal underpinning of English colonization was the fact that the colonial charters issued by the monarchy were patents or grants for their subjects to immigrate. The king then had oversight of each colony at large according to the specified terms in its particular charter. The land obtained by the colonists themselves, however, was owned by them and not the king. The colonists' property rights were secured by their own purchase and toil, protected by their own local representatives, and remained in the domain of their own families rather than any governing principality.

Land ownership, as it was understood in English colonial America, thus faithfully modeled the dominion mandate given in Genesis 1:28, where God commanded families to multiply and subdue the earth. That became the model of familial dominion in English America. God's mandate to subdue the earth still applies today to families – rather than to governments trying to subdue the property of families. Simply put, there is no biblical mandate for public representatives to do anything but safeguard the dominion that American citizens are to enjoy in what they own.

We can also learn from the mistakes of the early Pilgrims. They demonstrated that the communal or social ownership of property in general destroys both private incentive and personal industry, bringing any economy to ruin. In summation, only a godly respect for personal responsibility along with private property will secure the kind of genuine stewardship dominion ordained by God.

That idea of godly respect was also a bedrock principle at work in other New England colonies, as we will find in the following chapter.

9
A PURITAN NEW ENGLAND

The High Hand of Oppression

AS we have seen in previous chapters, from the beginning of the reign of James I in 1603 he had done his best to demonize the growing Puritan movement in England. At first, the king targeted its growing political influence by labeling Puritans' public policies as *"unable to be suffered in any well-governed commonwealth."*[1] In time, however, the king soon began to target the Puritans for their views regarding a further reformation of the Church of England. Through his bishops, James extended the Crown's persecution beyond the aforementioned Separatists. The bishops began to suppress Puritan ministers who used their pulpits to preach a truly life-changing faith or who decried the hollow rituals to which much of the Anglican establishment had been reduced.

Indeed, the king and his allies saw the whole Puritan movement as driven by the ever-persistent doctrines of John Calvin. James' ally, Oliver Ormerod, for example, scorned the persistent popularity of the long-deceased Calvin, whom he saw as the original driving force behind *"the old Puritans"*[2] of the prior century. This devoutly Royalist, High Church Anglican decried the practical style of Puritan ministers who vigorously engaged their pulpits to educate the nobility and peasantry alike. Ormerod thought the Puritans were as deluded as Calvin in thinking *"the church in the whole ...may be pure and unspotted."*[3] To Ormerod, the prestige of the king's Church was at stake, and by tolerating Puritans, there would soon be nothing left of the polished liturgy of the royal idea of Christianity.

Many Puritans likely agreed with Ormerod on that point. That is, many agreed that there was little that should be left of the purely ritualistic Anglican Church, as it had been corrupted by a pretentious king and his high-handed bishops. They saw in Calvin's writings a confirmation that

---

1 James I, *The Kings Majesties Speech,* leaf B4.
2 Oliver Ormerod, *The Picture of a Puritan* (London, 1605), included in Lawrence Sasek, ed., *Images of English Puritanism* (Baton Rouge: Louisiana State University Press, 1989), p. 254.
3 Ibid. Ormerod was here quoting the detested Calvin and mocking the like aspiration of Puritans.

there was no virtue in either the popish rituals or the centralized hierarchy of bishops who acted as though they were lords over England's faith.

These tensions did not end with the death of James I in 1625. His son, being even more devoted to divine right, was crowned Charles I and he immediately began to aggressively purge the influence of Puritanism. Soon after his coronation, Charles married the French Roman Catholic princess Henrietta Maria, deepening suspicions that the Reformed faith itself would come under the Crown's attack.

These suspicions were well-founded. Within a year of Charles' coronation, the powerfully influential Royalist Richard Montague began an open affront on the beloved Reformed doctrine of God's sovereign grace. After Montague engaged himself in a vigorous dispute with the leading Puritan clergy and members of Parliament on this point, he was appointed as a royal chaplain as a sign of Charles' personal approval.

Things worsened when in 1628 the no-less tolerant William Laud was appointed Bishop of London. Laud was driven by a belief in God's limited sovereignty in matters of grace along with the Anglican bishops' absolute sovereignty in all matters of Christian faith and living.

Anglican Archbishop Laud Forbids Puritan Publications

Archbishop William Laud and the title page of *A Decree of the Star Chamber,* banning Puritan books and forbidding all printing without his or the king's license.

Puritan illustration called *Rome For Canterbury,* indicating the Archbishop's affinity for the divine right of the king and his efforts to put England under *"Popish"* church government.

Laud, who was devoted to the king's divine right in all civil and ecclesiastical matters, moved quickly in the rigorous enforcement of his High Church dogma. Fines and/or imprisonment awaited anyone who dared speak out along strongly Reformed Christian lines in matters of either church or civil policy.[4] By the time Laud was promoted to Archbishop of Canterbury with its supposed apostolic primacy, he was in control of a well-oiled ecclesiastical machine bent on flushing out any open expression of Puritanism. Thus, many Puritans who had previously opposed the idea of Separatism on the principle of loyalty to their national Church were themselves forced into seclusion or driven into exile as "nonconformists."

The Puritan Vision of a City of God

By the late 1620s, many Puritans were beginning to believe that the Reformation had ultimately failed in England. Some even thought that under the regime of Charles, God's gracious hand had left England altogether. These devout patriots of God's kingdom saw America as the future hope for His work among the English people. Not many Puritans, however, saw that the solution was a complete separation from the Anglican Church in the manner of the earlier Pilgrims.

Reverend John White of Dorchester, England was the primary mover behind a sweeping and coordinated migration of Puritans to New England. On one hand, White opposed the aggressive and brutal centralized regime of Archbishop Laud; on the other, he opposed the complete Separatism of the isolated Plymouth Colony. White envisioned a vast colony of many faithful, like-minded communities working in unison to advance Christ's kingdom in New England. He was driven by the vision for an expansive American colony, and White also knew that such a monumental plantation must be an orderly effort conducted with careful planning and purpose.

The key was transporting large numbers of faithful English families as the stock of a godly New England in America. These families, as the basic societal building blocks, would then form themselves into like-minded congregations and towns. These local communities would then work

---

4 King Charles I used the Star Chamber as the royal court through which he suppressed opposition to his royal policies, especially to persecute and prosecute religious dissenters including the Puritans.

together under a coordinated, self-governed colonial government. Colonial society would therefore grow from the ground up. It would represent the antithesis of the forced, top-down, divine-right regime of King Charles in England. These would be a people who, at every level of government (whether of the family, or the church, or the town, or the colony at large), were free to maintain their overall identity as Englishmen while living faithfully in the dignity of a self-governed Christian society.

Such freedom incorporated the idea of a mutually cooperative civil environment – one that John White later recommended to his English Parliament as *"the advantages that the City of God and Church hath by uniting into a well compacted body."*[5] White's metaphorical *"City of God"* carried the historic Christian idea that God not only reigns as the Sovereign over the church, but also (and distinctively) over the state.

White's metaphor also carried the Reformed Christian idea that a godly civil body is made up of a free people. Thus, his metaphor of a *"City"* carried the idea of mutual citizens under a representative government rather than subjects under a regime of raw imperial power. To White and the Puritan patriots in the English Parliament, civil society must be composed of free towns and congregations spread across the English countryside, residing in brotherly cooperation. White explained that such a *"City of God"* is built upon localized authority, as *"in an orderly manner divided into streets or congregations, according to God's appointment."*[6]

The same idea of coordinated localized communities pictured in White's *"City"* analogy (that he recommended to Parliament) is what he had previously envisioned for a Puritan New England. White's idea of a godly New England pictured much larger colonies than New Plymouth, yet still composed of self-governed families living amid townships mutually dedicated to maintaining the people's liberty and property. New England would then be composed of colonies that respected the dominion that the people held in their own hands over their own land – those who were safe from the English Crown within self-governed communities.

---

5 John White, *The Troubles of Jerusalem's Restoration, or the Churches Reformation* (London, 1646), p. 51.
6 Ibid.

The First Massachusetts Settlement

Though he never immigrated to America, John White devoted himself to accommodate nearly all who desired to resettle there. White was, in that sense, a visionary in the manner of Richard Hakluyt who saw America as a field of the Lord's planting, but now in the seventeenth century he had much better means than Hakluyt to carry that vision through.

A prosperous New England colony certainly required a great number of godly souls willing and able to go. Under the oppressive regime of King Charles I, many were more than willing to migrate, and King Charles was more than willing to let them go.

As religious persecution was heating up in England in the later 1620s, White established a corporation called "The New England Company for a Plantation in Massachusetts Bay." Backed by generous financial support in England, White's company employed John Endicott to head the corporation's first mission of forming an expansive Puritan colony. Endicott, given the task of planting the seeds of White's vision for a godly New England, became the first resident governor of the newly named colony of Massachusetts Bay.

The settlers who accompanied Governor Endicott established the town of Salem. Similar to the Pilgrims' Combination of 1620, the citizens of Salem combined themselves by a general societal covenant. Salem's covenant, however, was primarily focused on the sphere of the church, as was stated: *"That the Reformation of the Church was to be endeavored according to the written Word of God."*[7] The point was that the Reformation which was being suppressed in England by a despotic regime of bishops would be advanced in Salem. And, in accord with White's vision of a cooperative City of God, Salem's Covenant included a pledge that it would walk in coordination with other congregations – to be in *"no way slighting our sister churches, but using their counsel, as need shall be."*[8] Salem was also committed in service to the local natives, pledging not to be *"a stumbling-block before any, no, not the Indians, whose good we desire to*

---

7 Mather, *Magnalia Christi Americana*, Book 1, p. 18.
8 Ibid.

promote; and so to converse, as we may avoid every appearance of evil."[9]

The appropriately-named town of Salem (or "peace") thus provided a model community for the host of Puritan families that would follow and also *"build houses ... [and] have a fair town."*[10] In fact, Salem's first minister, Francis Higginson, encouraged the faithful of England to join them, promising new colonists what was lacking under Charles I and his bishops, namely: *"plenty of preaching, and diligent catechizing."*[11] With this seed of John White's vision having been planted, the prospects of meaningful liberty awaited a host of faithful colonists in a land of promise.

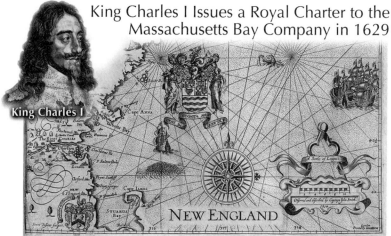

King Charles I Issues a Royal Charter to the Massachusetts Bay Company in 1629

King Charles I

NEW ENGLAND

Map of New England in the 1630s showing the coastline from Plymouth Colony northward past Salem

Despite his persecution of Puritans in England, King Charles I granted John White's Massachusetts Bay Company a royal charter, allowing White to organize a massive immigration to America – earning him the name "Patriarch White."

Self-Government for Colonial Massachusetts

On March 4, 1629 a royal charter was at last granted in the name of King Charles to *"the Governor and Company of the Massachusetts Bay in New England."*[12] This most prestigious charter formally secured

9 Ibid.

10 Francis Higginson, *New-England's Plantation. Or, a Short and True Description of Commodities and Discommodities of that Country,* 2nd ed. (London, 1630), leaf Db. (The first edition was published in 1629.)

11 Ibid.

12 Morison, *Builders of the Bay Colony,* p. 34.

Massachusetts' landholdings in the name of the Company. This ensured that competing companies could not stake a legally enforceable claim within its given territory. This immeasurable advantage, along with the prior success at Salem, translated into widespread confidence in the Bay Colony's future success. That, in turn, convinced a number of wealthy Puritan households and *"many deserving persons to transplant themselves and their families into New England."*[13]

Among those whom White convinced to emigrate was a prominent lawyer of considerable reputation. The devout Puritan John Winthrop had an impressive legal pedigree through his father and grandfather dating back to the days of Calvin and the English refugees in Europe. Well trained in theology and law, John Winthrop was a principled magistrate who the later New England historian Cotton Mather said admired Calvin more than the greatest legal minds of his time. Mather noted *"he would rather have devoted himself unto the study of Mr. John Calvin, than of Sir Edward Cook* [Coke]."[14] The Massachusetts Bay Company had thus appropriately named John Winthrop as its new resident governor. It would be because of Winthrop's distinctive civic service to the colony that Mather would honor him as *"the Father of New England, and the founder of a colony."*[15]

The fact that the Massachusetts charter failed to stipulate where the Company would hold its meetings was a significant but providential oversight by the Crown. Consequently, the stockholders were left to decide where to hold meetings and conduct their business, and accordingly, they took full advantage of this exceptional liberty. In a stroke of Solomon-like wisdom, the Massachusetts Company drew up the Cambridge Agreement in August 1629, stipulating that the colonists themselves would conduct the corporation's business in New England – provided, of course, that the governor and shareholders reside there.

Winthrop then took full advantage of both the king's charter and the Cambridge Agreement, finding it *"most convenient for the government*

---

13 Mather, *Magnalia Christi Americana*, Book 1, p. 17.

14 Ibid., Book 2, p. 8. Sir Edward Coke was the most famous early seventeenth-century legal proponent of the rights of English subjects under the Common Law.

15 Ibid., Book 1, p. 17.

with the charter of the plantation, to be transferred into the plantation itself."[16] With the colonists themselves having physical possession of the charter, they secured the Company's rights of self-government.

In effect, then, the civil government of the Bay Company and the Bay Colony became one and the same, meaning that the resident governor and local representatives of the colonists would govern Massachusetts rather than a corporate board across the ocean in England. The blessed result was that colonial Massachusetts would be ruled by a government based upon local elections conducted by the colonists themselves.

Applying the Dominion Mandate

Before departing England, Winthrop joined White in recruiting an impressive fleet of English families to emigrate. In 1629 Winthrop drafted a document entitled *Considerations for the Plantation of New-England*. Of its many points, the first directed the Puritans to a mission reminiscent of the earlier English forays into the wilderness of America: "*to carry the Gospel into those parts of the world.*"[17] This was the unmistakable Gospel calling – the Great Commission of their Savior whose concerns for His kingdom precede all other kings and governors.

Another key objective included in Winthrop's *Considerations* was to honor the biblical mandate by God to take possession of the earth. "*The whole earth is the Lord's garden,*" Winthrop reminded his fellow Englishmen, "*and He hath given it to the sons of Adam, to be tilled and improved by them.*"[18]

To Winthrop and many persecuted Puritans in England, now was the time to embrace such an opportune gift of Providence. The wooded hills and flowered fields of New England awaited those who both understood the genuine Gospel calling and were armed with the ancient dominion mandate. Once set free from the tethers of old England, such an industrious and self-governed people would not let the wilderness "*lie waste without*

---

16 Ibid., p. 20.
17 Ibid., p. 17.
18 Ibid., p. 18.

any improvement."[19] With a well-rooted appreciation for the blessings of liberty, they would cultivate a New England *"profitable for the use of man."*[20]

God's Dominion Mandate and the New England Colonies

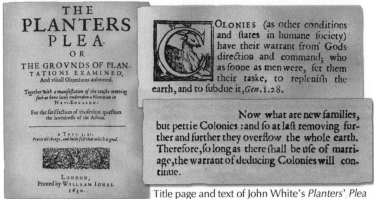

Title page and text of John White's *Planters' Plea*

❝ *Colonies (as other conditions and states in human society) have their warrant from God's direction and command; who as soon as men were, set them [to] their task, to replenish the earth, and to subdue it, Gen. 1:28.* ❞

❝ *Now what are new families, but petty Colonies: and so at last removing further and further they overflow the whole earth. Therefore, so long as there shall be use of marriage, the warrant of deducing Colonies will continue.* ❞

It was while Governor Winthrop was in the midst of recruiting a vast fleet of Puritans to accompany him to America that John White published a tract of significant importance. Like Winthrop's *Considerations for the Plantation*, White's *The Planters' Plea* began with the mandate that God gave to Adam, when *"men were ... set [to] their task, to replenish the earth, and to subdue it, Gen. 1:28."*[21] White then referenced Genesis 9:1, quoting Calvin's observation on that passage that the Lord had also directed Noah's family to *"multiply and subdue the earth."*[22] To White, the interpretation of the mandate in both Genesis 1 and 9 put families at the forefront of New England's colonization, with White explaining that families themselves are little colonies:

---

19 Ibid.

20 Ibid.

21 John White, *The Planters' Plea. Or the Grounds of Plantations Examined* (London, 1630), p. 1.

22 Ibid., pp. 1-2, quoting Calvin's Latin: *"Iubet eos crescere & simul benedictionem suam destinat."*

Now what are new families, but petty Colonies: and so at last removing [relocating] *further and further they overflow the whole earth. Therefore, so long as there shall be use of marriage, the warrant of deducing* [arriving at] *Colonies will continue.*[23]

White's *Planters' Plea* was a vivid example of the Reformed Christian approach to American colonization. It caused many faithful English families to look to God's great blessings in the West – and the dominative imagery of westward migration became an important part of America's sense of destiny, even following the American colonial era.

Liberty and Property in the Massachusetts "City" of God

The launching of John Winthrop's fleet in 1630 marked the first large migration of a significant number of English families. With over seven hundred English souls aboard eleven ships sailing within a few months of each other, the fleet doubled the population of American Puritans.

Many outpourings of prayer and blessing accompanied the embarkation of Winthrop's flagship *Arbella* on April 8. Of those outpourings, none was more poignant than the oration titled *God's Promise to His Plantations* by minister John Cotton. Cotton had traveled from Lincolnshire, England to preach a few words of encouragement to Governor Winthrop, and he reminded those departing that day that their calling was *"to plant a colony, that is, a company that agree together to remove out of their own country, and settle a city or commonwealth elsewhere."*[24] In other words, Cotton saw this band of faithful Englishmen leaving their nation to begin a distinctive work elsewhere in the cause of freedom. Cotton's use of the term *"city or commonwealth"* was indicative of much more than a vague idea or hope for liberty. These were a people (as free citizens rather than mere subjects) setting a course to see liberty's reality come to fruition.

Cotton's oration included an exhortation for them to walk humbly before their God who truly owned them and would rule the land they

23 Ibid., p. 2.
24 John Cotton, *God's Promise to His Plantation*. Recorded in Alan Heimert and Andrew Delbanco, eds., *The Puritans in America: A Narrative Anthology* (Cambridge: Harvard University Press, 1996), p. 78.

were soon to possess. God was to be their Lord in every tangible sense of the word: "[L]*earn to walk thankfully before him*," Cotton admonished the departing English colonists, "*defraud him not of his rent, but offer yourselves unto his service: serve that God, and teach your children to serve him, that has appointed you and them the place of your habitation.*"[25]

In Cotton's message, we see the connection of land ownership with the Puritan idea of a free "*city*." New England families were to be free in their government and to be freeholders of their property. However, they were never free from their true Landlord. The Puritan idea of a free "city" included a binding obligation to God. John Cotton called that obligation their "*rent*," meaning the direct obligations in their liberty and property that they owed distinctly to Him in all that they did. In other words, they were free from earthly or English lords, but they were always bound as vassals to their truly sovereign Lord, and they could not be proper renters when depriving Him of the payment in honor always due unto God.

Those were the same sentiments of Massachusetts Governor Winthrop, who delivered the most famous sermon preached on the occasion of this most noteworthy embarkation to America. His oration, commonly called *A Model of Christian Charity*, is perhaps the clearest description we have of the underlying principles of the great Puritan migration that extended throughout the 1630s. Winthrop employed the kind of characteristic phraseology that defined the Puritan idea of commitments, saying: "*We are entered into a covenant with God for this work.*"[26] He then spoke of their charge from heaven, saying: "*We have taken out a commission; the Lord hath given us leave to draw our own articles.*"[27] That idea of a "*commission*" spoke of the colonists' governing mandate; their "*leave to draw our own articles*" spoke of their representative government and local oversight of their laws. And together, their "*commission*" and the "*leave*" in their articles spoke of their privilege to be a self-governed people under God.

25 Ibid., p. 79.
26 John Winthrop, *Christian Charity, a Model Thereof*. Excerpt from Samuel Eliot Morison, *Builders of the Bay Colony*, p. 73.
27 Ibid.

That idea of liberty meant that the colonists were free from the immediate oversight of their English king, but not from the direct oversight of their true Sovereign. Winthrop therefore included the biblical mandate written in the book of Micah: *"to do justly, to love mercy, to walk humbly with our God."*[28] With that idea of humble and responsible liberty, the governor also used the metaphor of a "city" to describe the example of their witness before the world:

> *He* [God] *shall make us a praise and glory that men shall say of succeeding plantations, "the Lord make it like that of New England." For we must consider that we shall be as a city upon a hill.*[29]

Winthrop was warning his fellow immigrants of what lay ahead in either blessing or cursing. Their hope was that if they were faithful, God would fortify their *"city"* against every hazard. This idea of a fortified city of free people was a theme that stemmed back to the Reformation. Calvin, for instance, had noted *"the strength of the city,"*[30] in commenting on Isaiah 26:1: *"Let other cities rely on their fortifications, God alone will be to us instead of all bulwarks."*[31] Calvin was saying that a truly faithful *"city"* of self-governed citizens (such as his sixteenth-century city-republic of Geneva) must rely upon God Himself as their highest defense.

It should therefore not go unnoticed that in Winthrop's sermon, *A Model of Christian Charity*, he also warned conversely: *"if we shall deal falsely with our God in this work we have undertaken, and so cause Him to withdraw His present help from us, we shall be made a story and a byword through the world."*[32] Settling in a new environment with a foreboding ocean on one side and a hostile wilderness on the other, Puritan Massachusetts made sure to arm itself with the right kind of fortification in responsible liberty and property.

---

28 Ibid.
29 Ibid.
30 Calvin, *Commentary on Isaiah*, vol. 2, p. 209.
31 Ibid. (Indicating the free city-republic of Geneva and its protection under God at the time of the Reformation.)
32 Winthrop, *Christian Charity*. Excerpt from Morison, *Builders of the Bay Colony*, pp. 73-74.

10
THE GROWTH OF THE NEW ENGLAND PLANTINGS

The Blessing of Liberty Under Legitimate Public Authority

IN God's mercy, Massachusetts did not become the failed "byword" that John Winthrop warned would happen if the colony turned away from God. The colony, in fact, grew to prosper greatly because of its remarkable mindfulness of Him. It is always worth noting that the colonists were faithful not only in their homes and churches, but in their representative model of civil government and their public acknowledgments of the God who sustained them. In noting the remarkable success of the first several decades, historian (and maternal grandson of John Cotton) Cotton Mather recorded: "*'twas wonderful to see their dependence upon God, and God's mindfulness of them.*"[1]

Winthrop's fleet of 1630 had only been the beginning of a great migration of about twenty thousand Englishmen who came to the Massachusetts Bay Colony throughout that decade.[2] As the governor of a rapidly growing Puritan colony, John Winthrop had an opportunity that few leaders throughout history have been granted. He and his colonial council were in the position of applying the Reformed Christian principles of liberty and government to newly settled people forming themselves into a large civil society.

This essential relationship between liberty and proper civil government had been recognized since the early days of the Reformation. Calvin, for instance, had placed liberty within the context of well-constituted government, "*where liberty is framed to such moderation as it ought to be,*

---

1 Mather, *Magnalia Christi Americana*, Book 1, p. 22.

2 The migration that began with the Winthrop Fleet of 1630 continued until the English Parliament was reconvened in 1640, at which point the scale of migration dropped off sharply. The decade-plus oppressions by Charles I and Archbishop Laud were curtailed in 1641 with Parliament's condemnation of Laud and its concurrent Civil War with Charles. The massive Puritan exodus to America of about twenty thousand Puritans was considered a great migration not only because of the numbers, but also because of the high principles of the undertaking. The families who migrated were not vagrants or destitute English, but were generally well-educated and relatively prosperous.

and is orderly established to continuance."[3] Governor Winthrop described responsible liberty in the same manner as his Reformed predecessors, but added the typical American Puritan "federal" (covenantal) phraseology:

> [T]*here is a civil, a moral, a federal liberty, which is the proper end and object of authority; it is a liberty for that only which is just and good; for this liberty you are to stand with the hazard of your very lives; and whatsoever crosses it, is not authority, but a distemper thereof.*[4]

Massachusetts Governor Winthrop on "*Federal Liberty*,"
or Liberty Covenanted between the Rulers and People under God, Defining Legitimate Civil Authority (1645)

> there is a Civil, a Moral, a Federal *Liberty*, which is the proper End and Object of *Authority*; it is a *Liberty* for that only which is *juft* and *good*, for this *Liberty* you are to ftand with the hazard of your very *Lives*; and whatfoever Croffes it, is not *Authority*, but a *Diftemper* thereof.

John Winthrop, Governor of Massachusetts Bay, with excerpted quote from his speech in 1645 on responsible liberty – the kind worth taking a ❝ stand with the hazard of your very lives. ❞

Winthrop's remarks were not written in a book as political theory, but spoken before the council of Massachusetts amid the plain and often hard realities of colonial life. He was admonishing the representatives to respect the kind of tangible, responsible liberty that the people must enjoy with a mutually respectable, binding agreement between the rulers and the ruled – an agreement pledged before God.

That kind of "*a civil, a moral, a federal liberty*" required a vigilant stand by the magistrates themselves, and at times, required them to put their own lives on the line in the name of the people's liberty.

---

3 Calvin, *The Institution of Christian Religion*, vol. 2, leaf 624a, 4:20:8.
4 Mather, *Magnalia Christi Americana,* Book 2, p.13, recording Winthrop's 1645 speech.

John Cotton, who had himself finally fled the English inquisition of Archbishop Laud in 1633, went on to define what became known as the "New England Way." In numerous books and pamphlets, this well-published Boston preacher advocated godly societies in which the people's affairs were recognized as covenantal in nature. In his book *The Way of the Churches of Christ in New-England*, for example, Cotton explained the covenantal nature of all binding commitments by a free people:

> *There is no other way given whereby a people free from natural and compulsory engagements, can be united or combined together into one visible body, ... but only by mutual covenant; as appears between husband and wife in the family, magistrates and subjects in the commonwealth, fellow citizens in the same city.*[5]

Boston Preacher John Cotton on Binding Societal Relations

John Cotton, Preacher of Boston, Massachusetts, helped to define "The New England Way."

First page with excerpt of *The Way of the Churches of Christ in New-England* (1645)

For Cotton and his New England contemporaries, liberty did not mean autonomy from institutional authority – it meant people freely engaging in binding commitments dedicated to preserving their mutual good. In marriage, for example, the husband and wife were bound to their mutual

---

5 John Cotton, *The Way of the Churches of Christ in New-England* (London, 1645), p. 4.

care by their wedding vows sworn before God. In civil government, the magistrates were bound to safeguard the people's liberties by their oaths of office sworn before God. Therefore, the overall civil community's continued enjoyment of liberty depended upon those at every sphere of society maintaining their mutual commitments under the Lord, who alone gave proper dignity to all public institutions.

The Massachusetts Body of Liberties

In 1641 the government of Massachusetts Bay formally adopted a *Body of Liberties* after considerable preparation and deliberation. This important document was the first comprehensive statement of the liberties enjoyed by American colonials. The document's precedence was actually found in an earlier draft proposal prepared in the 1630s by Boston's preacher John Cotton, entitled *Moses, His Judicials*. In this treatise Cotton had tied colonial liberties directly with those of ancient Israel. For example, Cotton's *Judicials* concluded with a description of the Lord's authority in the three branches of civil government (as quoting from Isaiah 33:22): *"The Lord is our Judge, the Lord is our Law-giver, the Lord is our King: He will save us."*[6] Cotton's use of Scripture in this instance was more than a veiled acknowledgment of the colonists' dependence upon the King of kings rather than upon the English Courts, Parliament, or king.

Though Cotton's wording was not adopted per se as the *Body of Liberties* of 1641, it added much to the final document prepared mostly by the Ipswich, Massachusetts preacher Nathaniel Ward.[7] That document, based upon both Cotton's and Ward's contributions, included aspects of biblical Law and English Common Law as the final draft was *"revised, amended, and presented, and so established"*[8] by the Massachusetts body of representatives.

The expressed purpose of the Massachusetts *Body of Liberties* was to guarantee (as stated): "[T]*he free fruition of such liberties, immunities,*

6 Morison, *Builders of the Bay Colony*, p. 228.
7 Ibid., p. 229.
8 Ibid., p. 230.

and privileges as humanity, civility, and Christianity call for as due to every man."[9] Among its variances from England's Common Law was the prohibition of feudal dues,[10] which effectively eliminated the practice of lordships and feudal estates in New England.

Going a step further, this amazing document included the colony's written guarantee of every free man's life and liberty. The *Body of Liberties* stated that unless the *"equity of some expresse law"*[11] was violated, *"no man's life shall be taken away, no man's honor or good name shall be stained, no man's person shall be arrested, restrained, banished, dismembered, nor any ways punished, no man shall be deprived of his wife or children."*[12] The document also added the essential guarantees of private property under the government's protection of a free man's right, stating: *"no man's goods or estate shall be taken away from him, nor any way damaged under color of law* [the mere appearance of law] *or countenance of authority* [the mere appearance of authority]."[13] This celebrated document known as the Massachusetts *Body of Liberties* became an important precedent for the kind of God-given freedoms for which Americans have, until recently, been willing to risk life and limb.

Maintaining liberty and property under the law necessarily required a godly reverence for legitimate civil authority by the people. To that end, the early Puritan churches of New England were the greatest supports. These congregations, far removed from an oppressive Anglican regime, were vigorously employed in teaching the virtues of Christian liberty within the cooperative spheres of family, church, and state. John Cotton, for instance, taught the essential supportive role of the church to the civil sphere. *"Purity, preserved in the church,"* Cotton explained, *"will preserve well-ordered liberty in the people, and both of them establish well-balanced authority in the magistrates."*[14]

---

9 Ibid., p. 231.

10 Ibid., p. 232. In England, feudal dues were payments made in money or services to a member of the property-owning nobility in exchange for an entitlement to certain liberties granted on his lands.

11 Ibid., p. 231.

12 Ibid.

13 Ibid.

14 Thomas Hutchinson, *The History of the Colony of Massachusetts Bay* (London, 1765), p. 500.

The *Laws and Liberties* of Colonial Massachusetts, 1648

The *Laws and Liberties* of Massachusetts was enacted in 1648 and served as the basis
for civil and criminal law until the mid-1680s. It was a revision of the *Body of Liberties*
of 1641. Both documents reflected the Reformed Christian view of civil government,
and like the 1641 *Body of Liberties*, the 1648 *Laws and Liberties* protected
colonists' liberty and property through the due process of law.

This idea of *"well-ordered liberty"* in the people and *"well-balanced
authority"* in civil magistrates is essential to our understanding of the
orderly, balanced, biblical idea of a civilized society. Puritans such as
John Cotton understood that society at large depends upon sound biblical
principles enacted into civil law along with the church teaching the
principles of responsible citizenry. The role of faithful churches within
a civilized society is essential, for example, in maintaining the civil
government's God-ordained respect for the people's liberty and property
as well as for the people to respect the God-ordained authority of civil
government. This understanding of *"well-ordered liberty"* in the people
and *"well-balanced authority"* became cornerstone principles in Puritan
Massachusetts as well as in the other colonial commonwealths of New
England. And due to diligent, faithful men such as Boston's first preacher
John Cotton and Massachusetts' Governor Winthrop, the biblical idea of
liberty had deep roots within the colonial American legacy.

With that being noted, such a reverence for Christian liberty was
not reserved only for Englishmen. The idea of the liberating kingdom of

Christ played a key role in the methods of evangelization employed by the colonists as well.

The Establishment of Self-Governed Indian Towns Under God

As Governor Winthrop had warned the English immigrants regarding the work of God in America, the eyes of the world were watching. And indeed, the indigenous natives of Massachusetts had been carefully watching. By the 1640s the native Indians had not only witnessed an ever-growing English Massachusetts, they had also seen the same kind of repeated acts of divine mercy that the natives in and around the Plymouth Colony had earlier witnessed.

The Bay Colony took care to follow the practice of Plymouth Plantation in calling for days of fasting and prayer. John Cotton's grandson Cotton Mather recorded that the Indians in and around Massachusetts noticed the Englishmen's *"heaven-melting devotions, to fast and pray before God."*[15] The effect was also exactly as it had been in Plymouth, that *"on the very days, when they poured out the water of their tears before Him, He would shower down the water of His rain upon their fields; while they were yet speaking, He would hear them."*[16] Mather also recorded that when the glorious rains came, the Indians of Massachusetts *"would on that occasion admire the Englishman's God."*[17] To the colonists, it was clear that the heavenly outpouring was not only sent for their good, but also to provoke them into the mission field to declare His kingdom among the natives.

John Eliot, the preacher of the church in Roxbury, Massachusetts, was driven with a heart for evangelism. He would be given the allegorical title "Apostle to the Indians." It should be noted that Eliot's *"family-government"*[18] was ordered by the kingdom principles of Christ. Cotton Mather described this missionary's own home as *"a little Bethel, for the worship of God."*[19]

---

15 Mather, *Magnalia Christi Americana*, Book 1, p. 22.
16 Ibid.
17 Ibid.
18 Mather, *Magnalia Christi Americana*, Book 3, p. 185.
19 Ibid.

Eliot was certainly faithful in his primary mission field in leading "*his children, and his household after him, that they should keep the way of the Lord.*"[20] Only then, with a well-ordered home, was Eliot driven by a deeper sense of mission into the American wilderness and unto the wider harvest for Christ. Gripped with a wider Gospel calling, the mission-minded Eliot established close friendships with a number of Indians throughout the eastern regions of Massachusetts. He was careful to converse with them in their native tongue, and from that developed a phonetically-based text by which to teach the Indians to read and write in their own language. After then publishing the first native-language book of grammar, Eliot translated the Lord's Prayer and the Ten Commandments, and he finally began to catechize them in the great kingdom principles of God's holy Text.

Eliot's preaching had remarkable success, though many Indians mistakenly came to believe that the way to serve the Almighty was by becoming English. When the natives began placing their children on the doorsteps of English homes, Eliot began teaching the Indian parents to train their own children in the ways of God. He taught the indigenous natives of Massachusetts that the work of Christ was not in becoming English nor in becoming the subjects of a European monarch across the ocean. As a Puritan, John Eliot's goal was to have them come under the sole dominion of Christ and form themselves into the same kind of civilized, self-governed communities enjoyed by the immigrant English.

In Eliot's tract *The Further Progress of the Gospel Amongst the Indians in New-England*, he described the first such planting of an Indian town named Natick, Massachusetts in 1651:

> [W]*ith Prayer to God I read and expounded to them the 18th of Exodus, (which I had done several times before) and finally ... they first chose a ruler of a hundred, then they chose two rulers of fifties, ... and lastly for that days work every man chose who be ruler of ten, the rulers standing in order and every man going to the man he chose.*[21]

---

20 Ibid.
21 John Eliot, *Strength Out of Weakness. Or a Glorious Manifestation of the Further Progress of the Gospel Amongst the Indians in New-England* (London, 1652), pp. 10-11.

John Eliot's *Strength Out of Weakness*: Natives of America Form a Self-Governed Town Under God Rather than an English King in 1651

> *Strength out of Weakneß.*
> Or a Glorious
> **MANIFESTATION**
> Of the further Progreſſe of the
> **GOSPEL**
> AMONGST
> **THE INDIANS**
> IN
> **NEW-ENGLAND.**

They did enter into Covenant with God, and each other, to be the Lords people, and to be governed by the word of the Lord in all things. The words of which Covenant are theſe in Engliſh. *We doe give our ſelves and our Children unto God to be his people, he ſhall rule us in all our affaires, not onely in our Religion, and affairs of the Church (theſe we deſire as ſoone as we can, if God will) but alſo in all our works and affaires in this world, God ſhall rule over us.* Iſa. 33. 22. *The Lord is our Judge, the Lord is our Law giver, the Lord is our King, He will ſave us; the Wiſedome which God hath taught us in his Booke, that ſhall guide us and direct us in the way.*

Puritan Missionary John Eliot with title page and excerpt from *Strength Out of Weakness*

Similar to the model of the English colonists, the Indians joined themselves into a plan of self-government by choosing representatives. The natives then entered into a town covenant in order to serve the Lord according to the rule of Scripture. Eliot recorded their remarkable words:

> *We do give ourselves and our children unto God to be his people, he shall rule us in all our affairs, not only in our religion, and affairs of the church (these we desire as soon as we can, if God will) but also in all our works and affairs in this world, God shall rule over us. Isa. 33:22. The Lord is our Judge, the Lord is our Law giver, the Lord is our King, He will save us; the wisdom which God has taught us in his Book, that shall guide us and direct us in the way. Oh, Jehovah, teach us wisdom to find out thy wisdom in thy Scriptures, let the grace of Christ help us, because Christ is the wisdom of God, send thy Spirit into our hearts, and let it teach us, Lord take us to be thy people, and let us take thee to be our God.*[22]

---

22 Ibid., p. 11.

The Literature of Freedom for Indigenous Americans

Mural depicting missionary John Eliot preaching to Indians (Massachusetts State House)
with title pages of his *Indian Grammar* and the first Indian-language Bibles

This idea of the Almighty being the Lawgiver, Judge, and King became the model for the natives who sought to enjoy the blessings of liberty, independence, and property ownership. Put another way, the Christian Indians were governed with a conscious awareness of their direct dependence upon their heavenly Lord rather than becoming serfs of the English immigrants. This idea of the Lord of heaven as Lawgiver, Judge, and King then became the model for other independent Indian towns that took root in and around the Massachusetts and Plymouth colonies.

An independent Indian town, for example, was established on the island of Martha's Vineyard by 1652, where the missionary Thomas Mayhew recorded *"that they generally came in by families, bringing also their children with them."*[23] The Indians of Martha's Vineyard also entered into their own independent covenant to make *"Jehovah to be their God,*

---

23 Ibid., p. 31.

promising by his help to walk according to his counsels."[24] These were strictly self-governed native communities under God who were ruled by men of their own choosing and who thereby enjoyed the fruit of their own industry, property, and local representation.

Through the diligence of many mission-minded Puritan preachers, by 1674 there were an estimated four thousand "praying Indians" whose property holdings and independent settlements became known among themselves and the English alike as the "Praying Towns."

Perhaps the most endearing monument to the advancement of the true kingdom of Christ in America was Eliot's translation of the Bible printed at Cambridge, Massachusetts in 1663. As the first Bible printed in a native Indian dialect, *Up-Biblum God* became a testament to the wide success of the work of God among native-speaking Americans. Just as the practice of propagating God's Word in the common languages had freed Europeans at the outset of the Reformation, it proved successful in the wilds of America.

By the time John Eliot passed away in 1690, he had done much to propagate the Gospel that he deeply loved and to bring the realm of Christ's kingdom to thousands of native families amid dozens of "Praying Towns." So, whether English or Indian, the people of Massachusetts were ruled by the same heavenly Sovereign under whom many devout Christians found refuge and established homes and villages free from those who ruled under the pretense of divine right.

Reformation and Colonial Expansion in New England

As the plantings of New England branched out from Plymouth and Massachusetts in the later seventeenth century, succeeding towns and congregations embraced the same governing principles of the earlier settlers. And, as one generation gave way to the next, the same principles of life, liberty, and property became an enduring part of New England's vast landscape.

The idea of liberty with responsible self-government also continued to be an important part of public orations in later seventeenth-century New

24 Ibid.

England. For example, a 1669 election sermon preached by an elderly John Davenport (one of the early colonial founders) encouraged the current Massachusetts governor and legislature to *"see that your fruitfulness in good, answers the cost and pains that God has been at with you in his vineyard."*[25]

In other words, this new generation of magistrates must embrace the same obligations as their fathers in protecting the property the Lord had granted to the people of New England. God had seen the founding generation through many trying times and a new generation of civic leaders was now answerable to Him for the safety and security of the same precious vineyard. The seventy-two-year-old Davenport added that the colonial magistrates themselves were to bear this *"fruitfulness in good,"* lest they perish *"as he did with his ancient vineyard, Isaiah 5:1-8."*[26]

Continuing the Legacy of the Lord's Vineyard in America

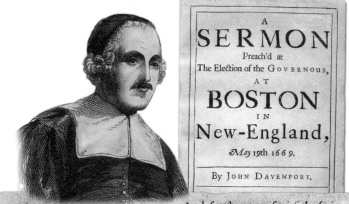

1669 Election Sermon delivered in Boston by New Haven, Connecticut founder John Davenport

Davenport tells the new generation: *❝ And see that your fruitfulness in good, answers the cost and pains that God has been at with you in his Vineyard....❞*

---

25 John Davenport, *A Sermon Preached at the Election of the Governor, at Boston in New-England, May 19th 1669* (Boston, 1670), p. 16.
26 Ibid.

Davenport was sternly warning that what God had done in His judgment of the ancient vineyard of Israel, He could certainly do to any generation of faithless Americans. These implications carried great weight with the colonists who still remained perched precariously at the edge of a restless frontier. And, not only would God's departing hand of favor overthrow their revered public communities, it would also lay desolate their beloved homes and private estates.

By the time the well-seasoned Davenport delivered his warning to the colonial magistrates in Boston in 1669, he had spent much of his adult life establishing another, more distant colony. Over three decades earlier, the same preacher had been one of the founders of Connecticut (the sister colony of Massachusetts) and he certainly knew the need for a colony's fidelity to God.

The idea of constant reformation had been part of Davenport's thinking when leading a large contingent of Puritans in 1638 to establish the New Haven Colony (in the region later known as Connecticut). At that time, Davenport was already concerned about the waning purity of many colonists in Massachusetts, explaining that *"whenever a reformation had been effected in the church, in any part of the world, it had rested where it had been left by the reformers."*[27] In other words, when there is biblical reformation and the reformers then become complacent, it marks the reformation's end. To Davenport, the settled comforts of Massachusetts had already led many into laxity, and to him the cause of further biblical reformation lay to the south and west of Massachusetts with a new plantation of Christ along the Connecticut shoreline.

Upon their arrival at the mouth of the Quinnipiac River in April 1638, the families of New Haven gathered under a canopy of trees to hear the first of Davenport's Sabbath Day sermons. Connecticut historian Benjamin Trumbull later recorded that the sermon by Davenport expressed their aim *"in a design of forming a civil and religious constitution, as near as possible to Scripture precepts and example."*[28]

---

27 Benjamin Trumbull, *A Complete History of Connecticut, Civil and Ecclesiastical, from the Emigration of its First Planters from England* (Hartford, 1797), p. 91.
28 Ibid.

Within a year, private homesteads were being established and New Haven's governing document called *Fundamental Articles* was formally adopted in June of 1639. With the stated purpose of *"the establishment of such civil order as might be most pleasing unto God,"* the *"whole assembly of free planters"* then engaged in a *"plantation covenant."*[29] Their first order of business was to legally secure the private landholdings of families by electing representatives for *"making and repealing laws."*[30] The one was to safeguard the other, with elected officials overseeing the legal protection of all families' property rights according to the particular *"allotments of inheritance."*[31] In other words, the landholdings of every free man (or "free planter") was secured and protected under law for his own family's perpetual inheritance. Moral integrity was also assured by the citizens of New Haven mutually pledging that: *"we would all of us be ordered by those rules which the Scripture holds forth to us."*[32]

To the east of New Haven, other similar settlements had already been planted, such as the 1636 settlement at Hartford along the Connecticut River. Hartford's first pastor, Thomas Hooker, envisioned their colony as part of fulfilling the dominion mandate of God: *"that they should turn the wilderness into gardens and fields, that they should plant and cultivate the earth."*[33]

To that end, Hartford joined with two other settlements (Windsor and Wethersfield) in adopting the first formally written constitution by a free people, or *"free planters,"* in the New World. Their stated purpose for entering into the January 1639 constitution called *The Fundamental Orders of Connecticut* was in framing *"an orderly and decent government established according to God."*[34]

The intent was to unify the settlements along the Connecticut River into a formidable colony that would eventually rival Massachusetts in its

---

29 Ibid., pp. 533, 534, 91.
30 Ibid., p. 91.
31 Ibid.
32 Ibid., p. 534.
33 Ibid., p. 57.
34 Ibid., p. 528.

scope and would similarly secure the people's liberty and private property. The constitution's *"first statute or bill of rights"* therefore included an historic *due process* clause stating: *"No man shall be deprived of his wife or children; no man's goods or estate shall be taken away from him, nor any wise endangered, under color of law..."*[35] This clause, by the way, was borrowed from John Cotton's proposed treatise *Moses, His Judicials*, and was first enacted by Connecticut two years before the Massachusetts *Body of Liberties* also included it in 1641. A similar bill of rights was adopted in New Haven as well. The inherent principles, though, were the same throughout Puritan New England. That is, the rule of legitimate laws passed by legitimate representatives secured the dominion of the people in their private homes against any arbitrary power.

The First Written Constitution by a Free People, 1639

Thomas Hooker:
founder of Hartford,
and promoter of the
*"Fundamental Orders
of Connecticut"* – the
first written constitution.

*THE original conſtitution of Conneɛ̆icut, formed by volunta-
ry compaɛ̆, 1639.*

FOR ASMUCH as it hath pleaſed the Almighty GOD, by the wiſe diſpoſition of his Divine Providence, ſo to or-der and diſpoſe of things, that we the inhabitants and reſidents of Windſor, Hartford, and Wethersfield, are now cohabiting and dwelling in and upon the river of Conneɛ̆icut and the lands thereunto adjoining, and well knowing where a people are gathered together the word of GOD requireth that, to maintain the peace and union of ſuch a people, there ſhould be an orderly and decent government eſtabliſhed according to GOD, to order and diſpoſe of the affairs of the people at all ſeaſons, as occa-ſion ſhould reauire : do therefore aſſociate and conioin ourſelves to be as one public STATE or COMMONWEALTH.

❝ [T]he Word of God requires that, to maintain the peace and union of such a
people, there should be an orderly and decent government established
according to God, to order and dispose of the affairs of the people
at all seasons, as occasion should require. ❞

---

35 Ibid., p. 98. The *due process of law* refers to the proper *"process"* that is *"due"* (or rightly owed) to have godly justice in the legitimate enforcement of laws. Due process, for example, prohibits the illegitimate use of governmental force against people suspected or accused of crimes. It is based upon the biblical principle that a quiet and peaceable people are to be secure in their private homes and property against injustices that are often done under a mere appearance (or so-called *"color"*) of law.

The planting of Christ's dominion continued on in Connecticut and throughout the later New England colonies. The overall point is that as the kingdom of Christ was going forth, families were taking possession of the land they settled. The three societies of family, church, and state each had their biblically prescribed roles. The families took possession and subdued the earth, the churches declared their Lord's highest kingdom principles, and the commonwealth protected His vineyard. Governments were endowed with biblical authority, but that authority was to protect the people's liberties and guard their private property. In other words, governments had a definitive role in the dominion of the earth, but it was to defend the vineyards of Christ by guarding the people's liberty and property.

These basic features of biblical dominion were fundamental to the American colonial character. It was the underpinnings of both the colonials' liberty and property that would eventually be challenged by Mother Britain. The eighteenth century would reveal Americans' ongoing struggle. It would reveal how America would be greatly challenged in her highest principles and how Americans would then rise up to *"travail in preserving and retaining"*[36] their God-given liberties and the vineyards of their Lord.

---

36 Calvin, *The Institution of Christian Religion*, vol. 2, leaf 623b, 4:20:8. Calvin on the principle: *"stoutly and constantly travail in preserving and retaining"* God-given liberty.

11
AMERICAN IDEAS OF LIBERTY AND PROPERTY IN THE EIGHTEENTH CENTURY

Dominion Stewardship in the 1700s

AS the dawn broke upon a new century, the blessings of liberty and property remained at the heart of Americans' cherished freedoms. The idea of property ownership, in which a typical man could enjoy the domain of his own private estate, was a reality in English America more than anywhere else in the world. The blessings of private property were certainly more widely enjoyed by the average English colonial than by the common peasant across the Atlantic in Mother England.

At the beginning of the eighteenth century, Samuel Willard pointed Americans to their blessed *"dominion over the works of thy hands."*[1] Willard, who was a lecturer as well as the acting President of Harvard College, quite pointedly reminded his fellow colonists that it was God Himself who had granted *"the first Charter given to man in his Creation."*[2] As he lectured, Willard also described God as *"the Creator and great Landlord."*[3] He was, of course, simply repeating the consistently-held American idea of God's sovereignty as it had been recognized since the first Englishmen set foot on colonial soil. Willard further explained that man *"was to be God's tenant, and hold* [stewardship] *under Him,"*[4] teaching his fellow colonists that their first and foremost duty in all that they possessed was to their ultimate Landlord.

Throughout the eighteenth century, American property ownership would continue to be seen as part of mankind's original Genesis mandate

---

1 Samuel Willard, *A Complete Body of Divinity In Two Hundred and Fifty Expository Lectures* (Boston, 1726), p. 686. Minister Samuel Willard was a colonial clergyman who served as acting president at Harvard from 1701 to the end of his life in 1707. His parents came to New England in the great Puritan migration and Samuel was born in Concord, Massachusetts in 1640. He graduated from Harvard in 1659 and was minister at Groton from 1663 to 1676. He was then pastor of the Third Church of Boston from 1678 until his death. Willard's massive folio book titled *A Complete Body of Divinity* was published by two of his former students in 1726, nearly two decades after his death and was the largest volume printed in colonial America.

2 Ibid.

3 Ibid.

4 Ibid.

decreed by the Creator. What they owned was known to be a sacred trust – an unchangeable, unchallengeable, well-documented biblical duty granted to them in the book of Genesis by their heavenly Sovereign. Their property could never be casually yielded to tyrants without the greatest offense to that truly sovereign Landlord. Consequently, private property was more than a secular possession; its care was a sacred duty for them to have, to hold, to use, and to defend according to their utmost obligation to God.

Private Property as *"A Dominion"* over One's *"Own Proper State"*

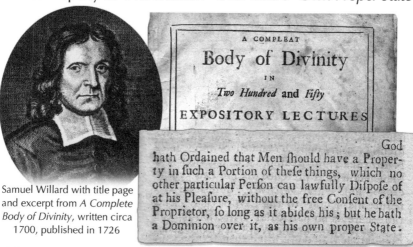

A COMPLEAT

Body of Divinity

IN

Two Hundred and *Fifty*

EXPOSITORY LECTURES

God hath Ordained that Men fhould have a Property in fuch a Portion of thefe things, which no other particular Perfon can lawfully Difpofe of at his Pleafure, without the free Confent of the Proprietor, fo long as it abides his; but he hath a Dominion over it, as his own proper State.

Samuel Willard with title page and excerpt from *A Complete Body of Divinity*, written circa 1700, published in 1726

❝God has ordained that men should have a property in such a portion of these things, which no other particular person can lawfully dispose of at his pleasure, without the free consent of the proprietor, so long as it abides his; but he has a dominion over it, as his own proper state.❞

Tyranny Defined

The misuse of governmental power was described in the colonial era as "arbitrary government."[5] It was called "arbitrary" when rulers acted on their own desires or impulses instead of acting within constitutionally defined limits of power. It was therefore an illegal use of power rather than

---

5 The term "arbitrary government" dates back to the early colonial era in Massachusetts. John Winthrop's defense of his governing principles was printed in a 1644 pamphlet called *Arbitrary Government Described and the Government of the Massachusetts Vindicated from that Aspersion*. In that work, Winthrop described the difference between biblical government under God's moral Law, and tyranny under man's arbitrary law.

legitimate authority, as Willard explained, rulers making *"their own will their law, in whatsoever may gratify their ambition or covetousness."*[6]

The English colonials knew that arbitrary power always targeted the people's liberties and their property. Tyranny therefore involved the invasive use of arbitrary power against the people as well as their property. *"Tyranny,"* Puritan Samuel Willard explained, *"is exercised, when men in power, without law, invade the liberties and properties of the subjects; and thereby oppress them."*[7] Similarly, *"tyrannical extortion"* was what John Calvin had long before called *"impositions"* that were made by rulers, *"wherewith to weary the poor commonality without cause."*[8]

Tyranny, according to Reformed Christians, was always put in terms of immorality as well as illegality – it was an illegal use of power in an immoral violation of the people's own obligations to God. It was the corrupt exercise of power against the legitimate model of dominion that He had authorized. In short, tyranny was understood as both the illegal and immoral exercise of power in violation of the people's liberty and/or property.

An Earlier Tyrannical Government in New England

Before the year 1700, New Englanders had already tasted the bitter fruit of tyranny during the reigns of King Charles II and his brother James II. England was developing a taste for expanding her empire and began consolidating power in the Crown. Standing in the way, however, were the charters granted to the independent Puritan commonwealths in New England. In the years before his death in 1685, Charles II began annulling the historic charters of the New England colonies, thus declaring their liberties meaningless. Then, upon Charles' death the newly crowned King James II replaced the former charters with a monstrosity of government called "The Dominion of New England."[9]

---

6 Willard, *A Complete Body of Divinity*, p. 650.

7 Ibid.

8 Calvin, *The Institution of Christian Religion*, vol. 2, leaf 626b, 4:20:13.

9 "The Dominion of New England" was a period of arbitrary rule that consolidated the New England colonies under a royal government. Charles II of England had begun annulling the various colonial

It appeared that the death knell of English Puritanism had arrived when the despotic Edmund Andros (who despised Puritans and their liberties alike) was appointed head of the new royal government in New England. With Governor Andros being accountable only to the king, the original land titles of the American colonials were called into question and property was subjected to arbitrary eminent domain.[10]

Christ's vineyards were suddenly being trampled underfoot. Just before the General Court of Massachusetts was dissolved by the new administration, it lodged its dying grievance: *"the subjects are abridged of their liberty as Englishmen, both in the manner of legislation, and in the laying of taxes..."*[11] This, the colonial representatives explained, *"we cannot give our assent thereto, yet hope shall demean ourselves as true and loyal subjects to his majesty; and humbly make our addresses to God."*[12]

A Wall of Separation

When local meetings were outlawed by Governor Andros, the voices of the colonial landowners were effectively silenced. Any outspoken protest was met with swift and often punitive reprisal. In a desperate move, Increase Mather,[13] the rector of Harvard College, was sent to London as

---

charters in the early to mid-1680s. Ascending the throne after Charles' death in 1685, King James II decreed the creation of the Dominion of New England. By 1686 all of New England was incorporated under one arbitrary government. In 1688, New York, East Jersey, and West Jersey were added to the Dominion. Governor Edmund Andros' administration (appointed by and answerable only to King James II) imposed the authority of the Church of England, banned town meetings, and destroyed many historic land titles. When news of the overthrow of James II in England's own "Glorious Revolution" (1688-1689) reached New England, the colonists rose up under the authority of their old charters and arrested Andros. The Dominion collapsed and chartered governments were restored under England's new co-monarchs William III and Mary II.

10 The power of eminent domain is a civil doctrine that at times permits public authorities to transfer the title of property from private ownership to the government with due compensation. Historically it was used only in cases of extreme necessity such as in obtaining specific parcels of land for forts or roadways, but never as a means of public plunder, for a government to make a profit or increase its revenue, or to arbitrarily punish or distress legitimate landowners – all corrupt uses of power.

11 Broadside: *The General Court's Answer* (Massachusetts Council, 1686).

12 Ibid.

13 Puritan minister Increase Mather was a most influential figure in the history of the Massachusetts Colony. Born in 1639 in Dorchester, Massachusetts, he was the son of Richard Mather (one of the colonial founding fathers) and upon his marriage became the son-in-law of John Cotton. He had degrees from Harvard College and schools in the British Isles, and was the minister at the North Church in Boston. Mather was also the administrator of Harvard College, and, as a colonial agent in London during the Dominion regime, he helped save the colonial New England charters. He was the father of the American historian and minister Cotton Mather.

the colonists' agent to relate their grievances to the king. Mather's 1688 tract, *A Narrative of the Miseries of New-England, by Reason of an Arbitrary Government Erected There*, was published for all in London to see the injustices being done to their American brethren. It explained the government's use of *"despotic and absolute power"* which was robbing England's loyal colonists of their *"houses which their own hands have built, and the lands, which ... they have for many years had a rightful possession."*[14] The problem in New England was new administrators who were playing the role of conquering masters rather than public servants.

The Dominion of New England in the late 1680s:
England's Assault Upon the Liberty and Property of Americans

A Narrative of the Miseries of New-England, by reason of an Arbitrary Government Erected there.

That a Colony so considerable as *New-England* is, should be discouraged, is not for the Honour and Interest of the *English Nation*; in as much as the People there are generally Sober, Industrious, Well-Disciplin'd, and apt for Martial Affairs; so that he that is Sovereign of *New-England*, may by means thereof (when he pleaseth) be Emperor of *America*: Nevertheless, the whole English Interest in that Territory has been of late in apparent danger of being lost and ruined, and the Miseries of that People by an Arbitrary Government erected amongst them, have been beyond Expression great.

Increase Mather and
*A Narrative of the Miseries
of New England*, 1689

Under arbitrary governmental power: **❝***their new masters tell them, that their charter being gone, their title to their lands and estates is gone therewith, and that all is the king's.***❞**

Through Increase Mather, the colonists petitioned the Crown against the government's use of *"Writs of Intrusion."*[15] These were arbitrary judicial orders by which colonists' land titles were annulled, their property was seized, and they were being *"told, that no man was owner of a foot of land*

---

14 Increase Mather, *A Narrative of the Miseries of New-England, by Reason of an Arbitrary Government Erected There* (1688). Published in *A Sixth Collection of Papers Relating to the Present Juncture of Affairs* (London, 1689), p. 31.

15 Increase Mather and Nathanael Byfield, *An Account of the Late Revolution in New-England together with the Declaration of the Gentlemen, Merchants, and Inhabitants of Boston and Country Adjacent* (London, 1689), p. 14.

in all the colony."[16] Another London petitioner argued for governmental safeguards that "*will perfectly secure us from slavery, and be a fence inviolable* [impenetrable] *to the liberty and property of the people.*"[17]

The idea of "*a fence inviolable*" meant that there was to be an impenetrable fence of protection around the liberty and property of the people. Put another way, there was to be a wall of separation between private dominion and the public authority – a separation that prevents governmental encroachments upon the sacred domain of private families. Godly civil governments should, in fact, secure people and families in their rightful possessions and never breach the sacred wall between private and public authority.

Providentially, the Andros regime came to an abrupt end in a most remarkable way. Upon New Englanders receiving news in early 1689 of the "Glorious Revolution"[18] and the overthrow of James II in England, the citizens of Boston seized the moment. At this singularly opportune time when England was being established as a constitutional monarchy, the merchants and magistrates of Boston interposed to forcefully remove Governor Andros as well. This, too, was a glorious deliverance! Then, acting in accord with their historic legacy of liberty, the people of Boston published a *Declaration* that rededicated them to the God who had saved them from tyranny – the God who required them to defend their land:

> *We commit our enterprise unto the blessing of Him who hears the cry of the oppressed, and advise all our neighbors, for whom we have thus ventured for ourselves, to join with us in prayers and all just actions for the defense of the land.*[19]

---

16 Ibid.

17 Anonymous, *A Letter to a Friend, Advising in this Extraordinary Juncture, How to Free the Nation from Slavery* (London, 1689), p. 15. This tract by an unidentified author was published together with Mather's *A Narrative of the Miseries of New-England*.

18 The Glorious Revolution was England's revolution of 1688-1689 involving the overthrow of King James II. It was conducted by Parliamentarians in an alliance with an invading army led by the Dutch Stadtholder William of Orange, and who, as a result, ascended the throne as William III of England in 1689. After the removal of James II, never again has an English monarch held absolute power, and the resulting *English Bill of Rights* of 1689 has become one of the most important documents in the political history of Britain. Its *Bill of Rights* laid out the basic rights of Englishmen and placed prohibitive limits on the Crown. These included freedom from royal interference with the law, freedom from taxation by royal prerogative without the representatives' consent, and freedom from a standing army during a time of peace, along with the people's right to own firearms, and so on.

19 Increase Mather, *An Account of the Late Revolution in New-England* (London, 1689), p. 19.

Such a devout commitment to defend their land would again serve the colonies later in the following century. The strict wall of separation between private dominion and illegal encroachments on liberty and property would again play an important part in the later deliverance of America that would result in her becoming a nation.

With chartered governments newly restored, the people of New England were thankful for the reestablishment of their sacred liberties and the rightful use of what they owned. From this point on, the colonists would be careful to guard their vineyards with an ever-watchful eye.

Faithfully Defending Colonial Interests

By the early 1700s, colonial America had become Britain's greatest financial asset. In 1721 Jeremiah Dummer,[20] the London agent of the Province of Massachusetts Bay, described the wealth in natural resources that the colonies sent across the ocean, including *"other and better returns than money itself they make in masts, the fairest and largest in the whole world, besides pitch, tar, turpentine, rosin, plank, knees for ships."*[21] Britain was gaining enormous prestige from her colonial assets and, as a result, she was becoming a respected imperial power.

The interests of Britain and America, however, often clashed. The commercial interests of London differed considerably from those of her colonies, and when they did, the constitutional guarantees of the colonial charters were often ignored.[22]

---

20 Jeremiah Dummer was an important colonial diplomat from New England in the early 1700s. He graduated from Harvard College in 1699 and received a Ph.D. in theology through further studies in Europe. In 1704 he returned to Massachusetts and became a preacher in Boston. After a few years, Dummer then went into diplomatic service and was appointed agent for the Province of Massachusetts Bay, a position that he held from 1710 until 1721. His most influential book, *A Defense of the New-England Charters*, was published in 1721 as a powerful defense of the self-government and trade of the northern colonies.

21 Jeremiah Dummer, *A Defense of the New-England Charters* (London, 1721). From the 1765 edition, p. 15.

22 The original, relatively lax administration of the colonial trade benefited both sides of the Atlantic. Controlled by Parliament's trade laws and the Board of Trade in London, colonial commerce was typically regulated to favor England. The trade policy was for England to receive recourses at below market rates and the colonies to purchase manufactured goods exclusively from England at full rate. The trade, however, also brought a considerable market and a healthy return on the abundant resources to the American colonists as well.

By the very nature of the Atlantic trade there always remained a division of interests on each side

That was the case, for example, with the notorious Pine Tree Act of the early eighteenth century. Britain had a growing need for the magnificent masts, massive timbers, and abundant planks used for building ships worthy of an imperial navy. The colonies had an abundance of trees perfect for that purpose, but those who owned colonial homesteads and estates naturally regarded their trees as their own private property.

Royal Claims to Colonial Private Property and Resources

The 1722 Pine Tree Act allocated American pine trees for the British Crown for harvest for the British Navy, violating the property rights of the colonists.

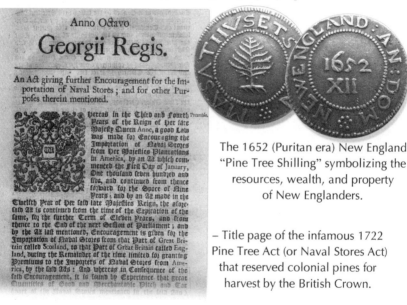

The 1652 (Puritan era) New England "Pine Tree Shilling" symbolizing the resources, wealth, and property of New Englanders.

– Title page of the infamous 1722 Pine Tree Act (or Naval Stores Act) that reserved colonial pines for harvest by the British Crown.

Britain's central government in England, of course, failed to see the colonials' perspective. In an overreaching pointed act of legislation from a

---

of the Ocean. London had its commercial interests and Boston, New York, and Charleston had their own. And, as the growing demands for revenue by the British government increased in proportion to its growing imperial status, the scale of the benefits from the commercial trade was gradually tipping more toward London. The Board of Trade administered the trade policies for the British Parliament while the colonial bodies of government were left to mind their internal colonial affairs. So, commercially speaking, Parliament and the Board of Trade ruled the waves. The colonies hired agents such as Massachusetts' Jeremiah Dummer to press their case, but without a vote in Parliament or membership in the Board of Trade their arguments seldom carried weight.

thousand leagues across the ocean, Parliament stipulated that all American white pines were reserved for the exclusive use of the British navy. The Pine Tree Act of 1722 stated bluntly that none *"shall presume to cut, fell, or destroy any white pine trees, not growing within any township, or the bounds, lines, or limits thereof, in any of the said colonies or plantations, without his majesty's royal license..."*[23] It was a clear intrusion into the rights of the property owners in America. Although the Act was careful to exempt trees within the confines of townships, trees beyond the immediate town limits were deemed the property of the king.

There was an added insult. In its method of enforcement, the same Pine Act (otherwise called the "Naval Stores Act") provided for agents of the Crown to keep tabs on the king's colonial resources reserved for the British Navy. That meant governmental agents could freely comb privately held tracts of land and not only mark selected trees for exclusive royal use, but confiscate cut timber at will. For all intents and purposes, this allowed British agents to plunder whatever suited their interests.

To the faithful British subjects in America, the idea of a distant governmental agency regulating private resources was outrageous enough. But, due to the fact that the British agents were completely unaccountable to any representative authority within the colonies, the colonists also regarded the whole scheme as an outright license to steal from – if not to terrorize – the people. In other words, by employing an agency authorized by a governing body not answerable to the landowners themselves, the people were not only deprived of their own resources, but they were denied any meaningful remedy to stop the nearly absolute governmental control of their property.

The colonists were, thankfully, not without their defenders. The Massachusetts colonial agent in London had cautioned against such abuses by Britain. In 1721 Jeremiah Dummer had published *A Defense of the New-England Charters*, arguing the case for equitable and mutually

---

23 Parliament of England, *Anno Octavo George II Regis. An Act Giving Further Encouragement for the Importation of Naval Stores* ... (London, 1722), p. 7 of the printed act, but paginated p. 207, (otherwise known as the Naval Stores Act or Pine Tree Act).

agreeable trade policies. His long list of arguments began with the fact that New England's planters did not use such unchristian methods to obtain the rights to their lands. *"The first planters,"* Dummer explained, *"far from using the barbarous methods practiced by the Spaniards on the southern continent, which have made them detestable to the whole Christian world, sought to gain the natives by strict justice in their dealings with them."*[24]

Whereas the Spaniards' methods were barbarous and cruel, the English methods were, from the beginning, virtuous in the eyes of the world. The English planters had, in fact, obtained a legitimate title to their land, coming not as conquerors, but they *"assured the Americans* [the Indians], *that they did not come among them as invaders but purchasers."*[25]

The point was that the colonists themselves did not steal the land – they gained a rightful title from the original owners. For God's blessing to be expected, they must have a legitimate title to the land. This was key to the prosperity of the colonists. To them, the idea of legitimate property ownership was equated with the blessings of wealth and the ability to create even more wealth. By diligent work, the families of colonial America both increased their private wealth and also increased their stake in America's blessings of freedom. In short, property ownership was the only means for gaining true prosperity, and it represented the best means of enjoying God-given liberty to its fullest extent.

According to Massachusetts' colonial agent Jeremiah Dummer, now was not the time to change the foundation of British policy toward America and begin treating the current landowners as conquered slaves. To the faithful colonists, the British administration should not now begin to use a harsh regiment to control the economy and trade. Such a policy change would display utter contempt for the loyal American subjects. According to Dummer, the British government should instead treat the plantation trade with the same care employed by the original settlers:

> *The trade of a young plantation is like a tender plant, and should be cherished with the fondest care; but if, instead of that, it meets*

---

24 Dummer, *A Defense of the New-England Charters*, p. 26.
25 Ibid.

with the rough hand of oppression, it will soon die. The proper nursery for this plant is a free government, where the laws are sacred, property secure, and justice not only impartially but expeditiously distributed. [26]

That visual imagery, we should notice, used the same biblical metaphors employed by the first colonists, and now was used to describe the commerce and trade of eighteenth-century provincial colonies. The picture of a *"tender plant"* under a *"rough hand of oppression"* served as a warning of what would lay ahead if the colonial commerce and trade were abused by Mother Britain. It also served as a warning of what would lay ahead if free government was not maintained and Americans' private property was not secured.

Defending America's Liberty, Property, and Trade in 1721

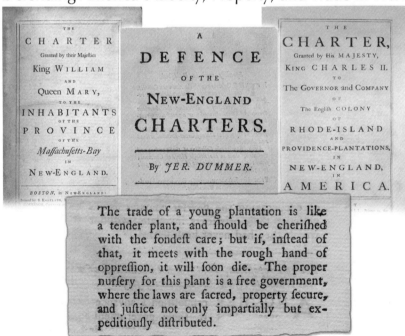

The charters of Massachusetts Bay and Rhode Island Colony are shown flanking the title page along with a text excerpt of Jeremiah Dummer's *Defense of the New-England Charters* (1721).

***

26 Ibid., p. 78.

It must be said that the same principle holds true today. A government that attempts to control the entire economy and trade of a nation crushes the "*tender plant*" of private business and free commerce. A nation that has governmental tentacles in every aspect of private life and private business has, in effect, reduced its citizens to the status of conquered slaves.

The historic idea of English colonial America as a planting of God would be a theme continued throughout the eighteenth century and the era of our nation's founding. To those who respected righteous law, private property, and free enterprise as the bulwark of a free people, the similar metaphor of the "*tender plant*" for free enterprise and trade would also remain profoundly significant in America's struggle against an increasingly overbearing British government.

12
LIBERTY RECONFIRMED IN THE EIGHTEENTH-CENTURY PULPIT

Recalling the Lessons of the Past

NOTHING expressed the sentiments – nothing shaped the sentiments – of eighteenth-century colonial Americans more than their preachers. Each Sunday was a time when the vast majority of Americans would hear an oration on the principles of life from Scripture. On a weekly basis, year after year and decade after decade, the typical American would be bathed in the principles of an abundant life and healthy living from a biblical point of view, and for the most part, they retained a strong biblical worldview. Yes, Americans certainly read newspapers for news, and kept track of the latest innovations in science, industry, and the arts through books and periodicals of all kinds, but we may safely conclude that nearly all English colonials received their basic ideas of life and living from a steady diet of God's Word from regular Sunday pulpit preaching.

Beyond the Sunday sermons (which could easily go on for over an hour) there were other sermons commonly added to the colonials' rich diet of Scripture application. As we have already seen, there were "occasional sermons" such as Fasting and Thanksgiving Sermons, Anniversary Sermons, Election Sermons, and other public sermons containing the highest regard for the principles of true biblical dominion. Sermons of all kinds throughout the mid-eighteenth century affirmed the original ideas of the colonial fathers regarding the dominion of God over His vineyard. They also affirmed America as a distinctive land of His blessings of freedom.

A Thanksgiving Sermon preached in Dedham, Massachusetts in 1738 on the one hundredth anniversary of the town's founding is a typical case in point. In the sermon called *Our Fathers' God, the Hope of Posterity*, preacher Samuel Dexter reminded his fellow townsmen to be thankful for the heritage of the "*Puritans*," of whom he said, "*by the care and zeal of these first planters, the kingdom of Christ was first planted.*"[1] These words

---

1 Samuel Dexter, *Our Fathers' God, the Hope of Posterity. Some Serious Thoughts on the Foundation,*

spoke of the heritage of the current Dedham, Massachusetts residents in 1738 whose ancestors had fled to America one hundred years earlier so *"that they and their posterity after them might enjoy the liberty of their consciences."*[2]

Standing on the Founding Principles of Colonial America

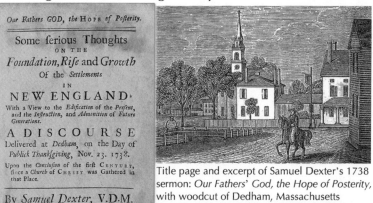

Title page and excerpt of Samuel Dexter's 1738 sermon: *Our Fathers' God, the Hope of Posterity*, with woodcut of Dedham, Massachusetts

    " *The inhabitants of this Province have always had a just value for their civil liberties, but the free and secure enjoyment of their religious privileges, has ever been most dear to them, and esteemed a plentiful reward of all the dangers and difficulties they have been struggling with, from their first plantation to this day.* "

Dexter also noted that their colony's blessedness was found in the nature of their representative civil government:

> [W]e in this land are favored with good rulers, and from among ourselves, such as are accepted of the multitude of their brethren, seeking the wealth of their people...[3]

Rise, and Growth of the Settlements in New England ... Delivered at Dedham, on the Day of Public Thanksgiving, Nov. 23, 1738 (Boston, 1738), p. 21.

2 Ibid.

3 Ibid., p. 42.

The Dedham preacher was describing the kind of civil government that seeks to keep the wealth of the people with the people. At the time of their town's founding in 1638, King Charles I was using the power of the state to confiscate the property and wealth of the people of England by arbitrary and abusive taxation. The colonial fathers set up a different kind of civil government – a representative government formed from among themselves – that respected the virtue of private wealth and encouraged the people of Dedham to prosper as individuals and families.

It was King Charles I, after all, who had driven John Winthrop, John Cotton, John Davenport, and the entire first decade of New England planters into the wilderness of America. The colonials' objective in the eighteenth century was to retain the blessings handed down to them from their forefathers. The small civics lesson preached by Dexter to the families of Dedham, Massachusetts in November 1738 was typical of the sentiments throughout the colonies – their own *"Hope of Posterity"* was in honoring their fathers' God by passing a heritage of liberty and property on *"to our children, and our children's children."*[4]

One of the key functions of the eighteenth-century public pulpit was to call the people into remembrance of their blessed civil inheritance. American preachers such as Pastor Dexter not only brought the people into remembrance of God's miraculous deliverances of His people in Scripture, but how the same Lord had also preserved their own forefathers in the fertile land of promise that they now possessed.

In 1750, on the occasion of the centennial anniversary of the fall of England's King Charles I, Boston's Jonathan Mayhew preached one of the most famous sermons of the colonial era. Mayhew's sermon was also one of a most important remembrance. The previous year had marked the one-hundredth anniversary of the downfall of the tyrant Charles I in England, who was now being idolized there as a supposed martyr to the cause of royalty. Jonathan Mayhew, who was the product of a family that had fled Charles' tyranny, would have none of that. His sermon, preached in 1750, called *A Discourse Concerning Unlimited Submission and Non-*

---

4 Ibid.

Resistance to the Higher Powers was a magnificent adaptation of the original reformational principles of civil policy.

Jonathan Mayhew on Limited Government and the Duty of the People's Representatives to Defend their Liberties

Boston Preacher Jonathan Mayhew and the title page of his sermon:
*A Discourse Concerning Unlimited Submission and
Non-Resistance to the Higher Powers* (1750)

Throughout the 1630s, Charles I had imposed a series of unconstitutional impositions, taxes, fees, and fines on the people of England without the people's representatives in Parliament having any say in the matter. He also imprisoned and confiscated the private property of individuals who opposed him. Mayhew's sermon described the king's tyranny as an affront to every idea of civil and Christian virtue. His message related the absolute necessity of resistance by the people's representatives in England's Parliament to stop the king's despotic ambitions:

> *Resistance was absolutely necessary in order to preserve the na-*
> *tion from slavery, misery and ruin. And who so proper to make this*
> *resistance as the lords and commons; the whole representative*
> *body of the people: guardians of the public welfare; and each of*
> *which was, in point of legislation, vested with an equal, co-ordi-*
> *nate power, with that of the Crown.*[5]

---

5 Jonathan Mayhew, *A Discourse Concerning Unlimited Submission and Non-Resistance to the Higher Powers* (Boston, 1750), p. 45.

That kind of godly interposition, whereby the English Parliament ("*the lords and commons*") intervened in the 1640s on behalf of the people's liberties and private property, had been the mark of their governing duty. Parliament passed laws that checked the king's ambitions and then led an army of faithful Englishmen to defeat the otherwise unyielding Charles I on the battlefield. This was indeed a just resistance that represented the triumph of biblical principle over the worst of despotic rulers, and it was an example to all free people of the benefits of a representative form of government.

Mayhew's point in 1750 was to remind Americans of the duty of any honorable statesman. It was clearly a reminder of the duty of their own lawfully-elected colonial representatives to interpose themselves on behalf of the people if and when their liberties and property were violated.

Such measured resistance stemmed from the Reformed Christian principle of lawfully defending the people's God-given liberties. Mayhew was therefore not preaching secular libertarianism – or undignified liberty apart from a due reverence for God's sanction of legitimate government. Mayhew was speaking of the kind of liberty that honors God as well as biblically-sanctioned governing authority. A ruler who respects the people's private and personal responsibilities under God, Mayhew reminded his audience, "*is God's minister to you for good.*"[6] He then lauded England's current King George II, adding: "*I am speaking of loyalty to our* [current] *earthly prince.*"[7] Mayhew concluded his oration by pointing to the only Authority that no one ought to resist – to the single Sovereign under whom all men must either submit or be found in rebellion:

> [S]*uffer me just to put you in mind to be loyal also to the supreme Ruler of the universe, by whom kings reign, and princes decree justice. To which King eternal, immortal, invisible, even to the Only Wise God, be all honor and praise, Dominion and Thanksgiving, through Jesus Christ our Lord. Amen.*[8]

---

6 Ibid., p. 10.
7 Ibid., p. 55.
8 Ibid.

Sermons of Humility and the Continuing Providential Blessings of God

Other colonial sermons were similar in their loyalty to legitimate authority. With godly rulers and the constitutional protections of their charters honored, the colonists were more than happy to be called British. When the policies of England did not encroach upon their charters or their rights as Englishmen, the colonies were the Crown's hearty supporters.

For example, when news arrived in 1739 that war had commenced in America between England and her old nemesis Spain, the northern colonies whole-heartedly aligned their patriotism with Britain's efforts. A Fast Day Sermon preached in Salem, Massachusetts in February 1741 was a powerful argument for New England to support England's efforts to defend her most southern colonies.

In the sermon, Salem's pastor Peter Clark admonished all Americans' need for humility before God, reminding them *"that God threatens to lay waste His Vineyard."*[9] He also recalled the brutality that Spain used in her dealings with Americans in the past, and reminded them of the *"Spanish monarchy which is deeply stained in blood of multitudes of innocents."*[10]

The situation looked grave. The survival of the colonies of Georgia and South Carolina rested upon repulsing the first organized Spanish invasion of English soil since the Armada appeared off the coast of England back in 1588. In the summer of 1742, another such moment came when a Spanish fleet appeared off the coast of St. Simon's Island, Georgia. It was a formidable force of fifty-two men-of-war, schooners, sloops, and galleys that landed a force of over four thousand Spanish troops.

The British defenders under the command of Georgia's founder, James Oglethorpe, won yet another miraculous victory for the English over their historic foe at the Battle of Bloody Marsh. With only eight hundred men, they miraculously outmaneuvered their surprisingly confused opponents in the field. The entire Spanish fleet then retreated back to Florida, never again to invade England's southern colonies. It was apparent that, once

9 Peter Clark, *Two Sermons Preached at Salem-Village on the General Fast Appointed on the Occasion of the War, February 26, 1741* (Boston, 1741), p. 41.
10 Ibid., p. 44.

again, the Lord of Hosts – the Lord of Armies – had defended the cause of liberty and put the favorable stamp of divine Providence on the success of Christ's true dominion in America.

Another equally remarkable deliverance by God came in the northern colonies just a few years later during the French and Indian War. In 1746 a massive French fleet assembled off the coast of the New England colonies in preparation for an armed invasion. Thomas Prince, then pastor of the Old South Church in Boston, described this force as an alliance between the French and certain Indian tribes, with the French ships supplying *"forty thousand arms, with proportionable ammunition … for the Indians."*[11]

New England's Miraculous Deliverance by God in 1746

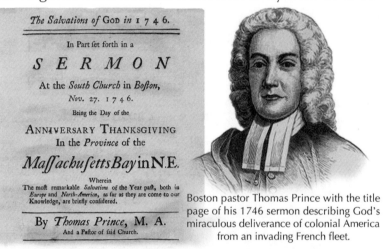

Boston pastor Thomas Prince with the title page of his 1746 sermon describing God's miraculous deliverance of colonial America from an invading French fleet.

Prince's sermon described the events during Massachusetts' Day of Fasting and Prayer:

❝ [T]hat very night ensuing, the glorious God entirely baffled their [the French invader's] purposes, and put a total end to their mischievous enterprise. He, the Mighty arose [in the tempest of a hurricane], and wrought a full salvation for us.❞

New England was completely unprepared to stave off such a massive attack. The colonists mustered their various militias on the Boston

---

11 Thomas Prince, *The Salvations of God in 1746. In Part set forth in a Sermon At the South Church in Boston, Nov. 27. 1746. Being the Day of the Anniversary Thanksgiving In the Province of the Massachusetts Bay in N.E.* (Boston, 1746), pp. 33-34.

Commons, but they knew this alone was wholly inadequate to repel such an organized onslaught. The colonists' only adequate defense was to call for another of their many public appeals to heaven. On October 6 the Bay Colony called for an emergency day of fasting and prayer. Prince wrote that on that particular day, *"we expressly cried to the Lord, as in Psalm 68:1-2 'Let God arise, let his enemies be scattered, let them that hate him flee before him.'"*[12] The same New England preacher then related the effect:

> *And that very night ensuing, the glorious God entirely baffled all their purposes, and put a total end to their mischievous enterprise. He mightily arose, and wrought a full salvation for us.*[13]

The colonists of New England witnessed an astounding deliverance on the very day that they gathered in their public venues to pray. Their deliverance from the French and Indians in 1746 came by a miraculous storm sent by God, as Prince's sermon related:

> *He sent a more furious storm of wind and rain and hail, than ever – which held to the next day noon – which they could not stand before – which so dispersed and broke them, they could never get together again.*[14]

New England's salvation that year was another confirmation that the Lord had made America a special object of His care – that she was intended to remain free and prosperous under His guiding hand. It was clear to the Americans and to the whole world that their deliverance was by a divine hand of mercy. Thomas Prince concluded his sermon with the appropriate praise: *"Sing unto God ye kingdoms of the earth."*[15]

That benign sense of divine purpose was nearly always present with the colonists. The objective was for them to remain as the faithful plantings of God, but also to defend His kingdom which had cast its gracious rays upon the fields and woodlands of America. Success, then, was a matter

---

12 Ibid., p. 32.
13 Ibid., p. 31.
14 Ibid.
15 Ibid., p. 35.

of remaining humble before their God, as the southern colonial preacher Samuel Davies would later remind the troops of Hanover, Virginia before embarking to successfully repel yet another French invasion in May 1758:

> *Remember to also put your confidence in God, who keeps the thread of your life and the events of war in His own hand. Devoutly acknowledge His Providence in all your ways, and be sensible of your dependence upon it.*[16]

Samuel Davies Called on Virginians to Forcefully Defend Themselves Against Invaders Intending to *"rob us of our property"*

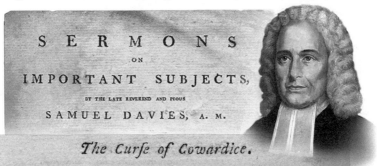

SERMONS

ON

IMPORTANT SUBJECTS,

BY THE LATE REVEREND AND PIOUS

SAMUEL DAVIES, A. M.

The Curse of Cowardice.

But when, in this corrupt, disordered state of things, where the lusts of men are perpetually embroiling the world with wars and fightings, throwing all into confusion ; when ambition and avarice would rob us of our property, for which we have toiled, and on which we subsist ; when they would enslave the free-born mind, and compel us meanly to cringe to usurpation and arbitrary power ;

❝... *when ambition and avarice would rob us of our property, for which we have toiled, and on which we subsist; when they would enslave the free-born mind, and compel us meanly to cringe to usurpation and arbitrary power; ... must peace then be maintained, maintained with our perfidious and cruel invaders, maintained at the expense of property, liberty, life, and everything dear and valuable? ... No: in such a time even the God of Peace proclaims by His providence: To arms!* ❞

Samuel Davies with an excerpt from his sermon *The Curse of Cowardice*, preached to the militia of Hanover County, Virginia in May of 1758.

---

16 Samuel Davies, *The Curse of Cowardice*, published in *Sermons on Important Subjects, by the late Reverend and Pious Samuel Davies* ... (Philadelphia, 1794), p. 545.

Time and again the American pulpits served a critical purpose in eighteenth-century English America.[17] First, the colonial ministers called hard-working families to the deepest appreciation for the tender kindnesses of the Almighty in ages past – that is, in remembrance of the Lord of mercies guiding their forefathers to such a land of promise and sustaining them. The colonial preachers then repeatedly drew from the same wells of duty, resolve, and courage of their fathers in directing the current generations through their own trying times.

Consequently, Americans were fortified with constant reminders that they were tethered by the same legacy of responsible liberty and stewardship of the land that defined the English colonial character. And, as the more distant sons of the earlier Reformation in Europe, these mid-eighteenth-century colonials had every reason to continue embracing the godly counsel of America's public pulpits and then imploring the same Lord's sustenance through some very trying times in the decades to come.

---

17 One of the most profound benefits of the American pulpit was the "Great Awakening," which commenced in the mid-1730s. This was a massive reawakening to God's Word, resulting in a profound sense of repentance on the part of those converted to Christ. It also resulted in a much greater cultural sense of godliness throughout the colonies and a widespread awareness that the Lord had a powerful and purposeful hand upon America as a land of His special favor.

13
DEFENDING MORAL GOVERNMENT

Constitutional Liberties

AS the eighteenth century progressed, the American colonies continued to enjoy the enormous cultural benefits of widespread pulpit preaching. The colonies, for example, were spared much of the widespread moral breakdown and cultural decay that was occurring at the time in mid-eighteenth-century Europe.

The Americans also continued to see God's gracious providence in the enormous benefit of limited government along with the abundance that accompanies the blessedness of liberty and private property. Until the 1760s, British Americans were mostly free to enjoy the increase of their own resources. For example, the enforcement of the Pine Tree Act that had caused so much concern in the 1720s, had lain virtually dormant for decades. From then on, it was a fairly rare event for the British agents to fine the colonists for felling or selling their own pines. The trees that were taken by the British Navy were purchased through the regular course of commerce rather than by confiscation. Another act, the Sugar Act (or Molasses Act) of 1733, which restricted imports and exports on the important commodities of sugar and molasses, also lay largely unenforced for decades.[1]

By 1760, however, the British colonial administration began to change. Its attitude and policies began to be more oppressive as Britain's need for revenue began to rise. In 1764, Parliament passed a new act that revised the old Sugar Act. That new act actually lowered the import/export duties, but toughened the enforcement of their regulation. The issue was therefore one of governmental *control* through taxation. If Parliament

---

1 For much of the mid-eighteenth century, Britain's political leadership had a hands-off policy of "salutary neglect," by which Crown officials laxly enforced Parliament's regulatory legislation. Custom officials turned a blind eye and allowed Americans to conduct their commerce in relative freedom with other nations in spite of the Sugar (or Molasses) Act of 1733, which required exclusive trade with Britain. Under salutary neglect, the colonial economy prospered, and Americans enjoyed the blessing of being subjects of such a freedom-loving monarchy as that of Great Britain.

could raise revenue by controlling one commodity, why not tax all other property along with the colonists' lands and homes? And further, since the laws were enforced through Britain's regulatory agencies and were not answerable to the colonial governments, the colonials would have no legal recourse but submission.

The days of regulatory laxity had come to an end. The new Sugar Act brought punitive penalties. American traders even suspected of sidetracking trade regulations were subject to severe fines and the confiscation of their ship's cargo as contraband. The private use of the colonists' trees and natural resources was again threatened when the White Pine Act was enforced with an all-new vigor by the British regulatory administration over the colonies. Taxes, restrictions, and regulations were gradually seizing control of the colonists' resources and placing outrageous burdens upon their private property – all by a centralized governmental regime beyond their reach in England.

The British government justified its actions by pointing to the fact that protecting and maintaining a multi-continental empire came at an enormous expense. As a gesture of submissive loyalty, the colonies should pay their part. The fact was that as Britain's overall debt was piling up, the unrepresented colonies were the most convenient targets from which Parliament could raise needed revenue. It was certainly easier to tax the Americans than tax the subjects in England to whom Parliament itself answered. The colonists argued that they had always benefited the mother country with resources at very advantageous rates, by generous contributions of troops in defending Britain's interests, and by faithfully conforming to the constitutional stipulations of their charters.

The colonists were, after all, Englishmen with all the inherent rights of other Englishmen across the Atlantic. For example, Mayor Daniel Dulany of Annapolis, Maryland argued in 1765 that the colonists were *"English subjects, who left their native country to settle in the wilderness of America,* [and] *had the privileges of other Englishmen."*[2]

---

2 Daniel Dulany, *Considerations on the Propriety of Imposing Taxes in the British Colonies, for the Purpose of Raising a Revenue, by Act of Parliament* (London, 1766), p. 39 (first edition was 1765).

Dulany's point was that one's specific residence, whether in England or America, did not affect one's standing as a freeborn Englishman. An Englishman across the sea had his own duly-elected representatives in Parliament, and an Englishman in colonial America had his own duly-elected representatives in his colony. The Americans would lose all their revered property rights if the British king and Parliament passed legislation regarding the colonists' property.

Private Property as the People's Greatest Security of Freedom

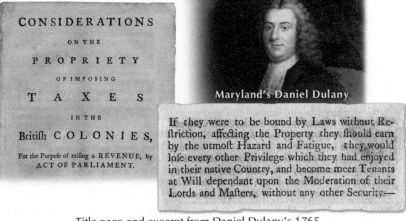

Title page and excerpt from Daniel Dulany's 1765
Considerations on the Propriety of Imposing Taxes in the British Colonies

Dulany explained that if civil rulers in England controlled the colonists' property, the colonists would lack any meaningful freedom. They would become vassal slaves to their lords and masters across the ocean:

> [I]*f they were to be bound by laws without restriction, affecting the property they should earn by the utmost hazard and fatigue, they would lose every other privilege which they had enjoyed in their native country, and become mere tenants at will dependent upon the moderation of their lords and masters, without any other security.*[3]

The safeguards in the colonial charters against British magistrates treading upon the colonists' property is what kept the colonists from

---

3 Ibid.

becoming vassals of abject despotism. Dulany's underlying point was clear: the people's right in their private property was the underpinning of all other rights. When a family's private estate is abusively regulated, overtaxed, or otherwise controlled by an unaccountable government or governmental agency, it not only loses its God-given dominion, but it effectively loses all other privileges of freedom with it.

Defending the Realm of the Home

From the time of the first English plantings in America, the family had been recognized as the foundation of colonial life. Samuel Davies, one of the aforementioned prominent southern preachers of the mid-eighteenth century, described the central importance of the "society" of the family amid the other social institutions:

> This [the family] was the society instituted in Paradise in the state of innocence, when the indulgent Creator, finding that it was not good for man, a sociable creature, to be alone, formed an help meet for him, and united them in the endearing bonds of the conjugal relation. From thence the human race propagated; and when multiplied, it was formed into civil governments and ecclesiastical assemblies. [4]

With that Genesis view of the family, the church and commonwealth were seen as its greatest beneficiaries. Hence, in American colonial life where all three societies were greatly valued, the family was revered as the most foundational. When the society of the family came under attack in the American colonies, that attack was an affront to the institution that was at the heart of all others.

At the beginning of the 1760s, British colonial policy did just that – it targeted the realm of private families. There was a new enforcement of a regulatory instrument called the Writs of Assistance. The writs were general warrants for governmental agents to search any suspect colonial dwellings for potential contraband or smuggled goods without any specificity in what they were seeking to find. With such a general writ in

---

4 Davies, *Sermons on Important Subjects*, p. 61.

hand, an agent of the British government could arbitrarily search any ship, wharf, dock house, shop, business, or even private residence for prohibited goods. For the colonists, the Writs of Assistance therefore represented not only a matter of increasing control, but also an unwarrantable attack on the sacred domain of the home.

In February 1761 the Massachusetts Superior Court convened in Salem to address the legality of such arbitrary writs. Boston attorney James Otis addressed the court in a powerful speech lasting over four hours. A young Boston lawyer named John Adams, who was privileged to hear it, later explained its monumental significance. Adams wrote: *"American independence was then and there born."*[5] He also recorded that *"Otis was a flame of fire!"*[6] The speech was a monument to American liberty because it exposed the British writs as being destructive to one of the most essential branches of all English liberty:

> *Now one of the most essential branches of English liberty is the freedom of one's house. A man's house is his castle, and whilst he is quiet, he is as well guarded as a prince in his castle. This writ, if it is declared legal, would totally annihilate this privilege.*[7]

For unaccountable government agents to *"annihilate"* the *"privilege"* of a quiet, faithful home undermined every idea of biblical dominion. It undermined the principle of a householder governing his own family's affairs as well as disregarded the domain of private property.

Otis' concern was not that a legitimate officer of the law might search a dwelling with due cause and a specific warrant. His grievance was with the writs' general warrant and complete lack of accountability to the people's duly-elected representatives.

Samuel Adams, one of colonial Massachusetts' most outspoken representatives, later argued that the whole idea of a general writ was an invasion of the colonists' most sacred possession:

---

5 John Adams, *Novanglus, and Massachusettensis; Or Political Essays* (Boston, 1819), p. 246.
6 Ibid.
7 Charles Francis Adams, *The Works of John Adams, Second President of the United States*, vol. 2 (Boston: Little, Brown, and Company, 1865), Appendix A, p. 524, referencing James Otis' speech.

*These officers may under color of law and the cloak of a general
warrant, break through the sacred rights of the domicile, ransack
men's houses, destroy their securities, carry off their property...*[8]

For Adams, Otis, and their fellow patriots, the home was a key line
of defense in the colonial cause. And, as governmental tyranny increased
throughout the 1760s, colonial homes continued to come under attack.

Government to Provide Security for Life, Liberty, and Property

James Otis

Title page of James Otis' 1764 book
*The Rights of the British Colonies
Asserted and Proved*

❝ *The end of government being the good of mankind, points out
its great duties: It is above all things to provide for the security,
the quiet, and happy enjoyment of life, liberty, and property.* ❞

Another outrage came when British troops were sent to America to
help enforce the new revenue laws. The Quartering Act that accompanied
the troops was an affront in every sense of the idea of English liberty.
This Act demanded the private "quartering" for British troops in any
unoccupied colonial dwelling (and later occupied homes). There was
an added problem. England's own Bill of Rights[9] did not allow standing

---

8 *The Votes and Proceedings of the Freeholders and Other Inhabitants of the Town of Boston* (Boston,
1772), p. 17, ref. Samuel Adams.

9 England's Parliament adopted the Bill of Rights in December 1689 as a list of statutory restrictions
on the powers of the Crown government of the realm. The bill was enacted partly as a response to the
events of the Glorious Revolution. With the expulsion of King James II, the bill's list of grievances

armies in times of peace without legislative approval in Parliament.[10] And, the Quartering Act not only condoned a standing army without the colonial representative's consent, it also demanded that American families provide British troops with shelter upon a military officer's command. An outraged Samuel Adams warned in a Boston Gazette article: "[L]*et any one consider whether this doctrine does not directly lead even to the setting up that superior officer, whoever he may be, as a tyrant.*"[11]

Adams' point was similar to that of Otis in that both patriots recognized that a criminal form of dominion was being progressively unleashed upon American soil. It was clear that the homes and private effects of colonial families were under assault by soldiers more like Spanish conquistadors than the dignified British who were to respect the dignity of peaceable dwellings. The Writs of Assistance and the Quartering Act were both outright affronts to the most foundational domain of colonial life, and they were also indicative of a much wider problem – one of a growing sense of a governmental entitlement to enslave the people themselves.

The Stamp Act Congress of 1765 and Private Property

In the mid-1760s, colonists were being confronted with a whole host of new and inventive governmental policies, each exceeding the former in its breach of justice and civic morality. For example, the Stamp Act of 1765 (also known as the Duties in American Colonies Act) was the first direct tax imposed by the British Parliament within the colonies.

The Stamp Act placed a fee on the production of American printed publications and manuscript public documents, and as its slang "stamp tax"

---

was presented to William and Mary as the terms under which they would become king and queen of England. The Bill of Rights enumerated certain rights to which subjects and permanent residents of a constitutional monarchy were entitled, including the right to an elected representative government, the right to petition their rulers, the right to keep and bear arms, and freedom from a standing army and the government stationing troops in private homes and businesses in times of peace.

10 Broadside: *The Public Grievances of the Nation, Adjudged Necessary, by the Honorable House of Commons* (London, 1689), side 1, point 6 stating: *"That the raising or keeping of a standing army within this kingdom, in times of peace, without consent of Parliament is against law."* Standing armies in times of peace were considered an intimidating feature of a despotic government without proper legislative approval. The House of Commons' list of grievances became the principled underpinning of the English Bill of Rights adopted in 1689.

11 Philip Kurland and Ralph Lerner, *The Founders' Constitution*, vol. 5 (Chicago: University of Chicago Press, 1987), p. 216. Citing Samuel Adams in the *Boston Gazette*, 17 Oct. 1768.

implied, a stamp with a royal seal was placed on documents for which the tax had been paid. The revenue collected, however, was sent to the British Isles to relieve the national debt rather than staying anywhere within the local vicinity of those being taxed. Patrick Henry, a member of Virginia's House of Burgesses, argued against the stamp tax because the British Parliament could never supercede the colonists' own representatives, *"who can only know what taxes the people are able to bear."*[12]

Only Representatives Who Are Themselves Taxed Will Be Sensible of the Real Burden That Their Taxation Imposes Upon the Property of Others

Resolved, That the taxation of the people by themselves, or by persons chosen by themselves to represent them, who can only know what taxes the people are able to bear, and the easiest mode of raising them, and are equally affected by such taxes themselves, is the distinguishing characteristic of British freedom.

Patrick Henry

Excerpt from the proposed 1765 Virginia House of Burgesses' Stamp Act Resolutions (as recorded from an original draft in Patrick Henry's handwriting)

The Virginia Burgesses' point was key to any just sense of taxation – that taxes ought to be legislated only by those who know the circumstances and burden of those being taxed. Accordingly, the various representative colonial assemblies such as Virginia's House of Burgesses sent petitions of protest to both the king and Parliament. Grassroots groups led by townsmen, merchants, and ministers also sprang up from New England to Georgia. Most of those were organized as independent, localized movements under the general name of the "Sons of Liberty."

In October 1765 a colonial "Stamp Act Congress" was organized. Composed of an assembly of representatives from nine American colonies,

12 William Wirt, *Sketches of the Life and Character of Patrick Henry* (Philadelphia, 1818), p. 57.

the Congress was the first organized joint response to Britain's increasingly despotic measures. The congressional petition to Parliament complained that the *"Commons, in Britain, undertake absolutely to dispose of the property of their fellow subjects, in America, without their consent."*[13]

In other words, the Stamp Act Congress questioned whether one group of Englishmen could rightly tax (*"dispose of"*) the property of another apart from their expressed consent. The issue of forced taxation was therefore one of immorality as much as illegality. The colonial charters, which reserved the right of imposing internal colonial taxes with each colonial legislature, answered the legal question. The British Parliament, as the sole representative body of the subjects in England, could not legally tax the subjects in Virginia any more than the Virginia House of Burgesses could tax the subjects in England, Pennsylvania, or anywhere else in the realm. Thus, Parliament's insistence upon taxing the colonies would always be an issue of immorality because when Parliament placed a tax upon the colonists without the consent of their own colonial representatives, that tax amounted to property theft.

The Moral Cause of Liberty and Property

The cause of the American patriots against Britain was always underpinned by moral considerations. For example, the first name chosen to identify the American patriots in the mid-1760s – "Sons of Liberty" – inferred that they were sons of something much greater than the immediate legal issues at hand. That something was also more than a philosophical ideal and more than addressing pragmatic or economic concerns of the day. The name "Sons of Liberty" embodied the same kind of responsible, manly, moral character that the colonists inherited from their Christian ancestors.

Silas Downer, one of the most prominent Sons of Liberty in Rhode Island, described the colonists' property rights in biblical terms, saying: *"we do not yield the Garden of God and our birthrights to the sons of*

---

13 *Speeches of the Governors of Massachusetts, from 1765 to 1775; and the Answers of the House of Representatives, to the Same* (Boston: Russell and Gardner, 1818), p. 38.

ambition."[14] Fighting for liberty and property in the mid-eighteenth century was therefore put in terms reminiscent of the first planters' understanding of the dominion mandate in Scripture. At the dedication of the Liberty Tree[15] in Providence, Rhode Island two years later, Downer also admonished the Sons of Liberty there, saying: *"let us with unconquerable resolution maintain and defend that liberty wherewith God hath made us free."*[16]

American Sons of Liberty Defend God's Dominion Mandate

❝ [W]e do not yield the Garden of God and our birthrights to the sons of ambition. ❞

– Silas Downer defending God's possession against the ambition of Britain, 1766 (Providence, Rhode Island).

– Late colonial-era cartoon depicting the defense of Americans' property (symbolized by a pine tree banner) against British aggression.

Such expressions of patriotism were bolstered by repeated appeals to moral duty. That was nothing new. The Sons of Liberty were repaving the same moral path that had been paved by Reformed Christians for over two

---

14 Pauline Maier, *From Resistance to Revolution* (New York: W.W. Norton and Company, 1991), p. 96.

15 A liberty tree was symbolic of the planting of liberty in colonial America, and it provided a rallying place for local American patriots. The earliest liberty tree was an elm in the Boston Commons that dated back to the era of the founding of Massachusetts Bay Colony in the seventeenth century, serving as a reminder of their original colonial principles of liberty and property. Other towns during the era of resistance to British encroachment in the 1760-1770s raised liberty poles or planted liberty trees as gestures of common patriotism toward the colonial cause.

16 Charles Hyneman and Donald Lutz, *American Political Writing during the Founding Era*, vol. 1 (Indianapolis: Liberty Fund, 1983), p.107.

centuries. When the colonists argued against Parliament's absolute right to tax them in the 1760s, they were restating similar arguments made by Scotland's Samuel Rutherford, who wrote more than a century before:

> The PP [Power of Parliament] *gives them but a poor deliberative power in subsidies* [taxes], *and that is, to make the king's will a law, in taking all the subjects' goods from them.*[17]

Rutherford was describing the limitations of any body of rulers, whether by *"the king's will"* or Parliament's *"deliberative power"* to claim dominion over the private *"goods"* of the people. In 1644, long before the Americans of the 1760s, Rutherford had explained the limitations upon Parliament's power to claim any absolute prerogative over the people's goods, much less to confiscate them under the pretenses of an entitlement. And, although taxation is a legitimate function of government, an absolute right to tax without limits can never be! To Rutherford and his contemporaries, any claim to legislate from a position of absolute right was immoral and unbiblical.

Rutherford himself was echoing the moral arguments made a century before him. At the time of the Reformation, John Calvin recognized that taxes were *"impositions"*[18] on the people which should be strictly limited. To Calvin, taxes or any governmental impositions should be used for limited public expenses, because private wealth, Calvin said, was *"the very blood of the people, which not to spare, is most cruel and unnatural."*[19]

Those who followed the Reformed Christian approach to civil government always considered taxes as a moral concern. Taxes, tributes, fees, and fines were all regarded as immoral and *"most cruel"* when taken either unconstitutionally or oppressively. A running principle from the time of John Calvin to Samuel Rutherford and on to the time of our nation's founding was that taxes or impositions of any kind were never to be regarded as governmental entitlements. Privately-held property was

---

17 Samuel Rutherford, *Lex, Rex: The Law and the Prince. A Dispute for the Just Prerogative of King and People* (London, 1644), p. 448.
18 Calvin, *The Institution of Christian Religion*, vol. 2, leaf 626b, 4:20:13.
19 Ibid.

off-limits to any taxation without the people's consent by representative legislation, because any *"cruel and unnatural"* taking of their property was recognized as a violation of God's commandment not to steal.[20] The same principle rings true today. Any government that thinks its idea of a greater social good somehow entitles it to unrestrained access to the private wealth of its citizens is immoral, if not outright tyrannical.

By the time of America's open resistance to British aggression in the later eighteenth century, God's moral restraints were built into the colonists' most fundamental understanding of good government. Moral government meant limited government, and strict limits on taxation had been a part of the colonists' Christian inheritance from the earliest times.

---

20 Exodus 20:15: *"You shall not steal."*

14
GODLY RESISTANCE TO INVASIVE TYRANNY

The Declaration of America's Dependence

THE most outrageous affront to the colonists' idea of moral government was the infamous Declaratory Act of 1766. In one sweeping piece of legislation, the British Parliament had granted itself *"full power and authority to make laws and statutes of sufficient force and validity to bind the colonies and people of America, subjects of the Crown of Great Britain, in all cases whatsoever."*[1]

Passed on the day after the repeal of the infamous Stamp Act, Parliament's Declaratory Act was a complete power grab – it was, in effect, a declaration of the colonies' total dependence on the central government of Britain. One body of English subjects was, in fact, subjecting another body to its arbitrary legislation, and that without limits. The Declaratory Act asserted that the British Parliament had an absolute power to impose its legislation *"in all cases whatsoever"* – thereby assuming full power to tax the colonists even though they remained unrepresented in Parliament.

Parliament's Declaration of American Dependence:
Unconstitutional Tyranny by the "Declaratory Act" of 1766

An Act for the better securing the Dependency of His Majesty's Dominions in *America* upon the Crown and Parliament of *Great Britain.*

Anno Regni sexto Georgii III. Regis.

That the said Colonies and Plantations in America have been, are, and of Right ought to be, subordinate unto, and dependent upon, the Imperial Crown and Parliament of Great Britain; and that the King's Majesty, by and with the Advice and Consent of the Lords Spiritual and Temporal, and Commons of Great Britain, in Parliament assembled, had, hath, and of Right ought to have, full Power and Authority to make Laws and Statutes of sufficient Force and Validity to bind the Colonies and People of America, Subjects of the Crown of Great Britain, in all Cases whatsoever.

Britain's King George III

1 Parliament of Great Britain, *Anno Regni George III. Regis Sexto. An Act for the Better Securing the Dependency of His Majesty's Dominions in America Upon the Crown and Parliament of Great Britain* (London, 1766), p. 4 of folio Act, paginated p. 248.

To the colonists, the Declaratory Act was a raw declaration of invasive power without either legal or moral standing. It was an illegal affront to their charters, but more than that, it robbed their colonial heritage in liberty and property of any tangible meaning. That being said, few complaints were made, at least initially, because the colonists were basking in the news of the repeal of the infamous Stamp Act.[2] And frankly, they considered the grossly licentious Declaratory Act as unenforceable.

Parliament, however, acted quickly on its newly claimed power over the colonies. Within a year it began enacting the kind of revenue taxes on colonial trade that would lead to open hostility within a decade.

The Rights and Sacred Responsibilities of Private Property

Another invasive affront to the private estates of the colonists was Parliament's new stream of revenue acts that followed the Declaratory Act. Britain's progressive attack on her colonies now came in the form of a series of taxes on the American trade, known as the Townshend Revenue Acts of 1767. These Acts, named for Charles Townshend, Chancellor of the Exchequer,[3] were a desperate attempt to control Britain's mounting national debt. The colonies, however, viewed them as a frontal attack on their liberties and countered with a round of protests against an ever-encroaching central government.

The Townshend Acts were denounced by the Massachusetts legislature on a similar moral basis as was Britain's previous taxation, describing this new revenue scheme as *"grievous to the subject, burdensome to trade, ruinous to the nation."*[4] The representatives' official letter of protest sent from Boston to London pointed out that it was not only the colonists' life and liberty that were essential blessings from the Creator, but that

---

2 The Declaratory Act of 1766 replaced the Stamp Act (passed by the English Parliament in 1765) that was discussed in chapter 13. Opposition to the Stamp Act was not limited to the colonies. British merchants, manufacturers, and many English lawmakers such as William Pitt who respected Americans' liberty and property pressured Parliament for its repeal. That Act was repealed on March 17, 1766 as a matter of expedience. The Declaratory Act was passed on March 18, 1766 as a matter of tyranny.

3 Britain's Chancellor of the Exchequer has for centuries been the Cabinet minister responsible for public revenues of the realm. It is a post similar to the United States Secretary of the Treasury.

4 John Adams, *A Dissertation on the Canon and the Feudal Law* in *The True Sentiments of America* (London, 1768), p. 62.

"property is a valuable acquisition, which ought to be held sacred."[5] With the fundamental purpose of government being to protect such a sacred holding, they argued that *"such measures as tend to render right and property precarious, tend to destroy both property and government."*[6]

This point is critical to our understanding of the patriots' grievance against Britain's aggressive taxation policies. To the American patriots, a government that undermines the people's source of wealth also undermines its own God-given purpose to safeguard the good of the people. Consequently, a government that does not avoid the temptation to make the people's property the object of its plunder undermines the value of the people's property (which is *"held sacred"*) and, ultimately, destroys itself. Conversely, a government that avoids such a temptation secures the people's God-given blessings and secures its own virtuous purpose under Him. The Massachusetts letter of protest declared in no uncertain terms: *"a man shall quietly enjoy, and have the sole disposal of his own property."*[7]

The People's Security in their own Private Property is the Essential Role of Civil Government!

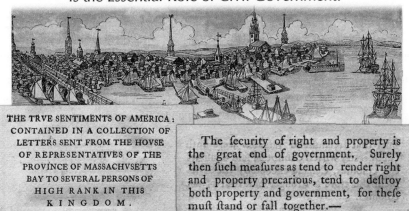

THE TRVE SENTIMENTS OF AMERICA: CONTAINED IN A COLLECTION OF LETTERS SENT FROM THE HOVSE OF REPRESENTATIVES OF THE PROVINCE OF MASSACHVSETTS BAY TO SEVERAL PERSONS OF HIGH RANK IN THIS KINGDOM.

The fecurity of right and property is the great end of government. Surely then fuch meafures as tend to render right and property precarious, tend to deftroy both property and government, for thefe muft ftand or fall together.—

Engraving of Boston in 1768 with excerpt from *The True Sentiments of America* (1768) in which Massachusetts protested Britain's new taxation regime:

❝ *The security of right and property is the great end of government. Surely then such measures as tend to render right and property precarious, tend to destroy both property and government, for these must stand or fall together.* ❞

5 Ibid., p. 63.
6 Ibid., p. 64.
7 Ibid., p. 61.

The Townshend Revenue Acts also resulted in the colonial Massachusetts legislature issuing its historic Circular Letter in 1768. Written to her sister colonies in America, this document also pointed to a *"fundamental law, ...held sacred and irrevocable"*[8] to all the colonists. That fundamental, sacred, and irrevocable law involved the godly necessity for a man to be secure in his property: *"that what a man hath honestly acquired is absolutely his own, which he may freely give, but cannot be taken from him without his consent."*[9] Although the Massachusetts Circular Letter was received throughout America with great applause, it was received with equal contempt in England. The first response in London was the outraged British colonial secretary demanding its retraction along with an apology. That outrage was followed by King George III's order that troops be sent to America to put the profitable port at Boston under his immediate subjection.

Like they had so many times in the past, the New England pulpits rallied to the American cause. In 1770, Cambridge, Massachusetts pastor Samuel Cooke preached a forceful sermon from the text of 2 Samuel 23:3: *"He that ruleth over Men, must be just, ruling in the fear of God."*[10] Cooke's sermon was a principled case defending Americans' property on both biblical and historical grounds. For instance, in drawing from the scriptural passage: *"Our fathers trusted in God, – He was their help and their shield,"*[11] Cooke made the historical application: *"Our fathers supposed their purchase of the aboriginals, gave them a just title to the lands – that the produce of them by their labor, was their property, which they had an exclusive right to dispose of."*[12]

To understand Cooke's meaning of the colonists' *"right"* to property, it is important to understand that the colonial idea of "rights" was more than

---

8 Ibid., p. 51.

9 Ibid.

10 Samuel Cooke, *Sermon Preached at Cambridge, in the Audience of His Honor Thomas Hutchinson, Esq.; Lieutenant Governor and Commander In Chief; the Honorable His Majesty's Council, and the Honorable House of Representatives, of the Province of the Massachusetts-Bay in New-England, May 30th, 1770* (Boston, 1770), p. 5.

11 Ibid., p. 31; referring to 2 Samuel 22:31: *"As for God, His way is perfect; the Word of the LORD is proven. He is a shield to all who trust in Him."*

12 Ibid., p. 33.

a legal matter. For the colonists, the whole idea of rights was also an issue of *moral rights* versus *moral wrongs*. In other words, the people's property *rights* were known as moral responsibilities, which they held directly under God. Consequently, a government could never have a *right* to do a *wrong* by interfering with obligations that the people owed to God. And, knowing that the people of colonial America had a moral obligation to the Creator in their property, Cooke defended the colonists' rights, "*which, had we any fears of being deprived of, we* [would have] *never wandered from our fathers' houses into these ends of the earth – nor laid out our labors and estates therein.*"[13]

The preacher's point was that the purpose of their colonial ancestors in fleeing the tyranny of their native England and establishing family estates in America was not to have their rightful estates now confiscated by another tyrannical regime. No indeed! To faithful pastors such as Samuel Cooke who dominated the New England pulpits during the colonial era, Americans' loyalty to their British king did not trump their duty to the King of kings. The colonists' obligation to the Lord's overriding truth and justice included their duty to defend their rightful estates against tyrants. Pastor Cooke concluded with the resolve: "*America now pleads her right to her possessions – which she cannot resign, while she apprehends she has truth and justice on her side.*"[14]

The Rights of Colonists as Men, as Christians, and as Subjects

As the colonists' grievances mounted, the tensions between Mother Britain and her colonies grew. In 1772 the Massachusetts legislature was under a new threat that their royal governor's accountability to them would be severed and he would become solely answerable to the Crown. Prior to that time, the governor's salary was set by the colonial legislature; though he was appointed by the king, he was in the colonists' employment and answerable to the concerns of their own colonial province.

The governor becoming a Crown employee was now a real threat

---

13 Ibid., p. 35.
14 Ibid., p. 44.

to their liberty, so the town of Boston organized an emergency town meeting. It was far from the so-called "town meetings" of our times where politicians often answer questions and patronize their audience in an orchestrated show of concern. The Boston town meeting of November 1772 was organized to hear from the people and to take action to address the real grievances of the colonies. Headed by Boston's most famous merchant, John Hancock, the town commissioned Samuel Adams to draft a statement of the *"rights of the colonists and of this province in particular, as men, as Christians, and as subjects."*[15]

Samuel Adams' Report of the Committee of Correspondence Stating the Rights of the Colonists (Boston,1772)

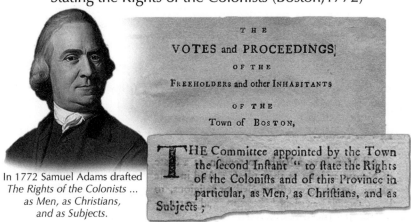

In 1772 Samuel Adams drafted *The Rights of the Colonists ... as Men, as Christians, and as Subjects.*

THE
VOTES and PROCEEDINGS
OF THE
FREEHOLDERS and other INHABITANTS
OF THE
Town of BOSTON,

THE Committee appointed by the Town the second Instant " to state the Rights of the Colonists and of this Province in particular, as Men, as Christians, and as Subjects ;

❝[I]f the breath of a British House of Commons can originate an act for taking away all our money, our lands will go next, or be subject to rack rents from haughty and relentless landlords, who will ride at ease, while we are trodden in the dirt.❞

When Samuel Adams explained their rights *"as men,"* he spoke of the foundational rights of men derived from the Creator: *"First, a right to life; secondly, to liberty; thirdly, to property."*[16] Adams included the essential duty that accompanies these particular blessings, which is *"the right to support and defend them in the best manner they can."*[17]

---

15 *The Votes and Proceedings of the Freeholders and other Inhabitants of the Town of Boston*, p. 1, ref. Samuel Adams.

16 Ibid., p. 2.

17 Ibid.

When Adams then turned his attention to describing their rights *"as Christians,"* he referred them to the *"Institutes of the great Lawgiver and Head of the Christian Church,"*[18] directing the colonists to read the Scriptures that were well-known as the foundation stone of all legitimate authority. When the patriot Adams also turned to the topic of the rights of colonists *"as subjects,"* he directed his fellow colonists to their stewardship responsibilities in what he termed *"the absolute rights of Englishmen, and all freemen."*[19] These he identified as *"personal security, personal liberty and private property,"*[20] and in echoing the same point of private dominion as had his colonial ancestors, Adams then declared that the *"legislative has no right to absolute arbitrary power over the lives and fortunes of the people."*[21]

Samuel Adams was simply arguing from the Puritans' earlier view of limited government – that true sovereignty is above the job description of any human government or potentate. *"Nor can mortals assume a prerogative, not only too high for men, but for angels,"* Adams explained, *"and therefore reserved for the exercise of the Deity alone."*[22]

That statement not only reconfirmed America's acknowledgment of an assertive, interactive Almighty God, but also spoke to the kind of limited government under Him that would be a core principle behind our nation's founding documents. Adams' meaning was clear regarding the security that a free people must have in their property. He pointedly warned about rulers who assume a governing power of *"taking away all our money,"* because, Adams added, *"our lands will go next; or be subject to rack rents from haughty and relentless landlords who will ride at ease, while we are trodden in the dirt."*[23]

Samuel Adams was describing the essential American idea that civil governments should never become the landlords of the people, lest with the

---

18 Ibid., p. 7.
19 Ibid., p. 8.
20 Ibid.
21 Ibid., p. 9.
22 Ibid.
23 Ibid., p. 12.

corruption that typically accompanies governments of men, they become lords in the cruelest way. That is a principle that is absolutely essential to our understanding of our nation's founders. Ideas have consequences, and unless we as Americans return to the recognition of God alone as our national Sovereign, we will either gradually or suddenly yield all we have to the very type of lords that Adams warned was ahead. He certainly cautioned his own generation of unaccountable agents who would "*break through the sacred rights of the domicile, ransack men's houses, destroy their securities, carry off their property, and with little danger to themselves commit the most horrid murders*."[24]

In looking back at the unflinching resolve of Samuel Adams, we can see why he was considered not only one of the most renowned Puritans of the later colonial era, but one of the key founding fathers of a blessed nation.

The Principles of the Reformation Reasserted

By 1773 it was apparent that the colonists' property was held precariously at best. The royal governor, Thomas Hutchinson, insulted the Massachusetts legislature by saying that all provincial lands were retained by "*the doctrine of the feudal tenure*."[25] He told them they had no sure title to anything – that all their property rights were "*held mediately or immediately, of the Crown*."[26] Hutchinson's point was that the land the colonists thought they owned either by right or by possession was an illusion, and in reality, the British government owned everything. In effect, all their bickering about punitive taxation on their property was without legal merit.

The indignant Massachusetts House countered the governor's absurdity by recounting the principles of the Reformation, explaining that medieval feudalism had been "*a most absurd form of government by which human*

24 Ibid., p. 17.
25 *Speeches of the Governors of Massachusetts, from 1765 to 1775; and the Answers of the House of Representatives, to the Same; with their Resolutions and Addresses for that Period and other Public Papers, Relating to the Dispute Between this Country and Great Britain, Which Led to the Independence of the United States* (Boston: Russell and Gardner, 1818), p. 384.
26 Ibid.

nature was so shamefully degraded."[27] They then drew a comparison between the old system of popery and the new royal policy, reminding their governor that feudalism had been "*calculated by the Roman Pontiff to exalt himself above all that is called God.*"[28] The colonists' association of Britain's new tyranny with Spain's old divine right pretenses was not only a clear appeal to England's Reformed Christian heritage, but it pointed to the failed ideas of dominion that "*prevailed to the almost utter extinction of knowledge, virtue, religion, and liberty.*"[29] In other words, a dominative control over the people's liberty and property by *any* government is an affront to the most basic virtues of Christian civilization.

The American patriots repeatedly drew from the deep well of their Reformed Christian heritage, which had previously prevailed against the divine right pretenses of despotic rulers. As a result, the Massachusetts House again redirected its governor's attention from the antiquated yoke of *divine right* to the glorious rays of the *divine light* of their true American inheritance:

> *But, from the time of the Reformation, in proportion as knowledge, which then darted its rays upon the benighted world, increased and spread among the people, they grew impatient under this heavy yoke; and the most virtuous and sensible among them (to whose steadfastness we in this distant age and climate are greatly indebted), were determined to get rid of it.*[30]

The point made by the Massachusetts representatives was that the *divine light* which had shone through the Reformation did not allow for the *divine right* of anyone – whether a pope, a king, or a legislature. By extension, that principle did not allow for the current King George III or his Parliament by way of their own pretensions to own the property of American colonists. A key reformational tenet of authority was that any absolute potentate, short of God Himself, was unbiblical. Certainly, an English king's claim of "*an absolute right to, and a perfect estate in, all*

---

27 Ibid., p. 385.
28 Ibid.
29 Ibid.
30 Ibid.

the land within his dominions," as the Massachusetts House observed with appropriate disgust, *"is a mystery which we have never seen unraveled."*[31] For them, there could be no absolute right over the property of the colonists by either Crown or Parliament: *"saving their actual purchase from the natives of the soil, the dominion, the lordship, and sovereignty, they had in the sight of God and man, no right of title..."*[32]

The first planters, of course, had purchased the titles to their land from the natives and secured their possessions with their own capital and personal sweat. The true dominion of America was by every reason of right, owned by those *"who hold estates clearly purchased at the expense of our own, as well as our ancestor's labor, and defended by them with treasure and blood."*[33]

No government that respected the dominion mandate given by God would dare to violate the sacred domain of private property and honest industry. The American representatives were quick to point to the obvious illegality of the new royal policy that *"could never be brought about but by foreign conquest and domestic usurpation."*[34]

Prayer and Unity in the Colonies

That kind of *"conquest and domestic usurpation"* commenced with fuller force in 1774 when Parliament passed a series of acts specifically intended to punish the colonies. These acts were figuratively known in England as the "Coercive Acts" and in America as the "Intolerable Acts." These acts came down particularly hard on the province of Massachusetts Bay. The Massachusetts Government Act,[35] for example, denied the Bay Colony its historic body of colonial representatives. With that single stroke of Parliamentary tyranny, the colony's heritage of self-government dating

---

31 Ibid.
32 Ibid., p. 389.
33 Ibid.
34 Ibid., p. 384.
35 The Massachusetts Government Act abrogated the colony's charter and instituted more direct royal control over the Bay Colony. Town meetings were forbidden without the royal governor's expressed approval (except for a single annual meeting), and the king was to appoint all members of the new Massachusetts Council to enact all colonial legislation.

back to John Winthrop in the 1630s now lay in ruins. Added to that was the Boston Port Bill which closed Boston Harbor and crippled the colony's commerce and trade.

Britain's military blockade of Boston Harbor was an unprecedented show of invasive power that shocked the sensibilities of all of her American colonies. It was also clear that what Britain was doing to punish Massachusetts could be done to all the other colonies. Upon receiving the news of the Intolerable Acts in early 1774, Virginia's House of Burgesses called for a day of fasting and prayer to "*devoutly implore divine interposition for averting the heavy calamity which threatens destruction to our civil rights and the evils of civil war...*"[36]

By asking for God's interposition through supplication and prayer, the Burgesses of Virginia were allying themselves with their Puritan brethren in Massachusetts. Calling for days of fasting and prayer had been a practice employed in England by the Puritans in Parliament itself against King Charles I when he had become tyrannical over a century earlier. The posture of prayer taken by the Virginia Burgesses in 1774, however, was seen by their royal governor, Lord Dunmore, as a gesture of rebellion aligned with that of Massachusetts. Dunmore promptly dissolved the Virginia Burgesses, which simply prompted other colonial legislatures to follow Virginia's lead by calling for days of fasting and prayer.

Meeting in a colonial convention (assembled without their governor's permission), Virginia's Burgesses then drafted *The Association of the Virginia Convention* in August of 1774, declaring their mutual resolve with "*our sister colony of Massachusetts Bay.*"[37] In this bold and magnificent gesture of colonial unity, the representatives of Virginia aligned themselves with Massachusetts against Parliament's "*unconstitutional taxation*" as well as in opposition to all British measures that "*violently and arbitrarily deprives them of their property.*"[38]

It was the Virginia Burgesses' common concern over the colonists'

---

36 Wirt, *Sketches of the Life and Character of Patrick Henry*, p. 95.
37 Ibid., p. 96.
38 Ibid., pp. 96-97.

property rights as well as their right to freely engage in commerce that caused them to rally behind their sister colony far to their north. Virginia's *Association* specifically condemned the Boston Port Bill by which the people of New England were being deprived of the *"wharves erected by private persons at their own great and proper expense."*[39] There was an ever-mounting sense in Virginia as well as in the other colonies that the government of Great Britain was acting immorally and illegally, in *"a most dangerous attempt to destroy the constitutional liberty of all North America."*[40] In all, it was the common cause of liberty and private property along with the rights of free commerce and industry that unified the colonies against a growing centralized government far distant from the people's concerns and their God-given freedoms.

The First Continental Congress

America's most formal gesture of unity was assembling the First Continental Congress, which convened in Philadelphia's Carpenters Hall on September 5, 1774. This historic course of action was intended to pursue America's colony-wide grievances against the invasive actions of Parliament and to preserve Americans' historic liberties.

New England was already under military siege. The Continental Congress' first letter of grievance was appropriately addressed to General Gage, Massachusetts' new military governor. General Thomas Gage had recently arrived from England to take charge of the ever-growing entrenchment of royal troops in Boston. Congress' appeal to him was a respectful (if not an understated) plea on behalf of the fundamental American cause: *"we hope, Sir, you will discontinue the fortifications in and about Boston, prevent any further invasions of private property,* [and] *restrain the irregularities of the soldiers..."*[41]

The Continental Congress recognized that Gage's encampment of British troops at Boston was merely at the forefront of a much broader

---

39 Ibid., p. 97.
40 Ibid.
41 Continental Congress, *Extracts from the Votes and Proceedings of the American Continental Congress, Held at Philadelphia, on the Fifth of September, 1774* (London, 1774), p. 13.

policy by a government bent on destroying Americans' long-enjoyed freedoms. Another letter that Congress circulated throughout the colonies addressed the wider concerns of Britain's Crusade-like policies toward all Americans:

Under pretense of governing them, so many new institutions, uniformly rigid and dangerous, have been introduced, as could only be expected from incensed masters, for collecting the tribute or rather the plunder of conquered provinces.[42]

Besides all of Britain's pretenses of good government, the colonists recognized that their mother country had become bent upon conquest and *"plunder"* rather than retaining any semblance of Christian civility.

The First American Continental Congress Defends the Life, Liberty, and Property of the Colonists in 1774

Peyton Randolph, President of the 1774 Congress.
Title page of the *Extracts* of the Congress (1774),
and opening page of *The Association.*

The 1774 Continental Congress organized the colonies under *The Association*:
❝ ❝To obtain redress of these grievances, which threaten destruction to the lives, liberty, and property of his Majesty's subjects in North-America.❞ ❞

The First Continental Congress then took the bold step of organizing the colonies under a formalized document of unity with the stated purpose: *"To obtain redress of these grievances, which threaten destruction to the lives, liberty, and property..."*[43] Much more broad and imposing than

---

42 Ibid., p. 55.
43 Ibid., p. 15.

Virginia's *Association* of August 1774, this Continental *Association* that
went into effect in December of that year formally established a colony-
wide boycott of the British trade by means of *"a non-importation, non-
consumption, and non-exportation agreement, faithfully adhered to."*[44]

This was real force meeting force. It was more than a political
gesture; it was striking the British trade in a way that would severely
affect the mother country's commerce and certainly bring the Crown's
disfavor and reprisal. But the Continental *Association* showed the level
of the Americans' fortitude and resolve, and this first formal action by
the Congress was taken seriously. Committees of Safety were established
throughout the colonies to enforce the directives of the *Association*, and
local communities published the names of those who defied the boycott
of British goods.

The organized boycott was also a tremendous act of continental unity
under the Almighty. By appealing to public humility and frugality, the
Association encouraged an inter-colony sense of reformation before God,
as was expressly stated in its closing words to all free Americans:

> *Above all things we earnestly entreat you, with devotion of spirit,*
> *penitence of heart, and amendment of life, to humble yourselves,*
> *and implore the favor of Almighty God: and we fervently beseech*
> *his divine goodness, to take you into his gracious protection.*[45]

Americans would soon come to rely whole-heartedly on the gracious
protection of that Almighty God. Though the public at large regarded
the First Continental Congress as an initial success, the delegates agreed
to convene the following May if the grievances had not been properly
addressed. The first meeting of the momentous Second Continental
Congress commenced in early May of 1775, and it continued to work
throughout the war years to eventually secure the independence of the
United States. Most providentially, the Second Congress met in the
immediate wake of the first two military battles of the war that commenced
with the first shots fired at the famed towns of Lexington and Concord.

---

44 Ibid.
45 Ibid., p. 65.

15
FROM PLANTATIONS TO A NATION

The Alarm of War

THE first alarm of war sounded on April 19, 1775 when volleys were exchanged in the Massachusetts towns of Lexington and Concord. Events came to blows when military governor General Gage sent seven hundred British royal troops from their quarters in Boston to confiscate the colony's stores of gunpowder and cannon at Concord.[1] On their way, a standoff with the Lexington Militia[2] resulted in the first American blood being spilled in what would eventually become a War for Independence.

When the British Regulars were forced to retreat back to Boston after a more extensive engagement with the colonials at Concord, patriot troops from across America rushed to Massachusetts' defense. The colonials were now forced to unite themselves in arms. Governor Gage and his troops were barricaded within the confines of Boston by regiments of Americans, all bearing weapons in an historic defense of their common homeland.

The regiments from various colonies flew colors, or standards (banners), typifying the American cause. The iconic phrase "An Appeal to Heaven" was emblazoned on many standards as a motto symbolizing the purpose of their firearms – that Providence would again come to their defense. Other standards and regimental flags featured a green pine tree symbolizing their defense of Americans' private property and resources. An article in the *New England Chronicle* reported the effect of Connecticut

---

1 Large amounts of ammunition were stored at Concord and elsewhere to be used in times of a necessary defense of the colony by the people. The British military governor Gage knew that by confiscating the stores of ammunition, the colonists would lose their ability to defend their colony against his military regime.

2 Defending the colonists' property by militias: the colonists had formed locally-trained militias since the mid-seventeenth century, at first primarily for the military defense of their homes and towns against Indian attacks. Earlier in the eighteenth century, provincial governments used militias in the French and Indian wars. The still-existent militias prepared to defend their colony again when in the 1770s the British Parliament dissolved Massachusetts' representative government and the liberties of the colonists were threatened. Under the guidance of the Committees of Correspondence, local towns began to muster on a regular basis to prepare their citizens against an armed British attack. It was the militias, first at Lexington and then at Concord, that encountered the British Regulars in April 1775 where the first shots of the war were fired.

General Israel Putnam's distinctive "Scarlet Standard" that was flown as
an encouragement just after America's losses at Bunker Hill in June 1775:

> *On Tuesday morning the standard lately sent to General Putnam
> was exhibited flourishing in the air, bearing on one side this motto,
> "An Appeal to Heaven,"and on the other, "Qui Transtulit Susti-
> net." The whole was conducted with the utmost decency, good or-
> der, and regularity, and to the universal acceptance of all present.
> All the Philistines on Bunker's Hill heard the shout of the Israel-
> ites, and being very fearful, paraded themselves in battle array.*[3]

These typical American sentiments aligned the patriot cause with
ancient Israel's struggle for freedom. The official Connecticut motto from
that time on depicted a shield with that standard's symbolic image of
fruitful vines surrounded by the Latin phrase *"Qui Transtulit Sustinet,"*
meaning: *"He who transported us, sustains us."*[4] At the time of the Boston
siege, the confident wording encouraged the patriots that God was with
them as He had been with their fathers earlier in calling them into the
harsh wilderness of America.

Being Sustained Throughout the Battle for God's Plantations: The Motto of Connecticut Featured the Vineyard of the Lord

The motto on the "Scarlet Standard" (military banner) of Connecticut's regiments
in 1775 became the state motto after 1776 (translated into English):
❝ He who transported us, sustains us ❞

---

3 George Henry Preble, *History of the Flag of the United States of America* (Boston, 1880), p. 201.
4 Ibid.

The Connecticut standard with its bold motto was yet another indelible symbol in America's long and confident celebration of Christ's plantings in America. As always, the cause was one of defending His precious vineyard – the very soil that they had inherited from the sweat and toil of their fathers. And, well-armed with an array of biblical metaphors denoting their cause, the patriots were fortified with a common purpose in "New Israel's" standoff with the "Philistine" invaders from Britain.[5]

A "Fair Possession Down to their Children"

Not long before an armed conflict commenced at Lexington and Concord, the Massachusetts Provincial Congress called for a Day of Repentance before God "*to supplicate His direction and assistance to recover and reform whatever is amiss.*"[6] From their history, the colonists were aware that they were not fit to engage any formidable foe without an ongoing moral reformation. The Fast Day Proclamation of March 1775 reflected on the humility of the colonists' "*pious and virtuous ancestors,*" and it called for a similar sense of humility and devout resolve before God. Like the "*pious and virtuous*" cause of their forefathers, the mission in 1775 was also framed in terms of a cause much greater than themselves. Americans' obligation was to faithfully "*transmit*" the blessings of their "*fair possession down to their children, to be by them handed down to the latest posterity.*"[7]

The mindset of passing along God's blessings to future generations has always animated the American character – that is, until recently with the onset of our abject dependence upon civil government. There is a truth born out in both Scripture and history that people are dependent upon the source of their blessings. With today's popular view that our civil institutions are the source of our blessings, we have nothing to pass down to future generations but a legacy of dependency upon that source.

---

5 The comparison of America with ancient Israel was not literal, but a metaphor for the identity of two distinctive peoples who each acknowledged their existence under the sovereign God of Scripture.

6 Broadside: *In Provincial Congress, Cambridge, February 16, 1775*; the Fast Day to be observed "*Thursday the sixteenth day of March*" signed "*John Hancock, President.*" The text appealed their cause against Britain to "*Almighty God, the just and good Governor of the World.*"

7 Ibid.

Maintaining Liberty as a Multigenerational Duty under God

In *Provincial Congreſs,*

Cambridge, *February* 16, 1775.

WHEREAS it has pleaſed Almighty GOD, the juſt and good Governor of the World, to permit ſo great a Calamity to befall us, as the preſent Controverſy between Great-Britain and theſe

WHEREAS it has pleaſed Almighty God, the juſt and good Governor of the World, to permit ſo great a Calamity to befall us, as the preſent Controverſy between Great-Britain *and theſe Colonies, and which threaten us with the Evils of War :*

to implore the Outpourings of his Spirit, to enables to bear and ſuffer, whatever his holy and righteous Providence may ſee fit to lay upon us ; and that we may again rejoice in the free and undiſturbed Exerciſe of all thoſe Rights and Privileges, for the Enjoyment of which our pious and virtuous Anceſtors braved every Danger, and tranſmitted the fair Poſſeſſion down to their Children, to be by them handed down intire to the lateſt Poſterity.

and virtuous Anceſtors braved every Danger, and tranſmitted the fair Poſſeſſion down to their Children, to be by them handed down intire to the lateſt Poſterity.

Signed by Order of the Provincial Congreſs,

JOHN HANCOCK, Preſident.

An early portrait of John Hancock, who signed Colonial Massachusetts' February 1775 *Fast Proclamation* imploring God's deliverance

> ❝ *... that we may again rejoice in the free and undisturbed exercise of all those rights and privileges, for the enjoyment of which our pious and virtuous ancestors braved every danger, and transmitted the fair possession down to their children, to be by them handed down entire to the lastest posterity.* ❞

Earlier generations of Americans were quite different from ours. They had a view of freedom and property as an ongoing legacy from God. Americans therefore honored civil government within its rightful limits. They, in fact, blessed God for government that stayed within its rightful bounds. Duty to Him obliged the colonists to pray for *"their rightful king and all the royal family"*[8] on one hand, but on the other to pray that God would *"recover and preserve our just rights and liberties."*[9] Civil government was therefore highly regarded as the means God uses to preserve the continued blessings of liberty and property for future generations.

We can be thankful, then, that on the brink of the armed conflict, which ultimately yielded America's formal independence, the colonials were not found looking to self-interest or a few favors they might curry from their earthly lords or governors. They were, instead, looking to *"Almighty God,*

---

8 Ibid.
9 Ibid.

the just and good Governor of the World," and for His infinite blessedness to be passed along even to those in their distant future, as the "*latest posterity.*"[10]

Firm Reliance on Divine Providence

Patriot leader John Adams also acknowledged that the colonists' duty was to honor God and pray for their British king. Adams noted that when the Second Continental Congress convened, they still fervently prayed to God on behalf of their earthly sovereign and all who ruled under that sovereign: "*they thought themselves bound to pray for the king and queen, and all the royal family, and all in authority under them.*"[11] The issue was always one of loyalty to both God and king.

On July 4, 1776, part of that obligation shifted. On that day an American nation was born with the announcement of the Declaration of Independence, stating: "*That these united Colonies are, and of Right ought to be, Free and Independent States.*"[12] The colonists were at last forced to reject a rebellious king that had repeatedly violated his limited chartered authority over them. The Declaration was a profound document, which explicitly pointed out those violations in exhaustive detail.

In 1776, Americans' obligations under the Crown of Britain may have ended, but certainly not their obligations under God. America's Declaration of Independence concluded with the expressed affirmation of their continuing dependence on God for all they possessed: "*with a firm reliance on the protection of Divine Providence, we mutually pledge to each other our lives, our fortunes and our sacred honor.*"[13]

---

10 Ibid.

11 John Adams, *Novanglus, and Massachusettensis; Or Political Essays,* p. 233. Citation from I Timothy 2:1-2: "*... that supplications, prayers, intercessions, and giving of thanks be made for all men, for kings and all who are in authority, that we may lead a quiet and peaceable life in all godliness and reverence.*"

12 Dunlap Broadside: Second Continental Congress, *In Congress, July 4, 1776 A Declaration by the Representatives of the UNITED STATES OF AMERICA in General Congress Assembled* (Philadelphia, 1776). The Declaration was a direct answer to Britain's arbitrary Declaratory Act of 1766 which declared that the colonies "*are, and of Right ought to be, subordinate unto, and Dependent upon the imperial Crown and Parliament.*" The 1776 Declaration stated instead: "*these united Colonies are, and of Right ought to be Free and Independent States.*"

13 Ibid.

What did not change at all in 1776 was America's reliance upon the Lord of nations – the God of armies, the Almighty Sovereign – who would ultimately crown them with success. John Adams said Americans' obligations to Him still required them to pray for all those in authority. But, he also explained the new circumstances in America: that *"when they saw those powers renouncing all the principles of authority, and bent upon the destruction of their lives, liberties, and property, they thought it their duty to pray for the Continental Congress and all the thirteen state Congresses, etc."*[14]

This, John Adams remarked, was the true American Revolution *"in the minds and hearts of the people."*[15] The Revolution was not a change in the Americans' attitude toward their ultimate Sovereign or in their duties toward civil government at all, but it was a change in those who now were bound before God to protect Americans' lives and liberties as well as their property. Though the biblical duty to pray for those in authority remained a constant fixture of Americans' civic duty, in 1776 the object of those prayers shifted from royalty to their fellow citizens. It also shifted from an obligation to pray for rulers who lived in a distant land to those who ruled exclusively upon American soil.

The Dominion of Providence

With these United States pledging their *"firm reliance on the protection of Divine Providence,"* it was fitting that one of the first publications following the Declaration of Independence was a pamphlet on that very subject. The pamphlet titled *The Dominion of Providence over the Passions of Men*[16] was published in Philadelphia by John Witherspoon, himself a signatory of the Declaration. Witherspoon was a powerful advocate of American liberty. He was also a direct descendant of John Knox, the

---

14 Ibid.

15 Ibid.

16 John Witherspoon, *The Dominion of Providence Over the Passions of Men. A Sermon Preached at Princeton, On the 17th of May, 1776. Being The General Fast appointed by the Congress through the United Colonies* (Philadelphia, 1776). The sermon was given less than two months before the Declaration of Independence was adopted, and printed immediately after its adoption.

Reformation-era liberator of Scotland (England's neighbor to her north),[17] who was a close ally of John Calvin.

Witherspoon was quick to point Americans to their historic legacy. It was *"the monarchy of Spain,"* Witherspoon reminded his readers, who *"was determined to crush the interest of the Reformation."*[18] He also related the *"violent persecution of many in England,"* whom he said *"carried the knowledge of Christ to the dark places of the earth, so they continued themselves in a great degree of purity of faith."*[19] By that, the great patriot, theologian, and historian was referring to the early English "planters" in America who had risked their all for the cause of the true Christian faith.

Witherspoon then brought the issue home for his current audience. God was now giving their own generation an opportunity to stand where their fathers had stood – to stand for the historic biblical faith and to stand for the historic cause of liberty and property. He warned his generation: *"If therefore we yield up our temporal property, we at the same time deliver the conscience into bondage."*[20]

Witherspoon was calling Americans of 1776 back to the dominion principles of their fathers. Duty to God involved both one's conscience as well as all that he owned. The true patriot could not afford to yield either conscience or property to any earthly masters, as Witherspoon stated:

> *Would any man who could prevent it, give up his estate, person, and family ... although he had liberty to choose the wisest and the best master? Surely not. This is the true and proper hinge of the controversy between Great-Britain and America.*[21]

In other words, no respectable patriot would disregard the responsibilities he personally owes to God in his family and private estate.

---

17 John Knox was a leader of the Protestant Reformation in Scotland in the mid-sixteenth century. Before that time, he had been exiled in Geneva where, under the influence of Calvin, he learned Reformed theology and civil polity. Upon his return to Scotland, Knox then led the Protestant Reformation in a powerful alliance with the Scottish nobility. As an active writer and minister, Knox continued as the leading voice of the faith in both church and state until his death in 1572.

18 Witherspoon, *The Dominion of Providence*, pp. 26-27.

19 Ibid., p. 28.

20 Ibid., p. 41.

21 Ibid., pp. 41-42.

If he does give up his responsibilities – even to the best and wisest earthly masters – he has still surrendered his most fundamental duties to his one, sovereign Lord and Master. That was true regarding government. No man's duties to govern his own family and estate could be yielded to even the *"wisest and best"* civil rulers, much less to the despotic lords of the British regime. That, to Americans, was the *"true and proper hinge of the controversy"* – or the true cause in defending their property.

The patriots of the founding era could hardly have imagined the carelessness with which Americans today now disregard those foremost duties. They could not have imagined a God-fearing householder allowing governmental institutions to overtake his leadership responsibilities and *"give up his estate, person, and family,"* nor yield his estate to even the *"wisest and the best master."*

The Scholar/Statesman of the Second Continental Congress Defines the Hinge of the American Controversy in 1776

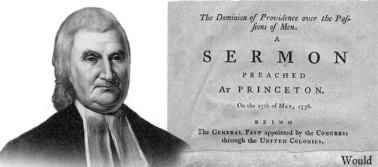

Dr. John Witherspoon with the title page and excerpt of his May 1776 Fast Day sermon: *The Dominion of Providence Over the Passions of Men*

Would any man who could prevent it, give up his eftate, perfon, and family, to the difpofal of his neighbour, although he had liberty to chufe the wifeft and the beft mafter? Surely not. This is the true and proper hinge of the controverfy between Great-Britain and America.

For Witherspoon and his fellow patriots, the time had come for Americans to rise to the cause of their ancestral fathers. It was a time for another great moment of courage and a time for the providence of God to again reign supreme over the passions of men. By engaging in an armed struggle with Britain, the now independent Continental Congress had a well-principled confidence of its own momentous place in the annals of American history.

Prayer, Prosperity, and Thanksgiving

An important feature in America's eventual success was her many thankful and penitent expressions of an ongoing reliance upon God. Time after time throughout the War for Independence, the Continental Congress appointed days of repentance with fasting as well as days of thanksgiving with praise. In each instance, gratitude was expressed for benefits received and supplications were made for the continuance of America's historic blessings of liberty and prosperity.

The first request for a Day of Thanksgiving throughout the thirteen new states was included in the minutes of the *Journal of the Continental Congress* in 1777. It was a request that the people of the various states not only *"consecrate themselves to the Service of their Divine Benefactor,"* but also pray *"that it please him to prosper the trade and manufactures of the people and the labor of the husbandman, that our land may yield its increase."*[22]

Congress' appeal on behalf of successful agriculture, manufacturing, and trade was indicative of America's original idea of national prosperity. The founders' principles of liberty included the blessings of healthy commerce and free enterprise that would cause their land to *"yield its increase."* God gave people liberty and property for that end. And, their governments were established for that purpose – that is, for the people to prosper free from the kind of regulatory regime that the British government tried to impose on American commerce and industry. The nation's greatness was seen in terms of the people's free and abundant use of their land – that the vineyard of God would indeed *"yield its increase."*

---

22 Broadside: Continental Congress, *A Proclamation For A General Thanksgiving* (Exeter, 1777). Text *"extracted from minutes"* from the Continental Congress for a general Thanksgiving Day to be observed December 18, 1777.

Conversely, without a continuing respect for such ideas behind America's independence, prosperity's abundance would "die on the vine."

The same gifted theologian and statesman, John Witherspoon, also drafted Congress' early Thanksgiving proclamations. His words were careful to address the means for genuine national prosperity, which was the standard Christian attitude of humility with hard work. Congress' 1778 Thanksgiving Proclamation was the first issued by way of a formal document sent individually to each of the states. This formal Proclamation included the nation's fervent gratitude toward God for the recent successes of the Continental Army: *"that it hath pleased Him in His overriding Providence in a just and necessary war for the defense of our rights and liberties."*[23] The concluding prayer was: that *"our trade be revived; our husbandry and manufactures increased, and the hearts of all impressed with undissembled piety, with benevolence, and zeal for the public good."*[24]

Proclaiming America's Dependence on Almighty God in 1778

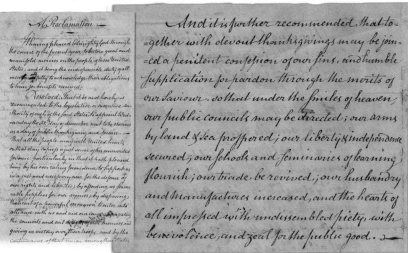

Congressional Thanksgiving Proclamation expressing America's dependence on God *"our Savior"* and prayer for the restoration of private enterprise, that:

❝our trade be revived, our husbandry and manufactures increased❞

23 Manuscript: Continental Congress, *A Proclamation* (Philadelphia, 1778), p.1, issued for a *"General Thanksgiving and Praise throughout these United States."*
24 Ibid., p. 2.

Those sentiments became the standard features of the proclamations that followed throughout the war years. There was a continual appeal that God would maintain their blessings of liberty – liberty that always necessitated the abundant use of the nation's resources in private agriculture, commerce, and industry. In our nation's founding era, it was the enterprise of hard-working people that made America strong rather than a prideful, powerful national government that made the people and the states its dependents.

It was that very sense of *"undissembled piety, with benevolence, and zeal for the public good"* that caused Americans to support the great cause of independence declared by their Continental Congress. They had already given generously of their sons and fathers to the militias that first battled the royal forces at Lexington and Concord. Many more sons and fathers then served their nation in the Continental Army under the command of General George Washington.

That army needed support and supplies beyond what the national Congress could provide and, quite notably, that support also came in the form of substantial contributions from American households. When the struggling army was near collapse at Valley Forge in the trying winter of 1777-1778, Congress requisitioned the states for desperately needed supplies. The states then requisitioned the citizens of their various counties and towns for help.

For example, Massachusetts issued formal requests for its families to provide *"shoes, stockings, and shirts, which cannot be immediately supplied from the public stores."*[25] It was a request prompting gratitude in return *"for the relief of those soldiers who are hazarding their lives in their defense."*[26] Thus, entire families whose land and estates were being defended also contributed in many ways to the American cause in the field. It should always be remembered with gratitude that many families voluntarily and sacrificially provided the fighting men, and equipped them

---

25 Broadside beginning with the text: *"Whereas the army are in present and pressing want of shoes, stockings, and shirts, which cannot be immediately supplied from the public stores ..."* (State of Massachusetts, 1778).

26 Ibid.

with the resources and supplies that secured the freedoms we Americans have since enjoyed.

The Liberty Pulpit

As the final years of war were playing out, there were many reminders of the first principles of godly civil government. None of those reminders were more expressive and to the point than the outpouring of civic sermons during the later era of the war.

Signal calls were made from America's pulpits reminding the new republican[27] magistrates to exclude any hint of tyranny or corruption in public office. Just such a sermon was preached in 1782 before Massachusetts' representatives and their first elected governor, John Hancock. Pastor Zabdiel Adams reminded the civic leaders that their government was not empowered to treat their electorate as a *"conquered"* people, nor to stoop to the methods of regimes that had *"frequently robbed the people of their dear earned wealth."*[28]

Such clearly defined lines were constantly being drawn between public power and private wealth, and between the people's well-guarded liberty and the limited authority of the state. Americans were certainly not a conquered people and their rulers were not to plunder their wealth. These were lines that had been sharpened by the Reformed Christians since the time of the Reformation. Pastor Adams then asked his magistrates to heed the warnings in two important examples of despotism in America's past:

> *What signified the mandatory letters* [divine right commands] *of Philip the Second* [of Spain], *to the people of the United States, when the design of them was to deprive that people of the unalienable rights of men and Christians? Equally unavailing were the laws of the British parliament, at the beginning of these times, when their manifest purpose was to despoil us of our chartered rights, and bring us into a state of bondage. Such acts are as little*

27 The term "republican" during the early era of our nation did not denote a political party; it indicated the American form of government, which was no longer under a monarchy but was formed as a confederation of several independent state republics.

28 Zabdiel Adams, *A Sermon Preached Before His Excellency John Hancock, Esq. Governor ... Council ... and House of Representatives of the Commonwealth of Massachusetts, May 29, 1782* (Boston, 1782), p. 23.

regarded as the bulls and thunders of the Vatican, at this enlight-
ened period of Christianity.[29]

The Massachusetts pastor compared the two vivid examples of tyranny in America's past as warnings to future American magistrates. Pastor Adams decried the divine right yoke imposed upon America by Spain (i.e. *"the mandatory letters of Philip the Second"*) and the equally pretentious yoke imposed by Great Britain in their lifetime. Those regimes were now as inconsequential as the old *"bulls and thunders of the Vatican"* that decreed complete sovereignty in the hands of human potentates. Adams therefore sternly warned America's current civil rulers not to become oppressive through licentious taxation:

> *If taxes are heavy, and people know not to what uses they are ap-*
> *plied; if they are left to vain conjectures, and finally conclude that*
> *they are swallowed up in a manner not beneficial to the public, no*
> *wonder there is a reluctance in paying them.*[30]

The American people had not been freed from one regime of grievous taxation only to be put under bondage to another. In other words, the old injustices of Spain and Britain must remain as vivid examples of failure to all public officials who desire to govern for the good of those they serve. Adams then pointed to the one noble objective of truly judicious public officials – that *"their laws, resolves and taxes must be agreeable to the eternal rules of right."*[31]

Those *"eternal rules of right"* were spelled out in Scripture. The *"eternal rules"* accommodated equal justice rather than the popular idea of "social" or weighted justice that is predominant in our time. Social justice (sometimes called "distributive" justice) favors one class (namely the underclass) over another (namely the wealthy), and it is by definition uneven and unequal justice. To our nation's founders, such an errant idea of justice would represent plain *injustice* and, in fact, be a sure sign of a corrupted government.

---

29 Ibid., p. 26.
30 Ibid., pp. 27-28.
31 Ibid., p. 28.

Our nation's founders sought to establish individual justice under the law rather than the unjust rulers making sweeping class distinctions by pitting the poor against the rich. Pastor Adams, for example, drew from the law of the ancient Hebrew republic in applying 2 Chronicles 19:6-7 to America's rulers: "*As on the one hand, they should not take bribes and favor the rich; so on the other, an idle compassion should not lead them to befriend the poor, and indulge them in measures iniquitous.*"[32]

Sermon Warnings Against Iniquity in Government Based Upon 2 Chronicles 19:6-7

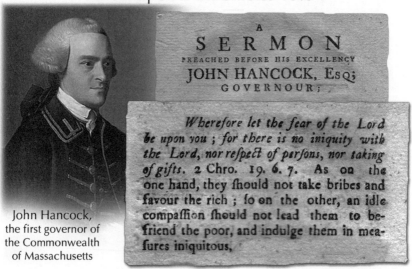

John Hancock, the first governor of the Commonwealth of Massachusetts

Title page and excerpt from Zabdiel Adams' sermon preached in 1782 before Governor Hancock and other elected officials of Massachusetts

The rich could not be set against the poor under the biblical model of justice. The founders who took the Bible at its word firmly believed that the role of civil rulers was limited to administering impartial laws rather than enforcing biased laws to redistribute the nation's wealth. The constraints of equal justice did not allow for civil magistrates to overreach their bounds and indulge "*in measures iniquitous,*" by taking the money

32 Ibid., p. 30.

that had been rightly earned by individuals and use it to make others dependent upon governmental redistribution.

The hallmark of any civil government was seen in the establishment of liberty rather than dependency. Thus, as Pastor Adams told the magistrates of our nation's founding era, "*idle compassion*" toward the people was sinful rather than virtuous. Creating dependents on the state is exactly the kind of "*iniquitous*" public abuse that comes when a government assumes authoritative control over a nation's people, resources, and economy.

Liberty, as it was known in our nation's founding era, had a dignity beyond our current, base understanding of the subject. Their idea of liberty did not allow for invasive governmental control of the people's goods or property, as the patriot Samuel Adams had explained in the 1760s: "*utopian schemes of leveling, and a community of goods, are as visionary and impracticable, as those which vest all property in the crown...*"[33]

In other words, socialistic tendencies toward "*a community of goods*" destroy the fundamental idea of freedom in one's private property. These redistributive tendencies create a governmental license to control the people's wealth on par with anything George III and his colonial administrators had ever envisioned. Either "*leveling*" the economy or creating "*a community of goods*" ultimately makes dependents of everyone except a few core potentates who oversee the land and control what little wealth it might still provide. In short, a socialized economy is the same old face of tyranny, yet perhaps with a more compassionate smile.

The principles of our nation's founders were set on standards higher than condoning corruptions of any kind. Approaching war's end, Americans had great confidence in their biblical course. "*We are now in sight of the promised land,*" Pastor Zabdiel Adams proclaimed, and he then encouraged his hearers to "*anticipate the rising glory of America.*"[34] By that, he explained: "*Behold her seas whitened with commerce; her capitals filled with inhabitants, and resounding with the din* [loud noise] *of industry.*"[35] But, as always, that hope was qualified by Americans honoring

---

33 House of Representatives, *True Sentiments of America*, p. 63, ref. Samuel Adams.
34 Zabdiel Adams, *A Sermon Preached Before His Excellency John Hancock*, p. 57.
35 Ibid.

the highest glory of all: *"and we would hope in the glory of Christ by a strict attachment to His gospel and divine institutions."*[36]

The liberty pulpits of the founding era continued to be instrumental in galvanizing the American public behind the first principles of freedom. Under her divine Sovereign, America was becoming recognized throughout the world as an independent nation and as the home of the free. Her multitudes – her millions – were free indeed! Her pulpits then continued to play a key role in keeping the historic association of America with the vineyard of the Lord alive in the minds of the faithful citizenry. By the time of Zabdiel Adams' sermon in 1782 and many others like it toward war's end, the fruits of victory and the expansion of that vineyard to the American West were near at hand.

36 Ibid.

16
THE FRUITS OF VICTORY

The Continuing Language of Liberty

FOLLOWING America's spectacular and providential victory over a seemingly insurmountable foe, the same biblical principles that carried her through the war were adhered to in the time of peace.

The Treaty of Peace (Treaty of Paris) Officially Recognized America's Sovereignty and Independence

THE

Definitive Treaty,

Between GREAT-BRITAIN and the UNITED STATES of America, sign-ed at Paris the 3d day of September, 1783.

In the Name of the most holy and undivided Trinity.

IT having pleased the Divine Providence to dif-pose the hearts of the most ferene and most po-tent prince George the third, by the grace of

the middle of the 0 id river into Lake Ontario ; through the middle if the faid lake until it ftrikes the communication by water between that lake and Lake Erie, fo 'X along the middle of faid communication, & Lake Erie & Through the mid-dle of faid lake, until it arrives at the water communication between that lake and Lake Hu-ron, thence through the middle of faid lake to

and that Congrefs fhall alfo earneftly recommend to the feveral ftates a reconfideration and revifion of all afts or laws regarding the premifes, fo as to render the faid laws or afts perfectly confift-ent not only with juftice and equity, but with that fpirit of conciliation, which, on the return of the bleffings of peace, fhould univerfally pre-vail ; and that Congrefs fhall alfo earneftly re-

ARTICLE I. HIS Britannic Majefty acknowledges the faid United States, viz. New-Hampfhire, Maffachufetts-Bay, Rhode-Ifland and Providence Planta-tions, Connecticut, New-York, New-Jerfey, Pennfylvania, Delaware, Maryland, Virginia, North-Carolina, South-Carolina and Georgia, to be free, fovereign and independent ftates ; that he treats with them as fuch ; and for himfelf, his heirs and fucceffors, relinquifhes all claims to the government, propriety and ter-ritorial rights of the fame, and every part thereof ;

In the 1783 treaty of peace (Treaty of Paris), the British Crown acknowledged *In the Name of the most holy and undivided Trinity* that her former colonies were now *free, sovereign and independent states.*

When news of a treaty of peace[1] with Britain reached America late in 1783, the Continental Congress appropriately called for another day of public Thanksgiving. Congressional Chaplain George Duffield saw their victory as so astounding that it could only be described in epic proportions. In his Thanksgiving Sermon preached at Philadelphia on behalf of the Continental Congress, Duffield spoke with an exuberant outpouring of praise in his application of Isaiah 66:8 by asking his audience: *"Who hath*

---

1 The treaty of peace by which Great Britain officially recognized that the United States of America were free, sovereign, and independent was signed in Paris, France. Consequently, it was generally referred to as *"The Treaty of Paris,"* or in other contemporary printed versions the final draft (signed in September 1783) was sometimes titled *"The Definitive Treaty."*

heard such a thing? Who hath seen such things?"

Duffield put the widely heralded American success in familiar biblical terms that were understood by all. He pointedly added: *"Zion shall here lengthen her cords, and strengthen her stakes; and the mountain of the house of the Lord be gloriously exalted on high."*[2] Duffield was making it clear that America, established on a godly foundation, was now free to expand further to the West (as in to *"lengthen her cords"*) and to more firmly anchor herself in the land (as in to *"strengthen her stakes"*).

The chaplain added that they were set free from *"the lusts of tyrannical landlords."*[3] Indeed! Americans had been freed by their *divine* Landlord from becoming what he called *"vassals at pleasure, and slaves to their lordly masters."*[4] Duffield was enthusiastic in his comparison of America with the Lord's freed nation of ancient Israel: *"Blessed be God, with Israel of old,"* the congressional chaplain exclaimed, *"We cried unto him in the day of our distress. ... He hath brought us forth into a large place; and established our rights; and opened before us a glorious prospect."*[5]

America's deliverance was typically put in terms of the Lord having miraculously saved their blessed country: *"he, and he alone, who says to the proud waves of the sea, 'Hitherto shall ye come, but no farther,' restrained the councils and arms of Britain from improving against us."*[6]

By this, Chaplain Duffield was relating the course of America's daunting military struggle against Britain, *"the most formidable power on earth, ... her fleets commanding the ocean; her troops numerous and veteran."*[7] America, on the other hand, had little strength of her own, save for *"her numerous husbandmen, her merchants and mechanics; ... strangers from the art of war."*[8] Duffield pointed out that in spite of circumstances,

---

2 George Duffield, *A Sermon Preached...in the City of Philadelphia, on Thursday December 11, 1783. The Day appointed by the United States in Congress assembled, to be observed as a Day of Thanksgiving, for the Restoration of Peace, and establishment of our Independence, in the Enjoyment of our Rights and Privileges* (Philadelphia, 1784), p. 17.

3 Ibid., p.16.

4 Ibid.

5 Ibid.

6 Ibid., p. 23.

7 Ibid., p. 8.

8 Ibid.

Providence had caused the actions of the heavens and seas to break against their British enemy and halt its advance. On many occasions the weather would suddenly turn and either give the American forces a way to escape, or amazingly, simply stop their foes in their tracks. According to Duffield, it was all *"the doing of the Lord; and marvelous in our eyes."*[9]

Congressional Thanksgiving for Victory, the Establishment of Liberty with Independence, and a Fruitful Country

A

S E R M O N

PREACHED IN THE

THIRD PRESBYTERIAN CHURCH

IN THE

CITY of PHILADELPHIA,

On Thurſday December 11, 1783.

The Day appointed by the United States in Congreſs aſſembled, to be obſerved as a Day of Thankſgiving, for the reſtoration of Peace, and eſtabliſhment of our Independence, in the Enjoyment of our Rights and Privileges.

By GEORGE DUFFIELD, A. M.

Paſtor of ſaid Church, and one of the Chaplains of Congress.

Congressional Chaplain George Duffield with the title page of his sermon delivered on the Day of Thanksgiving for Peace in 1783

66 *Almighty God has accomplished the whole in every part; and by his kind care, and omnipotent arm, has wrought out our deliverance; cast forth our enemy; bestowed upon us a wide extended, fruitful country; and blessed us with a safe and honorable peace.* 99

Over all, the congressional chaplain was full of optimism befitting the day. This formal Thanksgiving of 1783 was yet another in a series of public thanksgivings that accompanied the most marvelous series of deliverances that any people could have imagined. Through all the trials of the first "plantings" in the early 1600s, through the later attacks by the Spanish and French invaders in the mid-1700s, and through the culminating invasion by Britain in the 1770s, Americans' homes and property had been repeatedly preserved. Now, at war's end, God's continued blessing upon their land was greatly appreciated, as Chaplain Duffield prayed: *"may* [God's] *wisdom be given, to esteem and improve the invaluable blessing."*[10]

---

9 Ibid., p. 25.
10 Ibid., p. 16.

A Land of Promise

The citizens of the United States now saw themselves in possession of a land of nearly boundless promise. Again quoting from the book of Isaiah (as their Christian forefathers had so often done), Chaplain Duffield anticipated America's future prospects in terms of biblical promises:

> *Justice and truth shall here yet meet together, and righteousness and peace embrace each other: And the wilderness blossom as the rose, and the desert rejoice and sing. And here shall the various ancient promises of rich and glorious grace begin to complete divine fulfillment; and the light of divine revelation diffuse its beneficent rays, till the gospel of Jesus have accomplished its day, from east to west, around our world.*[11]

In noting these common sentiments of that era, we find that the idea of America as a land of plenty was linked with the advancement of godly principles. There was, in fact, a continuity of principle seen between the advancement of the kingdom of Christ westward across the country and America reaping the blessings of such a rich and bountiful land. Thus the metaphorical references of America as the Promised Land or the New Israel were far from mere enthusiasm. Americans had risked their very lives on behalf of their country's freedom and they were now rightful heirs of the promises attached to their convictions. They were also entitled to the fruits of freedom that accompanied such a miraculous success.

As we have seen, their convictions were nothing new. These were the same convictions of the first colonial planters who had also risked their lives for the sake of freedom and prosperity. Like always, however, the promises of future blessings came with warnings. William White, the Continental Congress' other chaplain, cautioned his generation of the *"passions that are continually exciting some members of the community."*[12]

---

11 Ibid., p. 18. The reference was to Isaiah 35:1-2: "*The wilderness and the wasteland shall be glad for them, and the desert shall rejoice and blossom as the rose; it shall blossom abundantly and rejoice, even with joy and singing*."

12 William White, *A Sermon on the Duty of Civil Obedience, as Required in Scripture* (Philadelphia, 1799), p. 7. Congressional Chaplain White had first delivered the same oration in November 1775, and again near war's end, and a third time on the occasion of a national "*Day of General Humiliation appointed by the President of the United States*" in 1799.

Chaplain White, as an Anglican (as were a number of Congressional representatives), was warning of the inherent leanings toward a sense of royal power by those in public office. White cautioned that there are always tendencies in rulers, even those in a representative Congress, to raise their personal prestige *"out of the public loss and misery."*[13] Here, White warned of the heavy burdens in taxes and regulations that were ahead for Americans if their representatives assumed a godless sense of personal prestige in their seats of power.

With this kind of *"loss and misery"* being the natural byproduct of men ruling apart from God, we can be thankful that Americans of the founding era were reverent toward their heavenly Lord and had no desire for their representatives lording over the national economy. We can also see the link between our nation's more recent disrespect for God and its current drift toward *"public loss and misery"* in overbearing taxes and governmental regulations. In fact, a governmental disrespect for private property, business, and economy has come in equal proportion to America's disrespect for the God who blessed her with such a vast, bountiful land.

The Wilderness Made to Rejoice

The first steps in the westward expansion of America were driven by a similar sense of evangelism as that of the prior colonial forefathers.[14] For example, the purpose of state-sponsored missionary work undertaken by Connecticut in the late 1700s was put in terms of a need to propagate God's Word among the indigenous tribes to the west. Connecticut's missionary workers in *"settlements as far north-westward towards lake Ontario,"*[15] reported an abundant success in bringing the Gospel to the *"Mohawk tribe*

---

13 Ibid.

14 The first state mission society was incorporated in 1787 by the Commonwealth of Massachusetts and was twofold in advancing the kingdom of Christ. First in *"Propagating the Gospel among the Indians"* (title page of *A Discourse Before the Society for Propagating the Gospel Among the Indians*, by Eliphalet Porter, D.D., Boston, 1808). That meant bringing *"the power of God unto eternal salvation to all who believe"* (p. 7). The other purpose was the missions' secondary civilizing effect: the Gospel also being *"the friend of public order, peace and prosperity, of domestic enjoyment, and individual happiness"* (p. 7).

15 State of Connecticut, *A Narrative of the Missions to the New Settlements According to the Appointment of the General Association of the State of Connecticut: together with an Account of the Receipts and Expenditures of the Money Contributed by the People of Connecticut, in May, 1793. According to an Act of the General Assembly of the State* (New Haven, 1794), p. 8.

southwest of the lake."[16] This particular effort to plant Christianity among the Mohawk tribes was productive enough that the 1793 mission report from the field enthusiastically stated: "*The wilderness has indeed been made to rejoice and the solitary place to be glad*."[17]

Civilizing the Frontiers Through State-Sponsored Missions

A 1788 Brief from Governor John Hancock encouraging Massachusetts citizens to support the state-sponsored Society for Propagating the Gospel Among the Indians

A 1793 account of the frontier missions sponsored by the State of Connecticut

Another purpose of the early state-sponsored missions was to provide itinerant preaching for American citizens who were establishing homes beyond the reach of established towns. As homesteads were established past the outskirts of Christian civilization, traveling missionaries brought needed assistance. Often settling in distant regions with their own families, ministers equipped the frontiers with regular biblical teaching "*to prevent their falling into error, a state of dissipation and forgetfulness of God*," as well as "*to instruct and animate them, till they shall be able to settle churches and a regular ministry among them*."[18]

---

16 Ibid., pp. 8-9.
17 Ibid., p. 13.
18 Ibid., p. 15.

These early state-sponsored missions were cooperative efforts. The state provided protective oversight, the various town churches provided the laborers and ministers, the families donated the funding, and Christian civilization moved westward taking possession of the earth.

This was all seen in terms of the long-promised advancement of the dominion of Christ. Dr. Jonathan Edwards,[19] who published Connecticut's first report called *A Narrative of the Missions ... According to the Appointment of the General Association of the State of Connecticut*, explained:

> *Never was there a happier opening for Zion, "To enlarge the place of her tent, to stretch forth the curtains of her habitations, to lengthen her cords, and strengthen her stakes." What a glorious service must it be, to plant regular churches and ministers, to promote Christian morals and diffuse the blessings of literature, civilization, regular society and undefiled religion, in the initial settlements through such extensive countries.*[20]

Once again, we see that advancing American civilization to the West was viewed in terms of continuing to plant the true kingdom of God. This idea of a figurative American *"Zion"* – the lengthening of *"her cords"* and strengthening of *"her stakes"* – was an important component of the idea of westward expansion in the early decades of America's nationhood. The missionaries and settlers of the new republic found themselves in a prime position to further carry out the original vision of their Christian colonial fathers. As families and communities began to spread westward, Christian civilization worked in concert with the mission of the Gospel, settling Christ's dominion over the fruited plains of the American Midwest.

The States' Protections of Private Property

Before the ink had dried on the Declaration of Independence, states were drafting constitutions to safeguard their beloved liberties. And central to

---

19 Dr. Jonathan Edwards, who assisted the state of Connecticut with its frontier missions in the 1790s, was the son of minister Jonathan Edwards who was used tremendously in the "Great Awakening," a famed colonial revival in the 1730s-40s. The senior Edwards had done considerable work in the 1750s as a missionary to the Housatonic Indians of western Massachusetts and Connecticut.

20 Connecticut, *A Narrative of the Missions*, p. 16.

the states' constitutions were governmental protections of private property and safeguards of the public worship of God. For instance, the first clause in the Declaration of Rights in the Massachusetts Constitution of 1780 began with "*the right of enjoying and defending their lives and liberties*" and "*acquiring, possessing, and protecting property.*"[21] The second clause added an essential public duty, saying: "*It is the right as well as the duty of all men in society, publicly, and at stated seasons, to worship the Supreme Being, the great Creator and Preserver of the Universe.*"[22] Together the clauses that stated the people's "*essential and unalienable rights*"[23] began with protections of private property and went on to describe the necessary public spirit.

The difference between that idea of a godly commonwealth and today's view of a secular state is glaring. Instead of embracing the kind of secularized governmental regime that relegates any meaningful idea of God to the closet and then assumes control of the entire economy, the founders stuck to higher principles. Our nation's founders envisioned commonwealths that publicly acknowledged God's superintending Authority. They framed governments that ensured the public recognition of that authority and then secured the people's rights derived from Him in their private homes and estates.

Long before the adoption of our federal Constitution in 1789, state constitutions expressed those essential principles of American liberty and independence. The Constitution adopted by Pennsylvania explicitly stated that among its objectives was to secure the "*blessings, which the Author of existence has bestowed upon man.*"[24] Pennsylvania's Declaration of Rights of 1776 identified those blessings as "*inherent and unalienable rights, among which are, the enjoying and defending* [of] *life and liberty, acquiring, possessing, and protecting property, and pursuing and obtaining happiness and safety.*"[25]

---

21 Continental Congress, *The Constitutions of the Several Independent States of America; the Declaration of Independence; the Articles of Confederation Between the Said States* ... (Boston, 1785), p. 6.
22 Ibid.
23 Ibid.
24 Ibid., p. 75.
25 Ibid., p. 77.

Virginia's Declaration of Rights of 1776 was similar, stating that the people cannot be deprived of certain *"inherent rights"* which were listed as *"namely, the enjoyment of life and liberty, with the means of acquiring and possessing property, and pursuing and obtaining happiness and safety."*[26] New Hampshire's Constitution of 1783 was worded nearly the same, speaking of the *"essential and inherent right,"* which it stated as *"the enjoying and defending* [of] *life and liberty – acquiring, possessing and protecting property – and in a word, of seeking and obtaining happiness."*[27]

Regarded as the "Magna Carta" of the United States: *The Constitutions of the Several Independent States* Defined and Defended Americans' Liberty in their Property[28]

Detailed map showing the lands of the United States as they existed in 1783

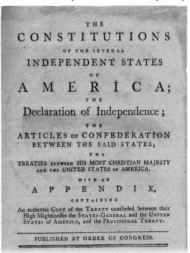

Title page of a 1783 edition of *The Constitutions of the Several Independent States of America* in which the American Congress published the constitutions of the state governments that legally secured the people's individual liberties and private property

---

26 Thorp, *The Federal and State Constitutions, Colonial Charters, and Other Organic Laws*, vol. 7, p. 3813.

27 Continental Congress, *The Constitutions of the Several Independent States*, p. 3.

28 Magna Carta (1215) was the most famous medieval statement of English liberties. It required kings to recognize certain liberties among the noble classes. The king was answerable to the nobility who generally controlled the land in England, and no landowner (or non-peasant) could be punished except through prosecution under the laws of England. In America, there was no peasant class, and under the various state constitutions, all free citizens were recognized as entitled to their God-given liberties.

Any imposition on the people's property was strictly limited to taxes or fees approved by their elected representatives. Massachusetts' Constitution qualified its power to tax by the premise that "*no part of the property of any individual, can, with justice, be taken from him, or applied to public uses, without his own consent, or that of the representative body of the people.*"[29]

Similarly, the Constitution of Pennsylvania expressed the same principle of limited taxation by beginning with the premise that "*every member of society has a right to be protected in the enjoyment of life, liberty, and property.*"[30] It also added, however, that he is "*bound to contribute his proportion towards the expense of that protection.*"[31] In other words, the reason that a member of civil society has a duty to "*contribute his proportion*" in taxes is simply for the government to cover its costs of protecting and defending the people's liberty and property. Therefore, similar to other states, Pennsylvania restricted public access to private wealth by saying: "*no part of a man's property can be justly taken from him, or applied to public uses, without his own consent, or that of his legal representatives.*"[32]

We can see when reading these early state constitutions that they were worded in ways which defended the dominion that the people themselves enjoyed in their private property and wealth. That was a core principle acknowledged before the state constitutions enumerated limited powers to their legislative, executive, and judicial branches of government. Even the power of imposing taxation was intended only to cover the costs of publicly administering that original purpose. Put another way, it would be a complete contradiction of the core purpose of their state constitutions for civil governments to then interfere in the management of the people's wealth, property, or private business.

In all, there was to be a well-revered wall of separation between private wealth and a government's "entitlement" to that wealth. The right

---

29 Ibid., p. 8.
30 Ibid., p. 78.
31 Ibid.
32 Ibid.

to private property by citizens was variously described as "essential," as "inherent," as "unalienable," as "inalienable," and as "blessings" from God in the original state constitutions of America.

The basic idea of being a free and independent nation relies upon people retaining God's mandated dominion in their homes, property, and estates. And the fact still remains that the original state constitutions recognized those rights – rights to which we now render lip service with little consequential understanding. To our nation's founders, the rights of *"life, liberty, and property"*[33] had real meaning under God, which must be preserved as the core of any idea of American independence or freedom.

Private Property and the "Power" of Families

The famed early American educator and scholar Noah Webster played an important role in the states adopting our nation's federal Constitution.

Published in 1787, Webster's small book *An Examination into the Leading Principles of the Federal Constitution* explained the necessary principles of a national Constitution, including *"life, liberty, and property."*[34] Webster considered property ownership as the central component of all American freedoms, saying that *"liberty of the press, trial by jury, the Habeas Corpus writ, even Magna Charta itself, although justly deemed the palladia of freedom, are all inferior considerations, when compared with a general distribution of real property among every class of people."*[35]

Such statements showed that widespread property ownership was at the heart of the American character. Property ownership was certainly viewed as the bedrock of Americans' freedoms. Like most Americans of his era, Webster viewed property ownership in terms of its importance to what he called the *"whole basis of national freedom."*[36] In other words, a

---

33 The constitutions of Massachusetts, Virginia, Pennsylvania, New Hampshire, Delaware, Maryland, North Carolina, and South Carolina all included liberty and property among the essential rights of citizens in their respective states.

34 Paul Leicester Ford, ed., *Pamphlets on the Constitution of the United States Published During Its Discussion by the People* (Brooklyn, 1888), p. 50. Quote from Noah Webster: *An Examination into the Leading Principles of the Federal Constitution*, published in 1787.

35 Ibid., pp. 59-60.

36 Ibid., p. 59.

nation that is truly free has the largest possible amount of its country's real estate in the hands of the largest number of its private citizens.

A nation of truly free people is one in which all classes of people are at liberty to enjoy the ownership of their own private domain. Therefore, in America there would be no select nobility that ruled over peasants, squatters, servants, and serfs. To the contrary, the entire American landscape was to be adorned with private estates, both of the rich and the poor alike with free holdings from the modest to the grand.

Widespread property ownership gave Americans a distinctive form of nobility within their representative republics.[37] Put another way, widespread property ownership provided an electorate that would vote for representatives who would then be forced to respect the people's own dignity and power in what they owned. Webster wisely observed of America's distinctive political landscape: *"Wherever we cast our eyes, we see this truth, that property is the basis of power; and this, being a cardinal point, directs us to the means of preserving our freedom."*[38]

In early America, liberty was never defined in terms of freedom *from* responsibility. Liberty was framed in the more solid terms of *owning* one's responsibility. That meant that the people were very vigilant in retaining the dominion in what they owned for themselves and their families. Dominion was power, and true dominion was to remain with the people in their own tangible assets. That was the original core idea of power in America, as Webster observed of our blessed nation: *"In what does real power consist? The answer is short and plain – in property."*[39]

The family was therefore known as the seat of power in America, and that power must be preserved in that most basic institution. Our founders recognized that for America to remain the epitome of freedom, familial estates must be freely passed uninterrupted to future generations. Webster explained that *"wherever the right of primogeniture* [familial inheritance] *is established, property must accumulate and remain in families."*[40] Thus,

---

37 Widespread property ownership was employed by the ancient Israelites when they entered the Promised Land of Canaan. First, the land was divided among the twelve tribes, then it was allotted to the various families for an inheritance. See Numbers chapter 34 and Joshua chapters 13-19.

38 Ford, *Pamphlets on the Constitution of the United States*, p. 59.

39 Ibid., p. 57.

40 Ibid., p. 58.

the full rights of inheritance must remain free and clear from governmental interference and confiscation because the true seat of power and dominion in America remains the institution of the family.

The People's Power is in their Private Property

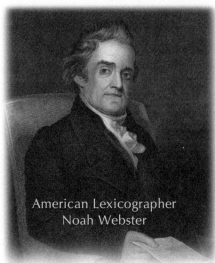

American Lexicographer
Noah Webster

    " *In what does real power consist? The answer is short and plain – in property.* "

    " *Let the people have property and they will have power – a power that will forever be exerted to prevent a restriction of the press, and abolition of trial by jury, or the abridgment of any other privilege.* "

Excerpts from Noah Webster's 1787
Examination into the Leading Principles of the Federal Constitution

Inheritance taxes, fees, and governmental confiscations run counter to the original idea of power in America. With private property kept safely in the hands of the people and families, Webster concluded that the other American freedoms would also be preserved:

> *Let the people have property and they will have power – a power that will forever be exerted to prevent a restriction of the press, and abolition of trial by jury, or the abridgment of any other privilege.*[41]

Private property ownership (including freely inheritable estates) was the key to America remaining a land of the free. In a government *by*, *for*, and *of* the people, familial estates must forever remain off limits from governmental control. Thus, Webster warned of the threat to the

---

41 Ibid., p. 60.

republic by a government that could legislate feudal restrictions upon the inheritance of the private estates of its citizens:

> *The power of entailing estates is more dangerous to liberty and republican government than all the considerations that can be written on paper, or even than a standing army.*[42]

Webster strongly opposed "*entailing estates*," or placing restrictions on citizens' full freedom to transmit property to their heirs or descendants. We can see the high regard our nation's founders had for the institution of the family and the full rights of familial property. In a republic, governmental infringement upon the free rights of inheritance represented an affront to the enduring estates of its citizens.[43] With property as the real seat of power in America, such an affront upon familial estates was considered an attack upon the very foundation of America's own integrity as a free republic.

Noah Webster was assuringly confident that the adoption of a federal Constitution would further safeguard the private estates of Americans. He stated quite assertively:

> *I believe life, liberty, and property is as safe in the hands of a federal legislature, organized in the manner proposed by the convention, as in the hand of any legislature that ever has been or ever will be chosen in any particular state.*[44]

The idea of a national government under a federal Constitution was therefore intended to reinforce the safeguards found in the state constitutions. The framers would not allow for a national government to destroy the people's life or liberty, nor to undermine the power and dominion they enjoyed in their property and possessions. The following chapter will briefly address some of the specific safeguards that are guaranteed in our nation's federal Constitution.

---

42 Ibid.

43 The 1777 Constitution of Georgia, for example, prohibited entailing estates, specifically stating: "*Estates shall not be entailed.*" (*The Constitutions of Several Independent States of America*, p. 165.) Virginia outlawed entailing estates in 1776.

44 Ford, *Pamphlets on the Constitution of the United States*, p. 50. (Re: Webster: *An Examination into the Leading Principles of the Federal Constitution*.)

17
THE NATIONAL CONSTITUTION AND THE BLESSINGS OF LIBERTY AND PROPERTY

Securing the Blessings of Liberty

THE purpose in the United States adopting a federal Constitution in 1789 was to establish an authoritative and respectable government on a national scale.[1] In other words, the national framers – those who drafted the federal Constitution – followed the states' prior practice of procuring formalized documents to secure the freedoms of a self-governed people.

The basic idea in drafting such a document was to grant certain authoritative powers of government on a national scale as well as to safeguard the states from a centralized, overreaching regime. For that reason, America's national government was described as "federal." That is, the national government was formed as a federation (from the Latin *foedus, foederis*, or "covenant") by an agreement of the already self-governed states that granted it an expressly limited amount of authority at the national level.

The federal Constitution was never empowered to depreciate the blessings of liberty that the citizens already enjoyed in their property or to deprive them of their rights already guaranteed by their state constitutions. The federal Constitution's Preamble which began with the indelible words "*We the People*," therefore included its equally indelible intention to "*secure the blessings of liberty to ourselves and our posterity*."[2]

As was already acknowledged in the Declaration of Independence and in the various state constitutions, these "*blessings of liberty*" were to be secured under God. Following the practice of the states in requiring oaths of office to bind state officials to their constitutional duties under

---

1 The United States of America was founded as a nation in July of 1776, and was governed very inefficiently under the *Articles of Confederation* adopted in 1781. The nation's sole governing body was the Congress of the Confederation, which represented each of the states and required a unanimous vote of all the states to pass any national legislation.

2 The United States Federal Congress: *Acts Passed at a Congress of the United States of America ... MDCCLXXXIX* [1789] (Hartford, 1791), p. 3.

God, federal officials were required to take oaths of office to bind them according to their own constitutional duties under Him. The Judiciary Act of 1789, for example, required all federal judges (including the Supreme Court justices) to take an oath that concluded: "*So help me God.*"[3]

Each federal judge was required to swear that he would adjudicate impartial justice – more precisely, to "*solemnly swear or affirm, that I will administer justice without respect to persons, and do equal right to the poor and to the rich…So help me God.*"[4] By such an explicit oath, no judge could bend the arm of justice to favor any class of people over another. In other words, by an oath sworn before the Judge of the universe, no court should favor one person's status as either poor or rich over another, nor should it validate laws that target the wealth of some unequally over others.[5] Put another way, no law that unequally taxes the rich ought to be upheld by a duly-sworn federal judge any more than a law that targets the poor![6]

The national government was neither intended to favor one state over another nor one class of citizen over another.[7] It was certainly not intended to have widespread or invasive involvement in the people's private business by creating financial entitlements given to certain people and then taxing others to supply the means to fund those entitlements.

---

3 Ibid., p. 131. All judges in the federal judiciary at any level, including the justices of the Supreme Court, are required to swear their oath ending in the phrase: "*So help me God.*" Although the Constitution *authorized* a Supreme Court as well as all inferior courts as they might be needed, the Judiciary Act of 1789 actually *established* the courts and required that an oath be taken by all federal judges.

4 Ibid. The phrase: "*I will administer justice without respect to persons, and do equal right to the poor and to the rich,*" remains part of the expanded oath still taken by all federal justices.

5 The justices' oath to treat the rich and poor equally before the law eliminates the idea of "social justice," or the creative use of uneven justice to obtain certain social goals. These techniques involve: unequal standards of "justice" among socioeconomic groups, the supposed leveling of economic opportunity by favoring the poor over the rich by governmentally funded social programs, and the redistribution of wealth from the rich to the poor through social legislation.

6 With regard to the judicial review of standing laws, the judges' oath requires them to rule impartially between the rich and the poor. "Judicial review" is the power under which legislative and executive action is subject to invalidation by the judiciary. Certain courts with the power of judicial review must annul any governmental act that violates any of the Constitution's enumerated provisions.

7 As the judicial oaths clearly indicate, equal protection of the rich and poor alike is a foundational principle of godly justice. 2 Chronicles 19:6-7 was often cited in the literature of the founding era regarding the equal protection of the rich and poor under law. See Zabdiel Adams, *A Sermon Preached Before His Excellency John Hancock, 1782,* referenced in chapter 15 of this book. Also see page 46 of this book where we saw that John Calvin warned that "*injustice is done*" when "*under the cloak of virtue*" judges "*misplace compassion*" for the poor and are "*liberal at another's expense.*"

United States Courts are Not to Favor the Rich over the Poor Nor the Poor over the Rich!

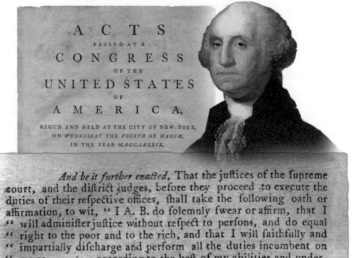

Title page and excerpt of the first federal Acts passed in the United States, with President George Washington who signed the 1789 Judiciary Act into law.

Reflective of 2 Chronicles 19:6-7: the Judiciary Act required all Federal Judges to swear an oath to ❝ *administer justice without respect to persons, and do equal right to the poor and to the rich ... so help me God.* ❞

Constitutional Separation of Family and State

Americans have often heard it noted that the word "church" is not in the federal Constitution. That is simply because the federal Constitution has granted[8] the national government no powers over the church.[9] And on that point, we should also note that the term "domestic family" does not appear for basically the same reason. The federal Constitution has very little involvement with private familial estates, and when private

---

8 Article 1 Section 8 of the Constitution lists the enumerated (or constitutionally granted) powers of federal legislation, stating: *"The Congress shall have power to lay and collect taxes, duties, imposts and excises, to pay the debts and provide for the common defense and general welfare of the United States; but all duties, imposts and excises shall be uniform throughout the United States."*

9 The First Amendment of the Bill of Rights of the federal Constitution mentions *"religion"* but only in strictly prohibiting the national government's interference with it, explicitly stating: *"Congress shall make no law respecting an establishment of religion, or prohibiting the free exercise thereof ..."*

homes or property of any kind are mentioned in the Bill of Rights, they are mentioned within the phraseology of guarded protections against governmental encroachments.

The point is that the central government's purpose was never intended to violate the fundamental separation between the private domain and public power. It was known by the founders' prior experience with a centralized British regime that any attack on private property is an attack on personal liberty and familial security. To remain secure as a private domain, a family was intended to be free to take risks (good or bad) with its private resources without the threat of governmental interference.

The framers recognized that a central government that controlled the citizens' private economy would also control the people and, in effect, destroy the foundation of a just civil society. The safeguard for the general, public good of the people was indicated by the term *"general welfare"*[10] as it is found in the Preamble of the Constitution. The original idea of *general* welfare excluded the idea of *specific* welfare as in the favoring of one particular state, social group, or family over others.[11] To the framers, any interference into a citizen's individual welfare would undermine the idea of a just government as well as the idea of a nation of free people.

Private Property and a National Bill of Rights

A unity of principle between the state and federal constitutions is strikingly evident by the fact that the national government proposed its own Bill of Rights in its first Congress.

Among the members of the 1789 federal Congress was a widespread move to amend the Constitution by adding protective clauses similar to the various state constitutions. For example, in proposing a Bill of Rights on a national scale, representative James Madison of Virginia, who had earlier

---

10 The Preamble of the federal Constitution includes the definitive clause: "[to] *promote the general welfare, and secure the blessings of Liberty to ourselves and our posterity, do ordain and establish this Constitution for the United States of America.*"

11 Article 1 section 8 of the federal Constitution also mentions *"general welfare"* as an enumerated power under Congress' ability to tax, but it cannot target certain families, social classes, or states for specific taxation, stating: *"all duties, imposts and excises shall be uniform throughout the United States."*

studied the principles of godly government under John Witherspoon, argued from the same principles of safeguarding the people's property as had the states. Madison, who was also tagged with the figurative title "father of the Constitution" because of his considerable contributions in the Constitutional Convention, reminded his fellow congressmen:

> *That Government is instituted and ought to be exercised for the benefit of the people; which consists in the enjoyment of life and liberty, with the right of acquiring and using property, and generally of pursuing and obtaining happiness and safety.*[12]

In other words, our nation's governing mandate is not only "*to be exercised for the benefit*" of the personal liberties of the people but for their enjoyment of the familial property they acquire and use for themselves. The safeguards of private wealth and property that had been central to the state constitutions were therefore central to our nation's Bill of Rights when it was incorporated into the federal Constitution in 1791.

James Madison on the Safeguards of a National Bill of Rights

James Madison with the draft proposal of Amendments to the federal Constitution

❝[G]overnment is instituted and ought to be exercised for the benefit of the people; which consist in the enjoyment of life and liberty, with the right of acquiring and using property, and generally of pursuing and obtaining happiness and safety.❞

12 Kurland and Lerner, *The Founders' Constitution*, vol. 5, p. 25. James Madison's August, 1789 proposition of Amendments to the United States Constitution, composing a Bill of Rights.

Constitutional Safeguards of Liberty and Property

We will briefly look at the first five amendments to see how the guarantees of liberty and property were expressed in the Constitution's Bill of Rights. It is not only important that we *know* the Bill of Rights protects our liberty and property, but that we know *how* it protects them.

1. The First Amendment

Congrefs fhall make no law refpecting an eftablifhment of religion, or prohibiting the free exercife thereof, or abridging the freedom of fpeech, or of the prefs ; or the right of the people peaceably to affemble, and to petition the government for a redrefs of grievances.

Excerpt from *Acts Passed at a Congress of the United States...*, 1791 Edition

❝ *Congress shall make no law respecting an establishment of religion, or prohibiting the free exercise thereof, or abridging the freedom of speech, or of the press; or the right of the people peaceably to assemble, and to petition the government for a redress of grievances.* ❞

Certain amendments of the Constitution are directed primarily toward personal liberties and others toward the ownership and use of private property. For example, the First Amendment guarantees a series of liberties regarding personal rights grouped together in a single article. We find them listed as, first, the guarantee of freedom of religion, or the right to worship God without governmental interference. The First Amendment also protects the freedom of speech, of publishing, of assembling peaceably in public, and *"to petition the government for a redress of grievances."*[13]

These are each liberties involving personal rights, or guarantees of personal acts in which every citizen is able to freely participate. These individual rights are grouped together in one amendment prerequisite to all the other amendments. The rights enumerated in the First Amendment are, each and all, important to acting responsibly as a citizen in a nation free from governmental tyranny.

---

13 Federal Congress, *Acts Passed*, p. 149.

2. The Second Amendment

A well regulated militia being neceffary to the fecurity of a free ftate, the right of the people to keep and bear arms fhall not be infringed.

Excerpt from *Acts Passed at a Congress of the United States...*, 1791 Edition

❝ *A well regulated militia being necessary to the security of a free state, the right of the people to keep and bear arms shall not be infringed.* **❞**

Besides the personal liberties protected by the First Amendment, other amendments specifically protect private property. For example, the Second Amendment guarantees that "*the right of the people to keep and bear arms shall not be infringed.*"[14] A defensive weapon is a very important piece of private property. Firearm ownership is thus at the heart of defending the people's other liberties and property, and Congress saw ownership of firearms as deserving of a specially enumerated amendment.

Britain's General Gage had previously attempted to call in all private firearms when he tightened his control over the citizens of Boston in 1775. Oppressive governmental regimes always have a tendency to restrict gun ownership and undermine the idea of citizen-integrity in a commonwealth. And, as might be expected, the constitutional guarantee of gun ownership also found its precedent in the newly formed states. Massachusetts' Constitution certainly made a point to include the right "*to keep and bear arms.*"[15] Pennsylvania's Constitution of 1776 stated: "*That the people have a right to bear arms for the defense of themselves and the state.*"[16]

In such language we can see that the states as well as the federal government acknowledged that individuals owning firearms was for the good of everyone, public and private. And, we can also see that the right to keep and bear arms is a most fundamental property right.

---

14 Ibid.
15 Continental Congress, *The Constitutions of the Several Independent States*, p. 9.
16 Ibid., p. 79.

3. The Third Amendment

No foldier fhall in time of peace be quartered in any houfe without the confent of the owner ; nor in time of war, but in a manner to be prefcribed by law.

Excerpt from *Acts Passed at a Congress of the United States...*, 1791 Edition

❝ *No soldier shall in time of peace be quartered in any house*
without the consent of the owner; nor in time of war,
but in a manner to be prescribed by law. ❞

The Third Amendment specifically protects the most sacred seat of all property – the domain of the home. As we have seen, a home was considered the centerpiece of domestic tranquility and must not be violated.

The "quartering" or stationing of governmental troops in private dwellings was a tactic of intimidation used by the British against the American colonials. Such tactics, however, denied the Americans of the private enjoyment of their property and, in effect, denied them of the peaceable, internal government of their families. The wording of the Third Amendment addressed the most threatening use of governmental force – that of subduing a private dwelling by force. It found its language in the former state constitutions, borrowing its text against soldiers "*quartered in any house without the consent of the owner*" – nearly word-for-word from New Hampshire's original Constitution.[17]

And further, when the Third Amendment is viewed in terms of its underlying respect for family dominion, it can be seen in principle as the prohibition against interference or domination by any forceful governmental agency upon a quiet and peaceable residence.[18]

---

17 Federal Congress, *Acts Passed*, p. 149. New Hampshire's Constitution adopted in 1783 read: "*No soldier in time of peace shall be quartered in any house without the consent of the owner; and in time of war such quarters ought not to be made but by the civil magistrate, in a manner ordained by the legislature.*"

18 The words "quiet" and "peaceable" were used during the founding era to describe the godly use

4. The Fourth Amendment

> The right of the people to be fecure in their perfons, houfes, papers, and effects, againft unreafonable fearches and feizures, fhall not be violated ; and no warrants fhall iffue, but upon probable caufe, fupported by oath or affirmation, and particularly defcribing the place to be fearched, and the perfon or things to be feized.

Excerpt from *Acts Passed at a Congress of the United States…*, 1791 Edition

❝The right of the people to be secure in their persons, houses, papers, and effects, against unreasonable searches and seizures, shall not be violated; and no warrants shall issue, but upon probable cause, supported by oath or affirmation, and particularly describing the place to be searched, and the person or things to be seized.❞

The federal Constitution's Fourth Amendment includes another key protection of the people's private dominion over their homes and property. The powers of civil government stop at the threshold of one's dwelling, or rather, at the property line of the land he owns. The fundamental premise of the Fourth Amendment was therefore for "*the people to be secure in their persons, houses, papers, and effects…*"[19]

Those words again express the historic wall of separation between the peaceable government of a home and the civil powers of the state. That wall had been expressed in the prior state constitutions. Pennsylvania's Constitution said: "*the people have a right to hold themselves, their houses, papers, and possessions free from search or seizure…*"[20] The principle was to prevent harassment by governing powers – that all homes, property, correspondence, and other possessions are off limits to governmental interference unless a specific law was credibly assumed to have been violated. In such a case, a specific search warrant should be drawn up by a

of one's home and property. The wording, of course, was from the Bible. In I Timothy 2:2, Christians were called to pray for "*all who are in authority, that we may lead a quiet and peaceable life in all godliness and reverence*."

19 Federal Congress, *Acts Passed*, p. 149.

20 Continental Congress, *The Constitutions of the Several Independent States*, p. 78.

court, *"upon probable cause,"*[21] with the Amendment stipulating: *"by oath or affirmation, and particularly describing the place to be searched, and the person or things to be seized."*[22]

In that way, the people's family possessions were to be free from all governmental interference unless those families broke clearly defined laws. It is one thing for people to use the domain of their home in illegal ways that invite the invasive policing powers of government in, and quite another for civil government to assume a right to regulate or police the concerns of a peaceable, law-abiding home. Thus, according to the principle of familial respect inherent in the Fourth Amendment, no law-abiding family should have any reason to expect invasive regulations on the peaceable use of their legal possessions.

5. The Fifth Amendment

No perfon fhall be held to anfwer for a capital, or otherwife infamous crime, unlefs on a prefentment or indictment of a Grand Jury, except in cafes arifing in the land or naval forces, or in the militia when in actual fervice in the time of war or public danger ; nor fhall any perfon be fubject for the fame offence to be twice put in jeopardy of life or limb ; nor fhall be compelled in any criminal cafe, to be a witnefs againft himfelf, nor be deprived of life, liberty or proper-ty, without due procefs of law ; nor fhall private property be taken for publick ufe without juft compenfation.

Excerpt from *Acts Passed at a Congress of the United States...*, 1791 Edition

❝ *No person shall be held to answer for a capital, or otherwise infamous crime, unless on a presentment or indictment of a Grand Jury, except in cases arising in the land or naval forces, or in the militia when in actual service in the time of war or public danger; nor shall any person be subject for the same offence to be twice put in jeopardy of life or limb; nor shall be compelled in any criminal case, to be a witness against himself, nor be deprived of life, liberty or property, without due process of law; nor shall private property be taken for public use without just compensation.* ❞

21 Federal Congress, *Acts Passed*, p. 149.
22 Ibid.

Our final example among the ten amendments of the Bill of Rights primarily protects both liberty and property according to the *"due process of law."*[23] An important clause of the Fifth Amendment recognizes safeguards against a governmental seizure of the property of those not convicted of crimes. It states that no one can be *"deprived of life, liberty or property, without due process of law; nor shall private property be taken for public use without just compensation."*[24]

In this wording, we find that any respectful administration of the law ensures the private domain of American citizens against unjust or vindictive encroachments by governmental powers. *"Due process of law"* in this amendment respects the historic wall of separation between private dominion and public authority by demanding that due constitutional processes are followed in the prosecution of anyone accused of a crime.

The separation between family and state is also implied in the underlying principle of private property acquisition for governmental purposes. In the rare case in which a given piece of private land must be acquired for the necessary purposes of government (such as for roads or defense), the rule is for generous compensation but never arbitrary confiscation. Arbitrary "eminent domain"[25] is not to be used as it was under England's Dominion government imposed upon New England in the 1600s when property confiscations along with punitive taxes and fees drove many lawful, peaceable people into abject poverty. The moral underpinning of eminent domain is that it should never be used for either expanding government or for increasing government revenues of any kind.

The Fifth Amendment also found its precedence in the prior state constitutions. For instance, the Connecticut Constitutional Ordinance of 1776 put the principle of the due process of law in terms of the protection of a man's role as a householder, stating: *"No man shall be deprived of his wife or children: No man's goods or estate shall be taken away from him,*

---

23 Due process of the law includes the right: 1) to be considered innocent until proven guilty; 2) to have the right to face your accusers; and 3) to be tried before an independent and impartial judiciary. These principles are based upon Deuteronomy 17 and Deuteronomy 19 in Holy Scripture.

24 Federal Congress, *Acts Passed*, p. 150.

25 See footnotes 9 and 10 in Chapter 11 of this book describing the Dominion of New England and England's arbitrary use of eminent domain to inflict tyranny upon colonial New England.

nor any ways damaged under the color of law..."[26]

The intent was to ensure one's possessions against harm from either governmental threats of prosecution or by any arbitrary use of the law. Put another way, any punishment that involves a fine or the confiscation of one's private property must *follow* the due process of a constitutional and legal prosecution in the courts of law. Any unjust prosecution might try to give the appearance of being legitimate (i.e. by *"the color of law"*), but if any proceeding lacks *"the due process of law"* on any point of law, it wrongly deprives the targeted citizen of his liberty and/or property.

Upon entering statehood in 1776, Rhode Island kept its original colonial charter in lieu of a written constitution, and its original *Act of Rights* of 1663 remained in force as the official statement of citizens' rights. It declared that no one *"shall be deprived of his freehold"* (his private property) except *"by the lawful judgment of his peers."*[27]

That original Rhode Island *Act of Rights* then explained the *"due course of law"*[28] by which a legal conviction must be obtained before the government could deprive any free man of his liberty or property. Rhode Island's 1663 *Act of Rights* thus provided a very early precedence for the Fifth Amendment. As we have already seen, the Puritans of the 1600s had also previously established the due process of law in both colonial Massachusetts' *Body of Liberties* (1641) and under colonial Connecticut's *Fundamental Orders* (1639). Each of these earlier Reformed Christian documents, grounded upon biblical principles and law, provided the sound legal precedents for our federal Constitution's Fifth Amendment.

Liberty under Constitutional Law

In summary, the fact that the federal Bill of Rights safeguarded liberty and property helped guarantee that we would have a nation ruled by laws rather than by the whims of men. The whole purpose of the Bill of Rights was to put shackles upon the reach of government into the private domain

---

26 Kurland and Lerner, *The Founders' Constitution*, vol. 5, p. 259.
27 *Acts and Laws of the English Colony of Rhode-Island and the Providence-Plantations, in New-England, in America* (Newport, 1767), p. 226.
28 Ibid.

of its citizens. This fact was clearly stated in the original Preamble that accompanied the proposed Bill of Rights passed by Congress in 1789.

To *"Prevent Misconstruction or Abuse"* of Constituted Powers
– The Preamble of the Bill of Rights as Proposed in 1789

> *The Conventions of a number of the States having at the time of their adopting the Con-*
> *stitution expressed a desire, in order to prevent misconstruction or abuse of its powers,*
> *that further declaratory and restrictive clauses should be added : And as extending the*
> *ground of public confidence in the government will best insure the beneficent ends of its*
> *institution—*

Excerpt from *Acts Passed at a Congress of the United States...*, 1791 Edition

❝ *The Conventions of a number of the States having at the time of their adopting the Constitution expressed a desire, in order to prevent misconstruction or abuse of its powers, that further declaratory and restrictive clauses should be added...* ❞

The Bill of Rights put *"further declaratory and restrictive clauses"* on the power of government. Accordingly, the Constitution incorporated the same foundation of limited power as had been asserted since the time of the early days of American colonization. The framers also respected the Scriptural underpinning of freedom, which mandates that liberty is to be enjoyed in a family's private property under the blessings of heaven.

From the earliest decades of our nationhood, a family's possessions were protected by the guardian nature of both the state and federal constitutions. Criminal and civil laws protected citizens and their property from the violence and evil of their fellow citizens. The federal and state constitutions, with bills of rights, protected citizens and their property from the violence and evil of those holding power. In spite of our generation's flagrant misuse of governmental power, it remains a fact that a citizen of the United States still has more constitutional authority regarding his own liberty and property than the entire force of any governmental administration or agency that might wish to encroach upon his God-given rights.

CONCLUSION
TO REMAIN FREE UNDER GOD

THE stacks of papers, books, and documents from our nation's founding era make it clear that the purpose of America gaining her independence was to preserve the blessings of freedom and private property. A serious question, however, remains as to whether this great nation conceived in liberty remains true to that original purpose.

A Summary of America's Original Cause of Freedom

In May 1776, less than two months before formally declaring independence, the Continental Congress passed a resolution requesting that the thirteen colonies prepare for statehood. Acting "*under the authority of the people of the colonies*," the resolution's preamble stated that the intention of the colonies adopting independent constitutions was for "*the preservation of internal peace, virtue, and good order, as well as for the defense of their lives, liberties, and properties, against the hostile invasions and cruel depredations* [plunder and pillage] *of their enemies.*"[1]

These thoughtful words spoke vividly of the original American character. They expressed the colonists' high regard for both the role of private responsibility and the obligation of legitimate civil government. The wording of the resolution's preamble also reflected the long-revered Protestant position of a biblically justified resistance to lawless, invasive force.[2] Since the time of Martin Luther, when hoards of Muslims were sweeping upon Europe in the 1520s, a war for the necessary defense of Christendom's institutions was considered legally justified and often morally obliging. The Second Continental Congress' defense against Britain's similar attempt to forcefully conquer Americans' homes and homeland was therefore far from any disrespect for the legitimate role of

---

1 Library of Congress, *Journals of the Continental Congress 1774-1789*, vol. 4 (Washington: Government Printing Office, 1906), p. 358. This was an otherwise untitled resolution.

2 See the principle of a morally justified defensive war in my reference to Martin Luther's *On War Against the Turks* on pages 33-34 in this book.

government. America's reaction to Britian's *"hostile invasions"* was an honest outpouring of patriotic duty and a moral obligation of the highest order.

When the British colonial administration first began imposing overbearing regulations and arbitrary taxes, responsible colonists dutifully petitioned their government for redress. When Britain's ill-governed regime then became more grievous and denied the colonists their legal voice within their chartered governments, responsible colonial representatives dutifully petitioned the British king and his administration with a unified voice of protest. It was only when Britain's encroachment upon the colonists' liberty and property was pressed to the point of demanding absolute submission to feudal tyranny under the force of lead and bayonets, that responsible Americans of every order were driven down the road toward independence.

A look at the historic struggle for constitutional liberty within England itself shows that the colonists were acting with the highest regard for their English inheritance of freedom. A distinctive honor in being called an Englishman was living within a Christian realm that strove to preserve the people's liberties under limited government. The distinctive honor of being called an English colonial American was enjoying private property apart from a lording nobility that oversaw the estates of its vassal subjects. Retaining both of these God-given blessings of freedom were primary objectives in the new states adopting limited forms of government – governments accountable to God and the people they served.

The American patriots did not immorally rebel. They did not illegally revolt. They did not defy any legitimate authority in order to obtain something they had not already constitutionally enjoyed. As most Americans were also the spiritual sons of the Reformation, they knew their *principles* were faithful, their *cause* was just, and their *objective* was to remain free in a land that the Almighty would again secure if they refused to give way to compromise. The point of it all was that patriotic Americans of the founding era simply desired to keep their time-honored responsibilities – responsibilities that they owed directly to the Sovereign of the universe rather than falling into the age-old role of being conquered vassals and then vying for the favors of petty tyrants.

On July 4, 1776, the same thirteen colonies that had lawfully resisted Britain's audacious show of force became independent states. They were then formally obliged to act upon the Continental Congress' May resolution to establish governments of their own. This, of course, was done with expressed acknowledgment of the only absolute Sovereign and with full appreciation for His overriding Providence. The states thus produced proclamations of prayer and thanksgiving; they produced documents of fortitude and resolve; and they also produced constitutions and bills of rights that displayed before the world their deep devotion to the principles of godly government upon which their nation was founded.

The expressed goal of the newly formed states was to legally secure the blessings of both liberty and property against any new domineering governmental regime – to ensure that actual power and dominion remained with the people in their own homes, possessions, and land. Independence from Britain certainly did not mean families becoming dependent upon new masters. It absolutely did not mean that the American people were to become subjects, tenants, or vassals of a new regime of lording lawmakers who oversaw the land and economy of a servile people. American independence, in fact, meant adopting a distinguished array of expressed constitutional safeguards, which ensured that individuals and families would remain dependent upon only one sovereign Landlord who truly deserved the designation "Lord."

The idea of a nation conceived in independence from tyranny was never intended to then turn against its own first principles and create dependents of its people. Any national government that was originally authorized to *"secure the blessings of liberty"*[3] was not empowered to then deny the people those very blessings by encroaching upon their private estates. To do so would simply make the whole nation dependent upon a new regime of ruling masters (albeit in the name of "social compassion") by stripping bare the very substance of the people's own liberty and dominion.

---

3 To *"secure the blessings of liberty"* was a stated objective in the Preamble of the federal Constitution.

Certainly, no federal Constitution would have been ratified by the states had it been seen as a threat to the liberty and property already secured by the states' constitutions. Lest we forget, the national Constitution did not replace the state constitutions. The *federal* framework was designed to give a further voice to *"We the people"*[4] on a national scale and to better enforce the prior guarantees of liberty and property by operating concurrently *with* the state constitutions. In fact, the people's enjoyment of their private land and possessions was to become all the more secure under a federal framework than it had been under the prior, loose constellation of states. The added Bill of Rights simply gave the Constitution its most vivid expression of our nation's original respect for liberty and property.

In all, the purpose of the colonists in resisting Britain's schemes of increasing governmental regulation and taxation, and then in adopting constitutions on both a state and national level, was to secure the same legacy of liberty and property that Americans inherited as God-honoring Englishmen. The original intent in America becoming a nation was to safeguard the blessings of peaceable homes and private industry for future generations of responsible Americans. Understanding this important fact is essential to our survival as a free nation.

Enjoying the God-Given Blessing of Quiet and Peaceable Homes

It is clear from the entire sweep of America's story that the people of our founding era did not invent new ideas of freedom or originate new notions of the people's power in their private domain. They had a rich inheritance in the soil and estates passed along to them by their colonial fathers. They also had a rich inheritance in the self-government of their towns, counties, and colonies upon which they enjoyed liberty in their property under law.

The whole idea of dominion as the colonists knew it did not stem from new ideas of freedom or innovative powers of government. Their ideas of private dominion poured from the timeless pages of Scripture –

---

4 *"We the people of the United States"* is the opening clause in the Preamble of the federal Constitution, indicating the source of the national government's delegated authority.

beginning with the Genesis mandate given by God Himself. That mandate included families multiplying, taking possession, and subduing the earth for the blessing of their own and future generations. That biblical idea of stewardship dominion along with responsible self-government drove the first English planters to settle in a distant wilderness under the banner of faithful Christianity.

The application of Holy Scripture to all human affairs defined both the private and the public responsibilities of our distant forefathers. When in the Bible, for example, the Apostle Paul called upon the faithful to pray for *"all that are in authority; that we may lead a quiet and peaceable life in all godliness and honesty,"*[5] he was pointing out that there is a godly responsibility attached to the private enjoyment of quiet and peaceable lives. At the same time, Paul was also driving at the point that those in public authority have a God-given role in securing that domestic peace and quiet within a safe civil setting.

In centuries past, such passages of Scripture have served Christians well, fortifying their faith in the knowledge that God uses civil rulers for that exact purpose – that He has, in fact, ordained civil government as a means to safeguard the blessings of life and liberty that we are to enjoy within the private realm of our homes. Reformed Christians since the sixteenth century therefore recognized that the biblical principles of godliness not only applied to individuals, families, and churches, but also to civil governments. We will recall that early Reformed Bible expositors such as John Calvin championed the cause of liberty under godly civil government. Calvin, for instance, further explained Paul's exhortation to pray for those in authority by adding: *"the true way of obtaining peace, therefore, is when every one obtains what is his own, and the violence of the more powerful is kept under restraint."* [6]

Such observations fortified the Reformed Christians' confidence in God's distinctive blessings upon private property and in the government's

---

5 1 Timothy 2:1-2 (full text): *"I exhort therefore, that, first of all, supplications, prayers, intercessions, and giving of thanks, be made for all men; For kings, and for all that are in authority; that we may lead a quiet and peaceable life in all godliness and honesty."* (King James version).

6 John Calvin, *Commentaries on the Epistles to Timothy, Titus, and Philemon* (Grand Rapids: Baker Books, 2005), remarks on 1 Timothy 2:2, pp. 51-52.

duty to defend the peaceable dominion of a faithful citizenry. This is exactly what our colonial forefathers and our nation's founding fathers understood, and it is exactly why they formed governments to safeguard the liberty and property of American citizens.

In Scripture, the Apostle Paul also used the word "quiet" to describe the character of our domestic work and private business, admonishing us in 1 Thessalonians 4:11: *"that you study to be quiet, and to do your own business, and to work with your own hands."*[7] This use of *"quiet"* in relation to our personal business expresses God's sanction of diligent, tranquil industry in securing His blessings upon our private homes.

This idea of diligent, tranquil industry became an important part of the legacy of the sixteenth-century Reformation that helped break apart the slavish feudal system of medieval Europe. Under the banner of Reformed Christianity, many households were freed from their former subjection to domineering lords in both church and state. The practical, everyday dominion of the earth was recognized as a heavenly blessing bestowed upon peaceable families who possessed their own responsibilities under God – families who knew that His favor was upon those who quietly went about their own business and who reaped the fruit of their own labor.

As sons of the Reformation, the English colonists in America reaffirmed the same principles of the dominion of peaceable homes and private industry. Americans today should have burned upon their minds that when the British government in the early 1760s took steps to encroach upon the peace and quiet of American homes that James Otis spoke out as a flame of fire, coining the famous phrase: *"A man's house is his castle, and whilst he is quiet, he is as well guarded as a prince in his castle."*[8] Otis was, of course, simply restating what his Reformed Christian ancestors had drawn from Holy Scripture. And, we should also not forget that Otis' good friend John Adams recorded that it was on this principle that American independence was born.

---

7 King James version with *"ye"* updated to *"you."*
8 Adams, *The Works of John Adams,* vol. 2, Appendix A, James Otis' speech, p. 524. Also see p. 155 of this book for James Otis.

We cannot fully appreciate the role of our national founders in preserving Americans' grand inheritance of liberty apart from appreciating the earlier colonial aspirations to plant godly freedom in the New World. We do ourselves a great disservice, for example, if in looking back at the sweeping story of Americans' freedom, we begin that story with the drafting of the federal Constitution in 1787. As we have seen, there were many expressions of sound self-government long before the phrase "*We the people*" was penned upon that particular document. There were many profound contributions to the right of the people to be safe in their houses, papers, and effects long before a national Bill of Rights was drafted. There were also many expressed declarations of the biblical principles of life, liberty, and the pursuit of happiness long before those God-given rights were recognized in the famous Declaration of July 4, 1776, which severed Americans from their political ties to Great Britain. There were, in addition, an untold number of contributors to America's enduring legacy of liberty and property long before the entire generation of men who gained our nation's independence were born.

For us to fully appreciate the monumental contribution of our nation's founders, we might consider their own perspective on their place in history. In his reflection upon the "*principles and feelings*" that led to America's independence, a very aged John Adams wrote in 1818: "*These principles and feelings ought to be traced back for two hundred years, and sought in the history of the country from* [which came] *the first plantations in America*."[9] John Adams, who from the early 1760s had participated in the momentous course of events that secured American independence, thus saw the *root* of that independence in the hand of Providence long before his own generation graced the earth.

For one thing, the former President Adams looked to the early English planters who had long before him hungered for liberty in England and who then toiled to settle their families in the wilderness of America. Writing in the mid-1760s, this same John Adams had recognized that the roots of liberty stemmed back even before the "*Puritans almost in despair ...*

9 Adams, *Novanglus and Massachusettenis*, p. 234.

resolved to fly to the wilderness of America."[10] Adams certainly revered his Puritan forefathers for planting their homes and houses of worship "*on the Bible and common sense.*"[11] He also saw the true vine of America's liberty stemming back even further to a time when "*one generation of darkness succeeded another, till God in His benign Providence raised up the champions who began and conducted the Reformation.*"[12]

These earlier European "*champions*" of the Reformation were those whom our nation's founders looked upon as having deciphered the principles of liberty and property long before those ideas spanned the Atlantic Ocean. It was the rediscovery of God's Word that first lit Europe aflame with its enduring principles which eventually illuminated England's pathway to America. It was particularly the Reformed Christian expositors of Scripture who deciphered the principles of genuine dominion amid the stifling darkness of European feudalism. It was the Reformed men of faith, particularly in England, who then drew the sharpest lines of freedom against tyranny and whose writings beaconed many subsequent generations of families to America as a land of the free.

Thus, neither John Adams nor his fellow freedom-loving Americans saw themselves as the innovators of liberty or the first to champion the clarion call of dominion in private property. They were conscientiously preserving the legacy of liberty, property, and the protective role of self-government that was theirs to pass along to other generations.

Civic Accountability Under God

Upon George Washington leaving office as the first federal President of the United States in 1796, his *Farewell Address* was printed in newspapers and pamphlets throughout America. This widely published, wildly popular address to his fellow citizens is a trove of sound political advice from the founding era. In it, President Washington urged Americans to preserve the original purpose for their federal government, warning his beloved nation:

---

10 John Adams, *Dissertation on the Canon and the Feudal Law*, published in The Massachusetts House of Representatives, *The True Sentiments of America*, p. 118.

11 Ibid., p. 121.

12 Ibid.

"resist with care the spirit of innovation upon its principles, however specious [deceptively alluring] *the pretexts."*[13]

The first president's point was that maintaining sound principles of government is necessary to retaining its originally constituted purpose. That purpose was to bind all Americans – private citizens and public officials alike – under a sacred authority. Without the Constitution being amended *"by an explicit and authentic act of the whole people,"* Washington said, its existing authority is *"sacredly obligatory upon all."*[14] This, of course, meant keeping power and dominion in the hands of a faithful electorate, rather than in the hands of *"cunning, ambitious, and unprincipled men"* who, Washington added, always seek to *"subvert the power of the people, and to usurp for themselves the reins of government; destroying afterwards the very engines which have lifted them to unjust dominion."*[15]

With power and dominion in the hands of a responsible citizenry, it was not enough for Americans to simply know *what* the Constitution said, but to know *why* it said it. It was certainly incumbent upon succeeding generations of lawmakers, judges, and presidents to understand the document they had sworn to uphold. It was equally important for the entire citizenry to be steeped in its original intent. It has always been necessary for the people to hold their elected officials accountable to their oaths to prevent *"specious"* (deceptively alluring) interpretations of the role of government that serve the ill intent of those who assume they are in positions of dominion.

Washington's *Farewell Address* did not stop with political warnings; he included sound moral advice for American citizens to preserve the blessings of government. *"Of all the dispositions and habits which lead to political prosperity,"* Washington advised his fellow Americans, *"religion and morality are indispensable supports."*[16] Once again, this president was speaking of citizens' responsibilities as self-governed people. Devout

---

13 Joseph Coe, *The True American; Containing the Inaugural Addresses, Together with the First Annual Addresses of all the Presidents of the United States from 1789 to 1839... also the Farewell Address of Washington...* (Concord, 1840), p. 309.

14 Ibid.

15 Ibid.

16 Ibid., p. 312.

citizens who had their feet planted upon God's timeless moral principles would not allow themselves to be seduced by political innovators who would lure them away from their sacred responsibilities. Consequently, President Washington punctuated his advice with an added warning to all duly-informed citizens: "*And let us with caution indulge the supposition that morality can be maintained without religion.*"[17]

Washington spoke here of the necessity of the people and elected officials alike being aligned with a meaningful faith. He was speaking of a "*religion*" that would benefit both the people and their civic institutions. Of what kind of religion would America's first president have been speaking? He was not speaking of any religion that would either promote or bow to the yoke of tyranny. He was certainly not speaking of any religion that would ever yield itself to progressive licentiousness or immorality, nor was he speaking of the kind of religion that was itself void of any meaningful contribution to the good of wider civil society. Judging from the sheer context of his *Farewell Address*, we can see that President Washington was speaking of the same Christian faith of his colonial fathers – the kind of faith that had yielded the gracious fruit of America's freedoms in the first place.

Such a devout sense of higher obligation was recognized as central to the prosperity of America's civic institutions. On this point, Washington's famed address made a particular reference to one important act that ties Americans to the Almighty in their civic capacity. Americans' obligations are directly tied to God by civil oaths – oaths which affect the security of all Americans' lives and property. "*Let it simply be asked,*" Washington questioned his fellow citizens, "*where is the security for property, for reputation, for life, if the sense of religious obligation desert the oaths, which are the instruments of investigation in courts of justice?*"[18]

This pertinent point gets to a key issue for all civic-minded Americans. The oaths that American citizens take in a variety of public matters directly tie them to a sacred fidelity under God. According to President Washington, without that level of an ever-present sense of accountability, there can

17 Ibid.
18 Ibid.

never be a sufficient sense of security in the citizens' lives, reputations, or property. Why? The people's security in their lives and property relies upon a heavenly accountability much higher than the praises, promises, and pretentions of mere people and politicians.

Whether we are speaking of the civil oaths by which foreigners become citizens of the United States, the oaths that citizens take in a variety of civil proceedings, or the oaths of office required by those entering public service, each oath is attached to a sacred trust. Simply put, civil oaths tie citizens and officials alike to faithfulness under God in their civic capacity.

Thus, completely aside from the sacred obligations of American families under God, and completely aside from the sacred obligations of American churches under God, American civil oaths directly bind all civil obligations under His overarching authority. Put another way, there can be respectable walls of separation between family, church, and state,[19] but never walls separating God's distinctive authority over each distinct sphere. A well-constituted nation will respect the difference between the God-given role of the church and the God-given role of the state, but *civil* oaths themselves hold citizens and officeholders alike to a *civic accountability* under God.

The original state constitutions typically required civil oaths of office that ended with the expressed affirmation: "So help me God."[20] In Washington's own oath of office upon becoming President, he concluded with the same affirmation: "So help me God."[21] Without such submissive affirmations by those who have been placed in positions of power, there

---

19 For further reading, see Robert Renaud and Lael Weinberger, *Spheres of Sovereignty: Church Autonomy Doctrine and the Theological Heritage of the Separation of Church and State*, Northern Kentucky Law Review 35 (2008).

20 The oaths under the constitutions of Georgia (1777), South Carolina (1778), Massachusetts (1780), and New Hampshire (1783) all required the affirmation "so help me God." The oath under the Constitution of Maryland (1776) required a profession of a belief in the Christian religion. The oath under the Constitution of Pennsylvania required the expression of a belief in the one God as Creator and Governor of the universe, an expressed belief in a future state of rewards and punishments, and an expressed belief in the Scriptures being given by divine inspiration. The oath under the Constitution of Delaware (1776) required a profession of faith in God the Father, Jesus Christ, and the Holy Ghost along with an acknowledgment that the Old and New Testaments were given by divine inspiration. The constitutions of New York (1777) and North Carolina (1776) required an unspecified oath. The Constitution of Virginia (1776) required an oath of fidelity.

21 The phrase "So help me God" not only acknowledged an officeholder's submission under God, but it also invited God's judgment if he was unfaithful toward his duties.

can be little public confidence that the people's rights will be respected and public wrongs will be avoided. Public officials are therefore sworn to uphold their state and federal constitutions, which safeguard the people's private obligations. Such a uniform sense of civic *"religious obligation,"* according to our first president, is essential to the security of all Americans' lives and reputations as well as their property.

As is plain to see, America's founders were not incorporating quaint expressions of pious religiosity just to prove to Americans two centuries later that they were a devout people. Their streams of purpose ran much deeper. Obedience to God was known as the essence of any well-anchored civil government, and the people of America knew they had a civic responsibility to hold their elected officials to their duly-sworn oaths.

If, in looking back over the centuries, we think that merely recognizing our nation's former acknowledgments of God is somehow sufficient for us, then we are incredibly blind. The vast collection of proclamations, declarations, and documents that our nation's founders passed along to us not only settle any question as to *their* acknowledgments of the Almighty, but those documents equally *place us* under the same terms of freedom.

The issue, then, for all Americans is rediscovering the underlying principles that fortified the constitutions which have been handed to us. Americans are, for example, the recipients of a well-principled federal Constitution and a Bill of Rights which express the highest regard for the people's responsibilities of liberty and private property. Americans must therefore *know* the inherent principles behind those responsibilities. Then, with due regard for the framers' original intent for a national government, Americans will certainly do themselves a great service in heeding the warning of our first federal president, who cautioned to *"resist with care the spirit of innovation upon its principles, however specious* [deceptively alluring] *the pretexts."*

Remaining as the Land of the Free

Our nation's founders knew the inherent principles of liberty and property and the source from whence they were derived. They knew how to draw the biblical lines between family government and civil government and between the private nature of true earthly dominion and the public nature of protecting that dominion.

All of this together was part of the legacy of liberty that shaped America's reputation throughout the world as a land of the free. The people had a meaningful property in their liberties when they had liberty in their property. The goal of the American governments – both state and federal governments – was therefore to get as much land into private hands as possible. The original idea of dominion in America was not for the federal government, much less the states, to own and control massive tracts of land and resources. It is today wrongly assumed as a "self-evident truth" that governments are entitled to regulate not only an unfathomable amount of public land, but also to regulate the internal affairs of private homes and estates. For example, governmental regulations are enforced to control the resources of peaceable, law-abiding citizens in the name of "the greater environmental good." Citizens' finances are constantly regulated and punitively taxed in the name of "the greater social good." Nearly everything else is regulated or controlled in the name of any other "good" except for the people to responsibly govern their own possessions freely under God.

The idea of public responsibility in the earlier days of our nation was quite the opposite. A vast wilderness bloomed when private industry was allowed to thrive under the encouraging hand of America's civil institutions. Our nation's founders had repudiated the whole idea of "Reserved Lands" when the British government attempted in the 1760s to control vast tracts of real estate and resources in the name of the Crown. In fact, in the 1800s, the federal government created "Bounty Lands" to encourage private citizens who desired to have a stake in land ownership to settle a homestead by tilling a plot of soil and making it productive. Earlier in America's history, huge tracts of federal territory along with their resources were thereby released into private hands in order to increase the blessings of private dominion. With such governmental encouragement of private enterprise, the forbidding wilderness flowered as a rose and the blessing of commerce yielded a nation richer and stronger than any feudal nation of the past. America then became revered all the more throughout the world as the land of the free.

The goal of that kind of freedom was not governmental ownership or control of the people's responsibilities. The goal was to safely secure as much land and as many natural resources as possible within the hands of the greatest number of responsible, productive citizens. As property was recognized as the basis of power, widespread private property ownership was recognized as a key to the people of America remaining free.

Instead of the government protecting the land *from* the people as if the American citizens were nothing but plunderers, the whole country was blessed when the citizens' dominion in land ownership was itself under governmental protection. At that time, America was not yet stifled by the kind of secular religion that regards untouched land as the ultimate goal of increasing governmental domination – religion that regards nature as a goddess to be worshiped from afar but never allowed to be embraced by human hands. In earlier times, it was the Triune God, who had mandated that families multiply, fill, and subdue the earth, who was honored as the *source* of all bounty and blessedness under heaven.

Recent history has shown that a nation that forgets the God who has always sustained it will spiral into slavery under artful masters of the state who claim for themselves god-like authority. At times in our past when productivity and commerce were regarded as God-given blessings, America was not crippled by the philosophy that the more resources, property, and people that come under governmental control, the closer we will come to an ecological utopia. Our forebearers would have recognized such utopian schemes as the very mark of dependency and serfdom. They would have seen any such attempt as the face of despotism that is always willing to barter ideas of an impossible, social utopia in exchange for the people sacrificing their liberty and independence.

Such impossible pretenses would certainly have been associated with the imperial policies of Spain over her vassal American colonies. Spain's failed colonial policy should remain as a vivid reminder of the failure of the kind of statism that assumes a government's right of dominion over the resources, economy, and land of a quiet and peaceable people. America's colonial era shows us that tyranny resonates from the *mere presumption* of governmental control over the people's lives, liberties, and happiness in their own property and possessions.

America's colonial experience under the dominance of Spain and later under Britain shows all Americans how liberty and property are inseparably linked. These oppressive governments of the past did not lay hold of the people's property without also laying claim to their liberty – neither did they lay claim to people's liberties without an assumption of dominion over their property and possessions. Liberty and property rise and fall together, and the sure sign of an already defeated people is when they suppose that they can give up either one in the name of expedience without yielding up the other and becoming slaves.

If the American story teaches us anything, it teaches that despotism is nothing new – its tentacles progressively attach themselves to the very substance of the people's lives. That same American story, however, teaches that the blessings of liberty and property are also nothing new. That story resonates with the blessings attached to the original promise by the Creator in expressing His goodwill toward the first man and woman. People of both the colonial and founding eras of our nation hung their hopes and futures on that promise, and in turn they founded perhaps the most blessed nation under God on the face of the earth.

The often-weighty mantle of liberty and property has now been placed upon another generation of Americans. This generation will either turn toward its rich inheritance and live in greater liberty or turn away and slip further into bondage. We will either rediscover and embrace the timeless principles of freedom and reclaim our nation's strength, or we will remain in ignorance and find ourselves vassals of artful masters. May Americans learn the priceless lessons of our past! May we reclaim the timeless principles that animated prior generations, and may we be as faithful as they were in passing the glorious legacy of liberty and property on to future generations.

SELECTED BIBLIOGRAPHY

Adams, Charles Francis, ed. *The Works of John Adams*. Boston: Little, Brown, 1865.

Adams, John. *Dissertation on the Canon and the Feudal Law*. Published in *The True Sentiments of America: contained in a collection of letters sent from the House of Representatives of the province of Massachusetts Bay*. London, 1768.

Adams, John. *Novanglus, and Massachusettensis; Or Political Essays*. Boston, 1819.

Adams, Zabdiel. *A Sermon Preached Before His Excellency John Hancock, Esq; Governor; ...Council, ... and House of Representatives of the Commonwealth of Massachusetts, May 29, 1782*. Boston, 1782.

Bradford, William. *Of Plymouth Plantation 1620-1647*. Ed. Samuel Eliot Morison. New York: Alfred A. Knopf, 1996.

Brown, Alexander. *The First Republic in America*. Boston: Houghton, Mifflin and Company, 1898.

Calvin, John. *Calvin's Commentaries*. 22 vols. Grand Rapids, MI: Baker Books, 2005.

Calvin, John. *The Institution of Christian Religion*. Trans. Thomas Norton. 2 vols. London, 1578.

Clark, Peter. *Two Sermons Preached at Salem-Village on the General Fast Appointed on the Occasion of the War, February 26, 1741*. Boston, 1741.

Coe, Joseph, ed. *The True American; Containing the Inaugural Addresses... also the Farewell Address of Washington*. Concord, N. H.: J. S. Boyd, 1840.

Continental Congress. *The Constitutions of the Several Independent States of America; the Declaration of Independence; the Articles of Confederation*. Boston, 1785.

Cooke, Samuel. *Sermon Preached at Cambridge, in the Audience of His Honor Thomas Hutchinson, Esq.; Lieutenant Governor and Commander In Chief; the Honorable His Majesty's Council, and the Honorable House of Representatives, of the Province of the Massachusetts-Bay in New-England, May 30th, 1770*. Boston, 1770.

Cotton, John. *The Way of the Churches of Christ in New-England*. London, 1645.

Cromwell, Oliver. *His Highness the Lord Protector's Speeches to the Parliament in the Painted Chamber*. London, 1654.

Davenport, Francis Gardiner, ed. *European Treaties bearing on the History of the United States and its Dependencies to 1648*. Washington, D.C.: Carnegie Institution, 1917.

Davenport, John. *A Sermon Preached at the Election of the Governor, at Boston in New-England, May 19th 1669*. Boston, 1670.

Davies, Samuel. *Sermons on Important Subjects, by the late Reverend and Pious Samuel Davies*. Philadelphia, 1794. (Includes: *The Curse of Cowardice*, and *The Necessity and Excellence of Family Religion* preached in the mid-eighteenth century.)

A Declaration of the Lords and Commons assembled in Parliament. London, 1642.

Dexter, Samuel. *Our Fathers' God, the Hope of Posterity*. Boston, 1738.

Dod, John, and Robert Cleaver. *A Godly Form of Household Government: for the Ordering of Private Families, According to the Direction of God's Word*. London, 1603.

Duffield, George. *A Sermon Preached... on... the Day appointed by... Congress... to be observed as a Day of Thanksgiving, for the Restoration of Peace, and Establishment of our Independence, in the Enjoyment of our Rights...* Philadelphia, 1784.

Dulany, Daniel. *Considerations on the Propriety of Imposing Taxes in the British Colonies, for the Purpose of Raising a Revenue, by Act of Parliament*. London, 1766.

Dummer, Jeremiah. *A Defense of the New-England Charters*. London, 1765.

Eliot, John. *Strength Out of Weakness. Or a Glorious Manifestation of the Further Progress of the Gospel Amongst the Indians in New-England*. London, 1652.

Elizabeth I. *A Most Excellent and Remarkable Speech, Delivered by That Mirrour and Miracle of Princes, Queen Elizabeth*. London, 1643.

Extracts from the Votes and Proceedings of the American Continental Congress, Held at Philadelphia, on the Fifth of September, 1774. Philadelphia and London, 1774.

Ford, Daniel J. *In the Name of God, Amen*. St. Louis: Lex Rex Publishing, 2003.

Ford, Paul Leicester, ed. *Pamphlets on the Constitution of the United States, Published During Its Discussion by the People 1787-1788*. Brooklyn, NY, 1888.

Hakluyt, Richard. *A Discourse Concerning Western Planting*. Ed. Charles Deane. Cambridge: Press of John Wilson and Son, 1877.

Hakluyt, Richard. *Diverse Voyages Touching the Discovery of America and the Islands Adjacent*. London: Hakluyt Society edition, 1850.

Hakluyt, Richard. *The Principal Navigations, Voyages, Traffics and Discoveries of the English Nation*. New York: The Macmillan Company, 1903.

Hariot, Thomas. *Hariot's Narrative of The First Plantation of Virginia in 1585*. London: Bernard Quaritch, 1893.

Heimert, Alan, and Andrew Delbanco, eds. *The Puritans in America: A Narrative Anthology*. Cambridge and London: Harvard University Press, 1996.

Higginson, Francis. *New-England's Plantation. Or, a Short and True Description of Commodities and Discommodities of that Country*. London, 1630.

Hutchinson, Thomas. *The History of the Colony of Massachusetts Bay*. London, 1765.

Hyneman, Charles S., and Donald S. Lutz, eds. *American Political Writing during the Founding Era*. Indianapolis: Liberty Fund, 1983.

James I. *The Kings Majesties Speech, as it was delivered by him in the upper house of the Parliament to the Lords ... 1603*. London, 1604.

Kingsbury, Susan Myra, ed. *The Records of the Virginia Company of London. From the ... Library of Congress*. 2 vols. Washington: Government Printing Office, 1906.

Kurland, Philip, and Ralph Lerner, eds. *The Founders' Constitution*. Chicago and London: University of Chicago Press, 1987.

Library of Congress. *Journals of the Continental Congress 1774-1789*. Washington, D.C.: Government Printing Office, 1906.

Luther, Martin. *Selected Writings of Martin Luther*. 4 vols. Ed. Theodore Tappert. Philadelphia: Fortress Press, 1967.

Maier, Pauline. *From Resistance to Revolution*. New York: W. W. Norton and Company, 1991.

Mather, Cotton. *Magnalia Christi Americana: or, the Ecclesiastical History of New-England*. London, 1702.

Mather, Increase. *A Narrative of the Miseries of New-England by Way of an Arbitrary Government Erected There* (1688). Published in *A Sixth Collection of Papers Relating to the Present Juncture of Affairs*. London, 1689.

Mather, Increase, and Nathanael Byfield. *An Account of the Late Revolution in New-England together with the Declaration of the Gentlemen, Merchants, and Inhabitants of Boston and Country Adjacent*. London, 1689.

Mayhew, Jonathan. *A Discourse Concerning Unlimited Submission and Non-Resistance to the Higher Powers*. Boston, 1750.

Morison, Samuel Eliot. *Builders of the Bay Colony*. Boston and New York: Houghton Mifflin Company, 1930.

Morton, Nathaniel. *New-England's Memorial: or, a Brief Relation of the Most Memorable and Remarkable Passages of the Providence of God*. Boston, 1727.

A Narrative of the Missions to the New Settlements According to the Appointment of the... State of Connecticut: together with an Account of the Receipts and Expenditures of the Money Contributed by the People of Connecticut, in May, 1793. According to an Act of the General Assembly of the State. New Haven: T. & S. Green, 1794.

Ormerod, Oliver. *The Picture of a Puritan*. London, 1605.

Preble, George Henry. *History of the Flag of the United States of America*. Boston, 1880.

Prince, Thomas. *The Salvations of God in 1746*. Boston, 1746.

Purchas, Samuel. *Purchas, His Pilgrimage*. London, 1613.

A Record of Some Worthy Proceedings in the Honorable, Wise, and Faithful House of Commons in the Parliament Holden in the year 1611. London, 1641.

Rutherford, Samuel. *Lex, Rex: The Law and the Prince. A Dispute for the Just Prerogative of King and People*. London, 1644.

Sandys, Sir Edwin. *A Relation of the State of Religion*. London, 1605.

Sasek, Lawrence A., ed. *Images of English Puritanism*. Baton Rouge: Louisiana State University Press, 1989.

Speeches of the Governors of Massachusetts, from 1765 to 1775; and the Answers of the House of Representatives, to the Same; with their Resolutions and Addresses for that Period and other Public Papers, Relating to the Dispute Between this Country and Great Britain, Which Led to the Independence of the United States. Boston: Russell and Gardner, 1818.

Suárez, Thomas. *Shedding the Veil: Mapping the European Discovery of America and the World*. Singapore: World Scientific Publishing Company, 1992.

Taylor, E. G. R., ed. *The Original Writings and Correspondence of the Two Richard Hakluyts*. London: Hakluyt Society, 1935.

Thorpe, Francis Newton, ed. *The Federal and State Constitutions, Colonial Charters, & Other Organic Laws of the States, Territories, and Colonies... Forming The United States of America*. 7 vols. Washington D.C.: Government Printing Office, 1909.

Trumbull, Benjamin. *A Complete History of Connecticut, Civil and Ecclesiastical, from the First Planters from England*. Hartford, 1797.

United States Federal Congress. *Acts Passed at a Congress of the United States of America* ... [1789]. Hartford, 1791.

The Votes and Proceedings of the Freeholders and Other Inhabitants of the Town of Boston. Boston: Edes and Gill, 1772.

Whitaker, Alexander. *Good News from Virginia*. London, 1613.

White, John. *Planters' Plea. Or the Grounds of Plantations Examined*. London, 1630.

White, John. *The Troubles of Jerusalem's Restoration, or the Churches Reformation*. London, 1646.

White, William. *A Sermon on the Duty of Civil Obedience, as Required in Scripture*. Philadelphia, 1799.

Willard, Samuel. *A Complete Body of Divinity In Two Hundred and Fifty Expository Lectures*. Boston, 1726.

Winslow, Edward. *Good News From New-England*. London, 1624.

Winslow, Edward. *A Relation or Journal of the Beginning and Proceedings of the English Plantation settled at Plymouth in New England, by Certain English Adventurers both Merchants and Others*. London, 1622.

Wirt, William. *Sketches of the Life and Character of Patrick Henry*. Philadelphia, 1818.

Witherspoon, John. *The Dominion of Providence Over the Passions of Men*. 1776.

Broadsides

Acts and Laws of the English Colony of Rhode-Island and the Providence-Plantations, in New-England, in America. Newport, 1767.

Continental Congress. *A Proclamation*. Philadelphia, 1778.

Continental Congress. *A Proclamation For A General Thanksgiving*. Exeter, 1777.

In the House of Representatives, November 1, 1776, [concurred] *in Council, November 2d, 1776*. Boston, 1776.

In Provincial Congress, Cambridge, February 16, 1775, [the Fast Day to be observed] *Thursday the sixteenth day of March*, [signed] *John Hancock, President*.

The Public Grievances of the Nation, Adjudged Necessary, by the Honorable House of Commons. London, 1689.

Whereas the army are in present and pressing want of shoes, stockings, and shirts, which cannot be immediately supplied from the public stores... . State of Massachusetts, 1778.

INDEX